The Lingering Eye

Wendy Swart

The Lingering Eye

by

Wendy Suart

Jacket illustrations and three drawings
by Peter Suart

Cartoons by Helen Shakespeare

The Pentland Press Limited
Edinburgh · Cambridge · Durham

First published in 1993 by
The Pentland Press Ltd.
1 Hutton Close
South Church
Bishop Auckland
Durham

ISBN 1 85821 103 4

Typeset by Elite Typesetting Techniques, Southampton.
Printed and bound by Antony Rowe Ltd., Chippenham.

For Brian
With love and gratitude

Acknowledgements

To Cable and Wireless plc for their interest and invaluable support and to the Cable and Wireless Archives.

To the many friends who read the typescript and helped with details, especially D. H. Law, K. V. Thompson, Marie Peters Cashmore, Nancy Summers Antliff and L. T. I. Tyson.

To the late D.E.M. Fiennes for permission to use family archives and to the following sources of information:

Cyril Alliston, *In the shadow of Kinabalu*

K.G. Tregonning, *North Borneo* (extract reproduced with the permission of the Controller of H. M. Stationery Office)

Cecilia Leong, *Sabah, the first 100 years*

Robert Hoebel, *Sabah*

Insight Guide, *Malaysia*

Jack Chen, *The Chinese Theatre*

Dick Horton, *Ring of Fire*

North Borneo Annual Report 1952

Duff Hart-Davies, *Ascension*

Jabatan Muzium dan Arkib Negeri Sabah

Finally to my six wonderful children for their unfailing support, love, encouragement and practical help.

Contents

Foreword

by
Lord Glenamara, C.H., P.C., D.C.L., D.Litt.
Sometime Chairman of Cable and Wireless Ltd.

When the Viceroy of India decided to invade Afghanistan in the 19th century, he did so without being able to consult his political masters in London, for the only links between India and England were by ship. The ensuing problems intensified the pressure for better communications within the Empire. These were first provided by a world-wide telegraphic system along marine cables laid and operated by a unique British company which eventually came to be called Cable and Wireless.

The cables often came ashore at remote places in the Colonies around the world where engineers, trained by the company, were sent to establish telegraph offices. One such was in British North Borneo (now Sabah) where 25-year-old Brian Suart was posted. There he met and married Wendy Law, a young Australian girl who had gone there in search of adventure.

In this delightful, nostalgic book Wendy – with total recall of every sight, sound and smell – has recorded their everyday lives in what was to them, in spite of all the hardships, an eastern paradise. Detail is piled upon detail until one can hear the water lapping on the home-made boat, smell the exotic cooking and see the swirling mist on the peaks of Kinabalu.

Like thousands of colonial servants and foreign service staff of Cable and Wireless and other companies, they were expected to go to whichever corner of the world they were sent without demur. Their salaries were far from princely and many postings, like theirs, were in places which lacked the most basis comforts. Heat, monotony, boredom, loneliness and often illness had to be endured as well as problems involved in their work.

But this, of course, is the life-blood of history, the intimate lives of the people who made it, their problems and how they coped with them, much more than the doings of the great and famous.

The story ends with Brian and Wendy preparing to go to Australia on leave. After this they went on to other increasingly important postings around the globe, Brian finally becoming General Manager in Hong Kong, the company's most prestigious post outside London.

It was my privilege to know him and count him a friend – and to see him launch, with the enthusiasm he had shown as a young man in Borneo forty years earlier, into a post-retirement career as a portrait sculptor.

Brian and Wendy Suart belonged to that breed of Britons who carried the good name and accomplishments of this country far and wide. They did so without pomposity or superior posturing but by serving the people among whom they lived and this book shows how well, and with what joy, they did it.

Prologue

'Cut! Feet out! GO!'

The Jump Master's commands ring out and I push myself out of the plane.

'Thousand and one, thousand and two, thousand and three, thousand and four, thousand and check canopy!' I bellow, the slipstream snatching the words from my mouth and whirling them back to the Jump Master at the yawning hole in the side of the Red Devils' aircraft.

Spreadeagled in the slipstream I fall.

Above me the colourful nylon canopy balloons and I drift silently down to the tiny patch of grass below. Suspended in a nothingness of blue and gold, riding the wind birdlike, my mind whirls exultantly.

Below me on the dual carriageway cars crawl like busy ants in a dedicated stream.

'Hope I miss those . . . and the trees . . .' I pull the right toggle to correct my drift. I must be mad! Why am I doing this? A fifty-nine-year-old Australian with an English husband and six children, living in retirement in the green depths of Hampshire.

I seem to look down the wrong end of a time telescope and see myself as a young, unsophisticated girl at the beginning of a long road which is to lead me to my husband and a fascinating life in countries across the world. I see my husband rising to a position of tremendous responsibility controlling the network of telecommunications in the Far East. I remember being an executive's wife, entertaining and being entertained, and seeing to the welfare of the dozens of Company wives on the station while bringing up our large family.

And now, my husband retired, we are able to pursue our own special interests, he to develop a second career in portrait sculpture, I to satisfy a frustrated urge to obtain a university degree. The guests we entertain now are our own friends and relations, not V.I.P.s swanning around the tropics to get away from northern winters.

Funny . . . I never thought I would end up in England. Australia is in my blood, my bones. My roots are in its dry soil and my soul akin to its grasses and aged mountains. So how has it happened? So many countries, so much travelling. By nature a tent-dweller with little regard for possessions, why am I settled now in an English cottage?

Two hundred feet. My feet clamp together, I flex my knees and prepare to land.

'Not bad,' says the course instructor, 'Let's run through it again and then we'll go to the airstrip and get kitted out.'

My body obeys his commands but my thoughts are far away, thinking of that June day in 1949 when the long journey started.

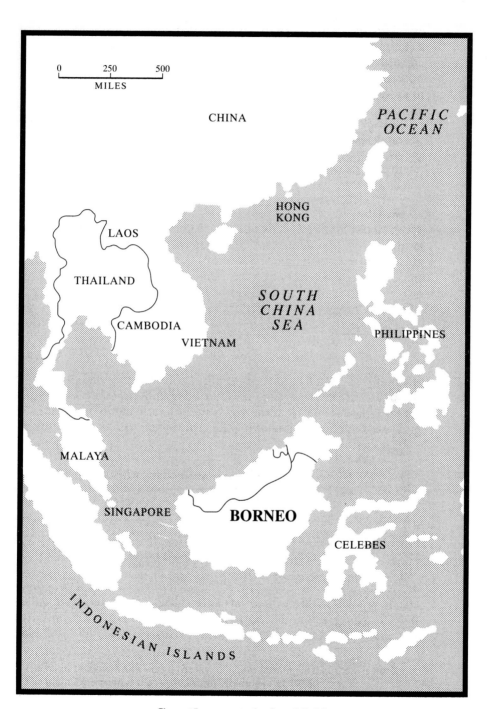

South-east Asia 1949

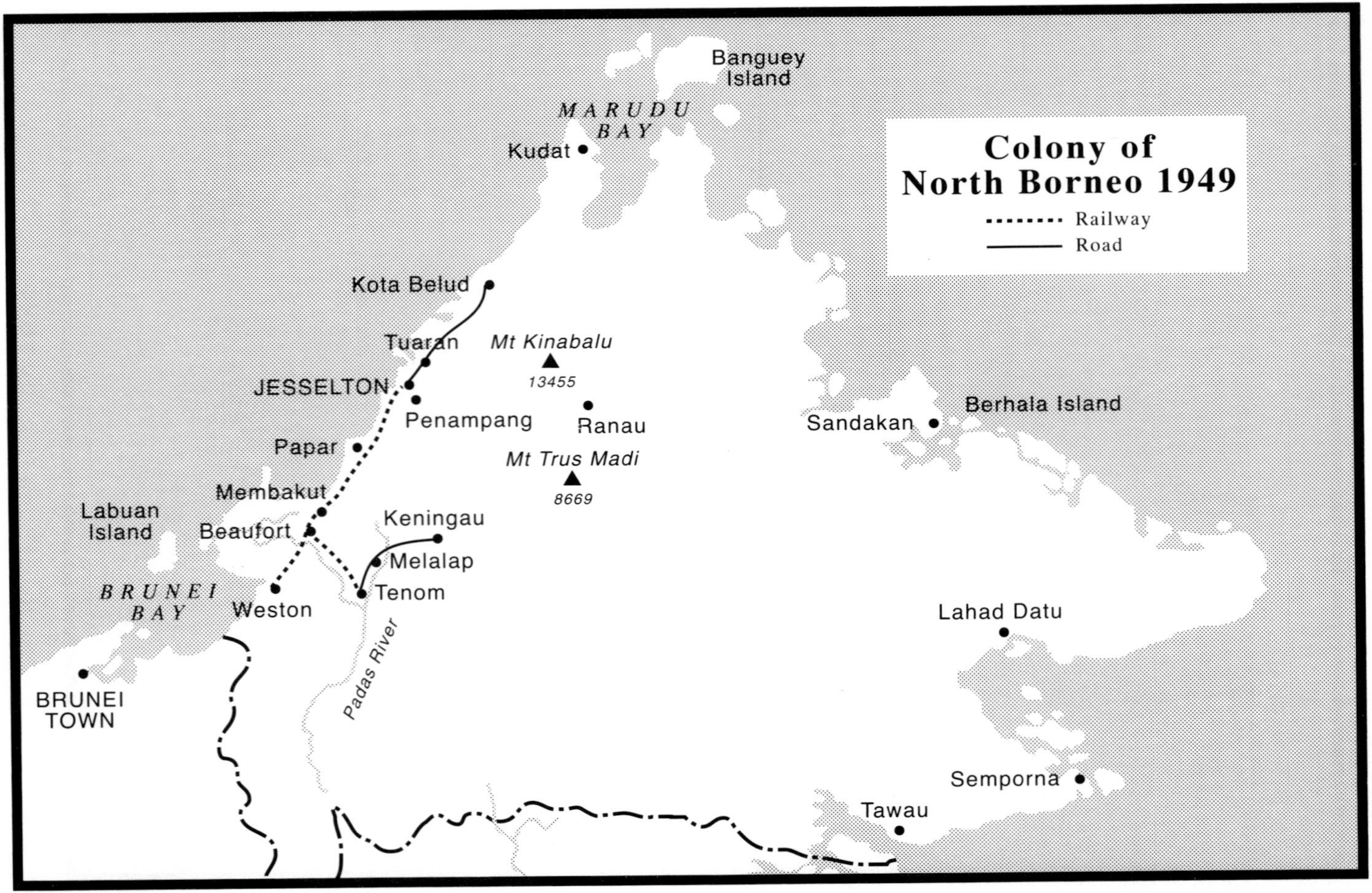

Colony of
North Borneo 1949

...... Railway
—— Road

Banguey
Island

Berhala Island

MARUDU
BAY

Kudat •

Sandakan •

Lahad Datu •

Semporna •

Tawau •

Mt Kinabalu
13455 ▲

Ranau •

Mt Trus Madi
8669 ▲

Kota Belud

Tuaran

Penampang

Keningau

Melalap

Tenom

Padas River

JESSELTON

Papar

Membakut

Beaufort

Weston

Labuan
Island

BRUNEI
BAY

BRUNEI
TOWN

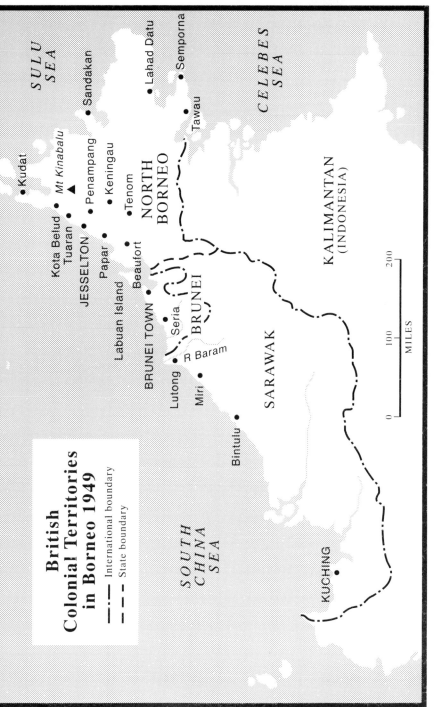

British
Colonial Territories
in Borneo 1949

—·—· International boundary
——— State boundary

*SULU
SEA*

• Kudat

Mt Kinabalu
▲

Kota Belud •
Tuaran •
JESSELTON •
Papar •

• Penampang
• Keningau
• Tenom

NORTH
BORNEO

• Sandakan

• Lahad Datu

• Semporna

Tawau •

*CELEBES
SEA*

Labuan Island
Beaufort •

BRUNEI TOWN •
Seria •
BRUNEI

R Baram
Lutong •
Miri •

• Bintulu

SARAWAK

KALIMANTAN
(INDONESIA)

200

100

MILES

0

*SOUTH
CHINA
SEA*

KUCHING
•

Chapter 1

Lion City – East Meets West

It was eight o'clock in the morning on the 3rd of June 1949 and we were lying in the Singapore roads waiting for the sea fog to lift. Passengers waiting for their breakfast lined the rails. How frustrating to be denied my first glimpse of a new world now!

I had just completed a three-year trip around Australia by bicycle with a girl friend and a dog. It had been rough going with few comforts and much hardship. Back in the bosom of my family in Melbourne, with a soft bed and three meals a day, I was tempted by the delights of a settled life and leapt precipitately into an engagement with a young man I had known since I was fifteen. My family wasn't happy about it and secretly I had my doubts too. After years of loneliness I was in love with the idea of love and when people asked me when we were to marry I thought: 'What's getting married got to do with it?' By formalizing an engagement with newspaper notices and a ring, I was trying to create an artificial state of happiness. As one of my friends said: 'Was getting engaged just another adventure to you?'

My brother Peter was working on the Shell oilfields in Seria in the State of Brunei on the island of Borneo. The nearest in age to me of my five older brothers and sisters, he invited me to Seria, over-ruling my protestations that I'd only just finished one trip, that I was enjoying being home, that I'd come and see him the following year. He said that everything was organized, accommodation arranged

1

and he'd never forgive me if I didn't come. My family added their weight to his persuasion and so a fortnight earlier I had left Melbourne on the night train to Adelaide.

Because the Australian States had never been able to agree on a common rail gauge, I had to change trains at Adelaide and Port Pirie before boarding the renowned Transcontinental train, the railway which holds the record for the longest straight stretch of rail in the world – 297 miles. This line crossed the Nullarbor Plain, the treeless stretch of gibber desert which was once an inland sea. It was quite different from that part of the Nullarbor which I'd ridden across eleven months earlier as the hard dirt road followed the coast and the railway was a hundred miles inland. There had been no aborigines near the coast but at the rail stops they clustered in pitiful groups proffering souvenirs to the travellers. They were dirty and unkempt, very different from the fine physical types I had seen in Northern Queensland and the Northern Territory.

Changing trains once more in Kalgoorlie, I finally reached Perth, that beautiful city loved by Englishmen, retired sea captains and Malayan Civil Servants, and there boarded the S.S. *Charon* which operated a shuttle service to Singapore with its sister ship *Gorgon*, calling at Geraldton, Port Hedland and Broome to load cattle.

Ships had always fascinated me. They smelt deliciously of tar and paint, they went to exotic, faraway places and I sensed the hidden danger inherent in the way they confronted the elements. I longed to make a voyage and whenever I boarded a ship to bid farewell to a friend or relative, it was heartbreaking to have to go ashore at sailing time. But now it was my turn. Tremendously excited, I found my cabin then set about exploring the ship.

It was a comfortable vessel, not so big that one didn't get to know everyone on it but large enough to move about, with plenty of room for deck sports. On board were about a dozen Shell employees also bound for Seria, some newly recruited, some returning from leave. One man in his thirties introduced himself as Roy Anderson and said Pete had asked him to look after me during the voyage. A quietly spoken, fair-haired man of stocky build from Toowoomba in Queensland, he was travelling by himself and was very lonely without his wife. I was feeling remote from family and friends, emotionally confused and more than a little nervous about the journey ahead of me. Although I was twenty-two, it was the first time I had travelled alone or left my country. Roy was as solid as a rock and became a reliable friend, adviser and confidant.

The rest of the Shell men were gregarious and lively. Apart from one man they were all bachelors. One young chap we nicknamed 'Walter Mitty' because he'd seemingly done everything in his short life. Mention any subject or activity, he could provide some personal experience of it. There was another young woman besides me, a quiet pretty girl who was going to meet her fiancé in Singapore. They were to be married there before going on to Seria. We formed a congenial group, playing deck sports or sitting on deck learning Malay. Those who had done a tour of duty in Borneo were fluent in the language and impressed us by giving orders in Malay to the Chinese stewards at meal times. They enthralled the first-timers with stories and jokes about life on the oilfield so that we felt we already knew the place.

As well as the oilmen there were tin-miners and rubber planters going to Malaya, Government officers bound for Singapore and Kuala Lumpur, and several wives rejoining their husbands in various outposts of Empire. Each had an interesting story to tell. The woman who shared my cabin mentioned casually one day that she had escaped from Singapore on a ship when the Japanese invaded Malaya. Her ship was bombed, she floated in a lifebelt till picked up by a raft and finally reached shore, only to be interned in prison camp for the duration.

A few days out of Perth my smallpox vaccination turned septic so I went to see the ship's doctor. I was pleasantly surprised to find him young and handsome. Tall and wiry in build, he had a lean face, light brown curly hair and blue, humorous eyes. He dressed my vaccination and told me to come back daily. I needed no encouragement. He seemed to be a kindred spirit and I was attracted by his lively interest in everything and his uninhibited love of living. Excited like me by the elements, he kept praying for a storm and rushed around the deck exulting when it rained. Together we rode the prow in heavy weather, soaring up, up on huge waves and crashing down into the seething green troughs. We met on deck early one morning to see 'the dawn come up like thunder' over the Indian Ocean and we tried to climb the mast until hauled down by an irate officer.

Along with the rest of the passengers we practised Malay. The doctor's method of learning was by an association of ideas. *Susu* (milk) he thought resembled the sound of a cow being milked into a bucket; *chuchi* (to clean) sounded like someone cleaning his teeth.

One day he said: 'Do you know how I remember the word for lavatory? It's *jamban* . . . well, you don't get jam there and you don't get buns there!'

I said that to me it suggested 'jump in' but he disagreed and it was always jam and buns after that.

Our leisurely voyage took us up the coast of Western Australia, past the ancient, flat-topped hills of Geraldton to Port Hedland where a stream of bellowing, wild-eyed, horn-tossing cattle plunged up the ramps and down into the hold, then on to Broome. This strange town with its background of pearl luggers and Japanese divers was very exotic to eyes used to anglicized Australian cities. The cemetery with its grave markers splashed with Japanese characters (so many pearl divers died in those waters!), the inescapable feeling in the town of clinging by a precarious toehold to a vast continent whose eastern coastline was over two and a half thousand miles of emptiness away, and the ludicrous tide which rises and falls thirty feet each day, all marked Broome with the stamp of improbability. When we left the ship in the morning it was tied up securely alongside the very large jetty running out from the shore. On returning in the afternoon we found it sitting despondently on its bottom on damp sand, like a child who has wet his pants. Of sea there was no sign. The ship looked obscene somehow with all its underwater parts exposed to public gaze . . . its large rudder, its stationary propeller. We walked around it marvelling. Gradually the tide came in and we sailed that night.

Once clear of Australia the spell of the tropics descended. We nosed our way through the jewelled string of Indonesian islands, passing through narrow Lombok Strait which separates Bali and Lombok and is overlooked by mighty Gunong Agung, the great Balinese volcano. The days were hot, the sea was calm and we became lethargic. The deck tennis courts seemed less inviting, the quoits and bullboard were as much as we could contemplate before subsiding into deckchairs with cold drinks. We began to adopt the habit so common in the tropics of wiping the sweat away from the dimple in the upper lip and the chin-crease below the bottom lip. We watched shoals of flying fish leaping from the water, gliding several yards then plunging into the waves. Near land the gulls were always with us, wheeling and shrieking as they dived for scraps of food flung from the galley.

The nights were sheer magic. The black velvet sky seemed within reach and the stars were at mast height, so many of them and so brilliant it was like watching rockets on Guy Fawkes Night. I spent hours leaning on the rail watching the phosphorescence in the water, liquid fire stirred by our creamy wake. The air was warm and balmy with light breezes that enticed me with Siren calls of tropical islands. My blood stirred with excitement and expectation.

One day out of Singapore we crossed the Equator and most of us were subjected to the traditional attentions of a string-bearded Neptune and his court who smothered our faces in shaving cream, shaved us with a large wooden razor and threw us into the make-shift canvas swimming pool.

And now we were waiting to dock, the engines barely turning over, the early morning mist lying on the silken surface of the turquoise sea. Suddenly the veils parted a little and I saw a magnificent Chinese junk, old as time, lying becalmed fifty yards away.

The huge, lumbering craft with its blackened timbers and patched batwing sails leaned on the swell like a foundering wreck. I was entranced. This was Asia. I was in Singapore at last.

•   •   •

Singapore. The very name was magical. It cannot be emphasized too much how very isolated Australians were in those days. In a vast continent, roughly 2,000 miles north to south and 2,500 miles east to west, we had to undertake a long journey to see a different kind of face or hear a different language. Very few Australians had seen an aborigine. Even if we crossed the Tasman Sea to New Zealand we still saw British descendants and heard English spoken.

The person who left the British Isles to go to the Far East by sea had Gibraltar, Port Said, Suez, Aden, Bombay and Colombo to acclimatize him gradually to a change of culture but the Australian, coming straight from Perth or Sydney, was catapulted straight into the bewildering, shattering milieu of Singapore, every sense feeding him impressions of mind-boggling differences: new sights, sounds, smells, tastes, all pouring into his brain in rapid succession.

Alien sights: the rich mix of nationalities – Malays, Chinese, Indians, Europeans; the flamboyance of their assorted dress – *sarong kebaya* (the *sarong* and neat voile jacket of the Malay women), *cheong saam* (the elegant high-necked Chinese sheath with side slits) and *saam fu* (the Chinese pyjama suit), saris and turbans, fashionable dresses; the springing luxuriant vegetation, gaudy flowers and improbable fruits. What a puzzling city of contrasts with squalor alongside wealth! Crowded Chinese tenements, plaster crumbling and paint peeling, sported brave Corinthian columns barely visible under the long poles of washing protruding from each window. Next to them rose skyscrapers of the latest American design. Trishaws (tricycle rickshaws) threaded their way through lines of luxurious limousines. An expensive European emporium stood cheek by jowl with fascinating Chinese markets and Indian bazaars where fabulous silks and brocades were piled in profusion in shabby little shops – gold and silver thread saris, butterfly-splashed *sarongs*, pure silk scarves and embroidered chiffons. I stood, apprehensive, in the back room of a poky Indian shop while the proprietor wound me round and round in seven yards of sari. I felt like screaming out of the window: 'Help! I've been draped!' I looked wistfully in the windows of the leather shops where croco-dile and snake-skin shoes and handbags were on display. Lambs-wool-lined ankle boots would be welcome in Melbourne's bitter winter but they were of no use to me now.

Wandering along the squalid back streets, I was astonished at the way life was lived in public – people eating, urinating, bathing, sleeping; children defecating in the gutter or doing schoolwork on the footpath; old women having their hair braided; men being shaved and having their nose and ear hair trimmed. There were notices plastered around the city in three languages forbidding spitting in the street, with a penalty of a Str. $25 fine. (Lee Kuan Yew many years later was to raise the fine to $500 for any kind of littering, even a cigarette butt or a bus ticket, and turned Singapore into a shining model, though perhaps less interesting, of what an Asian city can be.)

Strange sounds: whirring fans; the incessant ring of hundreds of melodious bicycle bells (really bells, not just whirrers or brazen clanks like ours); the rattle-bone clacking of Mah Jong tiles being swept across table tops and stacked noisily by urgent hands; the Cathedral bells ringing all Sunday morning without stopping; the cough, hawk, spit of the consumptive (known as the Chinese national anthem because one heard it almost unceasingly every-where); the clatter of wooden clogs; the cries of pedlars.

Unbelievable smells: the nose-twitching revulsion of dried fish and *durian* ('strawberries and cream with a strong overtone of drains' was how one writer described this fruit); the putrid smell of

the river at low tide, jammed with barges and sampans housing hundreds of families; the pungent aroma of exotic spices; the languorous scent of frangipani; the appetizing smell of Chinese food frying at wayside stalls.

And the tastes! What an undreamt-of world of tongue-tingling, palate-provoking tastes!

I ran into the ship's doctor while exploring Singapore and took him haggling down Change Alley. It was a noisy, narrow little lane and very exciting. On the crowded stalls we found Siamese silver jewellery, Chinese filigree, exquisite table linen, embroidered Mandarin coats, bolts of material from all over the Far East vying with the new nylon shirts from America and watches from Japan. It was a good place to try out our Malay.

'*Berapa harga itu*? *Wah . . . mahal lah!*' (How much is that? Too dear!)

We shouldered our way through the jostling crowd where slim Chinese girls in *saam fu*, magnificent bearded and turbaned Sikhs, Malay men in their black velvet *songkoks* (Muslim hat) and neat Malay women in *sarong kebaya* competed for attention with immaculate Chinese clerks and sun-tanned Europeans.

The doctor had telephoned the brother of a medical friend in Perth, a prominent lawyer called David Marshall (later to be Singapore's first Chief Minister after Independence), who told him to bring a friend that evening and he'd show him around Singapore.

'I'll pick you up at seven,' he said.

I went back to my room in the Adelphi Hotel, kicked off my tight shoes and put on the Chinese heel-less slippers I'd just bought. They were made of royal blue silk with embroidered peacocks across the toe and the soft cushioned sole brought relief to my weary feet. I would have to buy some open sandals. My feet had swollen in the heat and the humidity had made me very tired but after half an hour's rest and a shower I was ready to go out again.

I dressed in the tomato-red ballerina-length dress which suited my dark pageboy hair and we took a taxi to David Marshall's luxurious flat. He was about forty then, very dark, very Jewish and very rich. His thick black curly hair was streaked with grey and his heavy-lidded eyes looked deceptively sleepy. He actually had an exuberant personality, full of enthusiasm for all sorts of things. He said he intended to give up the law and start a course in medicine, just for the fun of it. He didn't want his money but enjoyed spending it lavishly on his friends. He introduced me to the tantalizing flavour of D.O.M., the Benedictine liqueur. I was no drinker and was always looking for something to drink at a party. D.O.M. was so strong I could sip only the tiniest drop but its heady fumes and exotic taste are forever Singapore to me.

David drove us to the tall Cathay building which housed a theatre, restaurant and Radio Malaya, but here again was contrast in the form of a notice outside the expensive restaurant: 'It is forbidden to bring dogs in here.' As if anyone would wish to! I had never been to a nightclub and I was naïvely impressed by the dance floor in the centre with tables grouped around it, and the orchestra on its dais. It played mainly sambas, rumbas and tangos which were very popular in Singapore and I danced in the arms of the young doctor to the romantic rumba 'Reflections on the water'. The atmosphere was sophisticated and cosmopolitan. Malay, Chinese and Indian girls in their national dress mingled with Europeans in evening dress. I felt I was on another planet, worlds away from the Australian outback. We dined sumptuously, dancing in between courses, and at about eleven o'clock drove out to the Swimming Club.

A long cream building with horizontal balconies, concealed green lighting making it eerie and interesting, bordered an inviting pool. We walked through the imposing entrance and up a marble stairway to the restaurant and ballroom on the first floor where under soft lights people were dancing to a sensuous tango. Leading off the ballroom were the balconies where others were sitting enjoying the lovely night. No Asiatics were there, of course, only Europeans. We found a table which looked over lawns sloping down to the sea. Out in the moonlit harbour were hundreds of small craft and the festooned lights of large liners. I couldn't get over the delicious warmth of the evening. The heavy heat of the day had gone and the night enveloped us like cotton wool. There was no need for jackets or wraps. We danced till after midnight then decided to cool off in the pool. Downstairs were well-equipped changing rooms and as I walked out through the foyer in my swimsuit I passed incoming guests in evening wear and jewels. We swam and lazed in the warm water for nearly an hour then changed back into our clothes.

David said: 'I feel peckish. Let's go and have some supper.'

We drove through the narrow backstreets of Singapore and came to one which despite the early hour (it was nearly 2 a.m.) was bustling with activity. Beneath flaring acetylene lamps there were trestle tables with low stools around them every twenty yards or so down the street. By each table a Malay squatted beside a small brazier of glowing red charcoal.

'This is *satay* row. We always eat *satay* at this time of night.'

I watched, fascinated. The food vendor crouched by his fire on which were balanced dozens of bamboo slivers with pieces of meat impaled on them. He fanned the gleaming coals of his fire vigorously with a palm-leaf fan, turning the sticks with dexterity and basting them with spices and sauces. A plate with two dozen of them slammed down on the table.

'Dip them in this sauce and then pull the meat off the stick with your teeth,' said David, demonstrating.

I ate my first *satay*. The heavenly taste attacked my palate: beef, curry, peanut and a lot of mysterious unknown flavours clamouring for recognition. My mouth on fire, I reached for the chunks of cold clean cucumber on another plate, the perfect antidote. Plate after plate arrived, prawn and chicken alternating with beef, and when we all declared we could eat no more, the man counted the empty sticks and proffered the bill. I have eaten hundreds of *satay* since then but have never quite recaptured the magic of that first experience in *satay* row with the warm, velvety Singapore night, brilliant stars and a full moon overhead, the lamps hissing, the charcoal glowing and an extremely attractive young man by my side.

•   •   •

Next morning I awoke and stretched contentedly in my vast double bed. A 'Dutch wife' – a plump bolster – lay along the bottom of the bed. Why was it at the foot of the bed? I learned later that one is meant to rest a leg, or both legs, on it so that one's skin is not in close contact with the hot mattress.

My suite was huge, the enormous bedroom leading into a sitting alcove overlooking the street. To the rear of the bedroom was the bathroom, itself the size of a normal bedroom. Overhead the ceiling fans turned silently. Through the open windows came the clamour of the street.

There was a soft knock at the door and in came the room boy clad in *sarong* and high-buttoned jacket, black velvet *songkok* on his head and bare brown feet. How beautiful the Malays are!

He smiled. '*Selamat pagi misi! Mahu makan-kah?*'

I quickly summoned my wits and tried to remember the vocabulary I had learned on the trip up from Australia.

'*Ya, terimakasi.*'

He placed a tray by my bed and, lifting the mosquito net in snowy armfuls, stowed it neatly above. He removed soiled towels from the bathroom, left clean ones and took my shoes for cleaning.

I sat up. On the tray was what I later discovered to be the standard Malayan early morning snack. Segments of pomelo, a very large citrus fruit like an outsize grapefruit but very sweet, slices of *papaya* with segments of lime on the side, and beautiful little bananas, *pisang mas*, golden and sweet. I ignored the pot of tea on the tray and devoured all the fruit.

The phone rang. It was the doctor.

'What, not up yet? Come on, I've only got today to see the rest of Singapore. I'll call for you in half an hour. David's lent us his car and *syce* (driver).'

The day passed in a whirl of new experiences. We saw the Jade House, home of the multi-millionaire maker of Tiger Balm, the panacea of the East, and I learned that jade isn't always green but comes in pink, lemon and mauve shades as well. We ate pungent curry puffs at the Seaview Hotel, sitting in a circular dining room open on all sides and overlooking the sea. We drove to a Hindu temple, marvelling at the ferocious, hideous gods which threatened from all sides, then paused to watch a Chinese funeral making its noisy way along the street. The long retinue wound past us, para- doxically white-clad professional mourners wailing loudly, the large photograph of the deceased borne in state on the hearse, the family clothed in woven palmleaf 'sackcloth', the coloured umbrel- las and the musicians crashing brasses, tooting on trumpets and pounding drums. How the Chinese love noise! We escaped to Ob- servatory Hill and saw Singapore, its harbour and the surrounding islands spread out before us and then made our way to the Botanic Gardens. Monkeys capered over the grass, orchids drooped in showers from overhead branches and huge poinciana, cassia and frangipani trees drenched the air with perfume.

'Now what?' asked the doctor.

The driver looked at us enquiringly. 'You like see Great World, *misi*?'

I nodded excitedly. I had heard about the Singapore Worlds, vast amusement parks with every conceivable entertainment. At the Great World we found Chinese and Indian shops, sports facilities, dance halls and plenty of excellent Chinese cafés and restaurants where one could eat anything from a small satisfying dish for fifty Straits cents to an expensive twelve-course banquet.

There was also a Chinese theatre and the noise from it attracted us from the other side of the park. We found seats and were imme- diately transported to Imperial China. I was spellbound by the superb costumes and extravagant make-up of the actors as they portrayed some legendary tale of Princes and Princesses, Emperors and concubines. I watched the Princess make her impressive entrance in a sumptuous gown of brocade and satin encrusted with gems, her lily-like hands lost in the folds of the long, hanging

sleeves, her huge head-dress spangled with jewels and pendant pearls. Without moving a muscle of her enamelled face, she delivered an oration in the high-pitched nasal whine of Chinese opera and as she began to subside gracefully on the floor, a little old man, emaciated and consumptive in appearance, wearing a holey faded singlet and patched shorts, pattered in from the wings and tossed a velvet cushion onto the floor a second before her bottom touched it. When she arose seconds later, he removed the cushion and exited. No one paid any attention to him but my jaw dropped. This really called for suspension of disbelief. How astonishing the Chinese are! Their theatre is pure escapism and they close their eyes to necessary adjuncts like scene shifters and props men.

I found the whole production incomprehensible, although the foreign language wasn't the only reason. Had I known then what I know now, I might have followed the plot fairly well because Chinese opera is full of the heavy symbolism which marks Chinese classical theatre. The appearance of the hero and the villain immediately tells the audience which is which, the hero wearing red make-up and the villain having a white-painted face. Costume too is significant. Yellow robes indicate a member of the Imperial House; honourable people wear red, the virtuous blue. Good officials wear square hats, scoundrels wear round ones – rather like the way the good guy in Western films always wears a white hat. There are fifty different kinds of sleeve movement. The long 'rippling water' sleeve can show embarrassment or weeping, it can signal the orchestra to be ready, and held before the face it can indicate that the actor is hidden from others on the stage.

Then there are the props. We were puzzled by the short stick with four silken tassels on it which a character carried round and round the stage rapidly to the accompaniment of loud clonks on the wood blocks. I found out years later that it represents a horse!

As for the noise, it would shatter glass. The orchestra sits in the wings and every line of dialogue seems to be accompanied by deafening crashes on the cymbals. Some of the performances continue for several days and you aren't expected to watch it all, so when we could bear the din no more we came out and wandered hand in hand past the various stalls.

A little Chinese girl, no more than six years old, came up and without speaking stretched her hand up and tucked a rose in my belt. Charmed, touched, I went to give her twenty cents but she insisted on forty and I spied her tiny, grubby fist clutching a handful of notes.

We dined in a scruffy restaurant in a side street. I had already decided not to worry too much about the hygiene in the kitchen. Chinese food is cooked at such high temperatures that it is unlikely any bacteria survive.

Afterwards we dismissed the *syce* and walked round and round the block, talking endlessly and postponing the hour of separation. I was really smitten by this young man and he seemed quite interested in me but the engagement ring on my finger was a barrier which stopped all intimate conversation.

We parted at my hotel and although we wrote sporadically for a few months I never saw him again.

Chapter 2

Brunei – Abode of Peace

I left the hotel early next morning and drove to Kallang airport with Roy Anderson. The other Shell people returning from leave were to go on to Borneo by ship but Roy and I were in a hurry to reach Seria.

On the plane a charming Chinese air hostess fluttered around us providing barley sugar, copies of the *Straits Times* and palm-leaf fans. The fans were indispensable until we reached 9,000 feet when I was glad of a blanket.

My thoughts were in a turmoil. I felt dreadfully sad at leaving the compatible doctor. My fiancé had not sent letters to Broome or Singapore but I felt surprisingly uninterested. If I could feel so involved with another man, did I really care for my fiancé? More and more I was inclined to doubt it. With sudden resolve I took the ring off my left hand and put it on my right. I looked up and saw Roy watching me. He didn't miss much.

'Is that the way it is?'

I smiled ruefully and turned my head to look out of the window. I felt choked with all sorts of conflicting emotions but above all a sense of release. Roy was a very restful sort of person and left me alone with my thoughts.

After two hours flying over the sea we crossed the Borneo coast. It was a wonderful sight. There were mountains everywhere, but what mountains! The whole landscape looked as though it had

17

been thrown up in mighty convulsions so that each hill was not so much part of a range but an individual eruption on its own. All had weird shapes, humps and jagged peaks, thickly wooded with no sign of settlement.

At 11 o'clock we landed at Kuching, the capital of Sarawak. The very name was redolent of exotic history. Vague memories of White Rajahs and Dyak headhunters stirred in my mind. We got out to stretch our legs and I was relieved to find the climate seemed good. No humidity, just hot sun. Singapore's climate had been enervating.

The countryside around us was still very mountainous and I couldn't imagine how anyone had managed to find a valley in which to build an airstrip. It was alarming on take-off to see the jungle rushing towards us.

As we flew north-east up the length of Sarawak we passed over dozens of rivers and tributaries, splashings of native villages then more sea. Roy nudged me and pointed to the oil settlements of Miri, Lutong and Seria strung out along the coast. I felt rather disappointed. Seria was so different from what I'd imagined. Instead of being mountainous it looked flat and uninteresting from the air. The bungalows were built in V formations and all I could see were these long zigzags dotted with dolls' houses. There seemed to be very little vegetation and no hills. I was also surprised to see its proximity to the sea. Although Pete had spoken of swimming, I had had a strange idea that Seria was inland.

At half past two we landed at the island of Labuan off the west coast of North Borneo and were met by a Shell representative. Our flight was the first of the new civil service operated by Malayan Airways, replacing the old post-war service run by the R.A.F., and groups of curious people had turned up at each airfield to see its arrival. There was also the disturbing presence of a fire cart and an ambulance which seemed ominous.

The Shell man, Mr Shannon, drove us to the Company's Rest House. It was situated amongst light timber facing the sea and a scattering of small wooded islands. We were shown to a bungalow consisting of a front verandah from which led two bedrooms side by side. Behind these and leading from each of them was the bathroom. The interesting thing about the bungalow was that all the surfaces, walls and doors, were made of woven palm leaf. The Malays make great strips of the stuff like rugs and then nail them onto the wooden framework of the house. It is called *kajang* and as well as being cheap is certainly cooler than a non-porous wall. There were no ceilings in the rooms. I could look straight up at the rafters under the thatch and at the *chichaks*, those quaint little flesh-coloured lizards about five inches long which chase each other over the walls and rafters and carry out their reproductive functions frequently and obviously. A loud splat! The long-suffering female hits the deck and scampers away, climbing to her perch in the roof with a curious side-waddling movement. All this happens to the accompaniment of a loud chirping noise which sounds like its name. When threatened by an enemy, the *chichak* drops its tail which jerks and twitches to distract the pursuer while it makes its escape.

Mr Shannon couldn't tell us when a Landing Craft would be available to take us across to Seria and cheerfully spoke about our being in Labuan for several days. I was downcast as I knew there were to be great celebrations in Seria on the King's Birthday, two days hence. However there was nothing to do but wait. I consoled myself with the thought that I could improve my Malay by speaking with the *amah* who cleaned my room. She was a sweet-faced Chinese who came in while I was resting before tea, stood shyly in the middle of the room and proceeded to chatter. I hastily went through the *'Chakap perlahan-perlahan'* (Speak more slowly) routine and after that we became quite matey.

Another Shell employee asked if we would like to go for a run around the island so Roy and I climbed into his truck with him and his 'housekeeper', a rather ugly but good-tempered Chinese girl who acted as go-between with the natives. We drove through the picturesque *kedai* or bazaar. These are identical throughout Malaya and are miniature replicas of a Singapore side street with about a dozen poky little shops on each side of the road. Each one is like its neighbour, selling anything from dried fish and '100-year-old' eggs (eggs preserved in their shells by covering them with a thick black mud – three to six months old but no more) to exotic *sarongs*, sandals and toiletries.

We drove several miles into the interior of the island along quiet roads bordered by thick jungle. As in Singapore everything was luxuriantly green, almost as though one were wearing green-tinted glasses. Every now and then we passed people whom I took to be Malays but who, I learned, were Kedayans. There were men on bicycles; girls and women, colourfully dressed in *sarong kebaya* and carrying baskets; naked children, the colour of honey, playing in the ditches on each side of the road; a young man, resplendent in clean white clothes and a smart *songkok* carrying his beautifully-saronged girl-friend to a wedding on the carrier of his bicycle. (In the Far East, girls always ride pillion sideways, never astride.) There were workers from the paddy fields going home after the day's labour, leading their teams of water buffalo or *kerbau*. These animals are quite repulsive, seen for the first time. They are rather like a hippopotamus with a dark grey, tough, leathery skin, usually caked with mud from their wallowings in slimy ditches, and their squat legs seem to have difficulty supporting the heavy rotund body. Their ridged horns curve horizontally to the rear in a wide arc and a ring in the snout enables them to be led by their driver.

We turned off the road and bumped along a rough track till we reached a group of native houses in a small clearing. They were built up on stilts and hens scratched in the dirt underneath. A woman came out of one with her little daughter, a solemn-eyed youngster with silky hair curling around her shoulders. Our Shell man asked a question.

'*Sana!*' replied the mother, pointing with her lips in the Malay fashion.

The little girl was despatched as our guide to find watermelons and squirrels. These animals are popular with the Chinese who make a succulent dish from them. Apparently they are very destructive, gouging holes in the coconuts and draining the milk. Clever little things! I hoped we wouldn't find any.

The small clearing in the jungle was the most delightful place with lush grass and groves of graceful coconut palms screening the few thatched houses. The pandanus provides leaves for thatching. The leaves are arranged in overlapping layers attached to four-foot lengths of wood which are then fastened to the battens on the roof. It is called *attap* and the standard pattern of bungalow found throughout Borneo and the *kampongs* of Malaya is called *kajang* and *attap*.

It would be hard to imagine a more peaceful spot so far removed from the turmoil of the outside world, yet it was only four years since it was a Japanese stronghold. Our guide told us that they were so firmly entrenched here, defying all attempts to shoot them out, that the Australians got a bulldozer and ploughed them in. A shadow fell over the sunny clearing.

On the way back to the Rest House we stopped to pick gardenias from wayside bushes. Remembering the cost of a single bloom whenever I went to a Ball in Melbourne, I picked and picked, intoxicated by the heady scent.

I wore some in my hair that night when we dined with the Shannons. It was a large dinner party and included some men from Singapore. One of them promised me a job whenever I wanted one. It was a tempting idea. Singapore had completely captivated me. But first I had to get to Seria.

In the morning I woke and raising myself on my elbow peered sleepily over the windowsill. The sun was just rising, pouring molten gold over the horizon, the sea was running with gold, the islands were ingots and the sand was gold dust. A few yards away was a tawny bungalow and a golden-skinned boy was sweeping the verandah with a coconut-fibre broom. I sank back with a contented sigh and went back to sleep.

Roy woke me with a shout of exultation and said there was a Landing Craft at the wharf which could take us to Seria. We packed hurriedly, drove to the wharf, boarded the small vessel and embarked on the most delightful voyage.

Chugging out of Labuan harbour past native huts built in the water, we spent the next four hours weaving through islands which would suddenly materialize out of the heat haze. Labuan was only five miles off the North Borneo coast but it was more like twenty miles to the mouth of the Brunei River. This wide and placid waterway was bordered by steep, wooded hills with native villages coming into sight as the river turned. The Malays here are essentially a river-bred race and are expert boatmen. We saw every variety of craft skimming past us and I was particularly tickled by the sight of a long *perahu* or canoe being paddled by three large coolie hats, all that was visible of its occupants.

The Landing Craft was to load stone for five hours at Brunei Town, the capital of the Sultanate of Brunei, and would then return down the river to the open sea to follow the coast south for eleven hours to Miri, Seria's port. From there we would have several hours by road to Seria.

However, as soon as we docked at Brunei Town a radio message was handed to us which said that a jeep tool-truck had left Seria at noon to pick us up and take us there by road. We were jubilant! I guessed correctly that Pete was doing all he could to get me there in time for the King's Birthday celebrations so that the orchestra would have a pianist. His usual pianist was married and didn't like leaving his wife alone during the night's dancing.

We disembarked, passed through Customs and had a quick look around the town. Brunei Town was quiet and peaceful and had a perfect example of a *kampong ayer* or water village. On one side of the river on the slopes of a green hill were the homes of the British Resident, the Public Works Engineer and the Doctor. On the other side was the astounding conglomeration of river houses built on high stilts in the water and jammed together so closely that I shud-

dered at the thought of what one dropped match might do. Why did they build there when there was so much room on dry land? Easy sanitation is one explanation but perhaps it was also a simple historical matter of defence, a moat with drawbridges of bamboo. Even when a house became decrepit and fell down, another was built on the same spot. Boats of course were the only means of transport.

We went to the Rest House for a clean up, a Rest House apparently being the Malayan equivalent of a hotel or boarding house. I was shown to the bathroom and there had my introduction to bathing in Borneo. It was a square room with a concrete floor and in one corner a large waist-high ceramic jar about ten feet in circumference. It was glazed a rich brown with an ochre dragon coiling around the outside. It was full of cold water. I undressed and with difficulty clambered over the rim of the jar and into the water. This

was the way to bathe, I thought, feeling like an ancient Roman. Sitting up to my neck in the cold water I bathed slowly, soaping away the fatigue of travel, then climbed out and dressed. Much later I learned that the receptacle is called a Shanghai jar and is used merely as a reservoir of water. Bathing is done by dipping water out of it, pouring it over oneself, soaping and rinsing off with more water. I still blush when I think how I immersed my hot and sweaty body in all those gallons of clean water!

At six o'clock our jeep arrived. We left just as the sun was setting. Right down the west coast of Borneo there is a nightly vision of such magnificence that words are unable to describe it. Take an artist's palette, daub it with scarlet and crimson, streak it with gold, draw paths of turquoise and black through it and you may get an idea of a Borneo sunset.

It was only ninety miles to Seria but the trip usually took three or four hours because the unsurfaced road was bad in places. At eight o'clock we reached a wide river and had to wait over an hour for a ferry to come from a village three miles away. This was the Danau ferry and it consisted of a tiny motor launch pulling two *perahus* lashed together with a platform of planks. The jeep drove onto this and we sailed away upstream to the village. Only the sputtering of the launch engine broke the heavy silence of the wide river, the jungle black along each bank.

Leaving the ferry on the opposite bank we followed a track to the beach and covered the remaining forty-five miles along the hard sand, splashing through small creeks or *sungeis* which flowed into the sea. It was quite exciting as the tide was coming in fast and we had only about ten yards of firm sand on which to drive. Our headlights cast a beam ahead of us and our *syce* drove like Jehu, spinning the wheel madly in order to avoid logs or creeks but rarely slackening speed to less than forty miles an hour. Little crabs scurried sideways, skittering across the sand to avoid our wheels. Always in front of us, like the Israelites' pillar of fire, was a bright glow on the horizon. It came from the flares on the oilfield where surplus natural gas is burnt. Soon we could smell oil and after splashing through the last *sungei*, hit a bitumen road. A little further and we could see the flares burning fiercely against the dark sky. They will always remain my dominant memory of Seria with their angry red glow and flickering shadows every night.

We were now on the outskirts of the oilfield. An approaching truck skidded to a halt amidst loud shouts and Pete leapt out to greet us.

'G'day Roy! How are you, Wen?'

I hugged my brother with joy. My constant companion when I lived at home, I missed him dreadfully when he went abroad. I looked at him in the light of the flares. His lean body was dressed in oilfields uniform – open-necked shirt, shorts and sandals. He was very suntanned and his brown hair was bleached by sun and salt water. He told us excitedly how he'd been pulling strings to speed up our arrival.

'Thank God you're in time for King's Birthday! We'll have some great music tomorrow.'

He looked at me closely. 'You're looking pretty tired and wan, Wen. I'll take you to the Brockfields'.'

It had been a very long day. The excitement and stimulation of the journey suddenly left me and I just wanted to sleep. We drove to the *kajang* bungalow of Ken and Audrey Brockfield who were to be my hosts. Ken was small and nuggety. He supervised the maintenance of mechanical equipment on the field and was also Pete's drummer. Audrey was blonde and pretty and I recognised her as having been at school with me. They had a young baby, Susan.

'You can see her in the morning,' said Audrey firmly. 'You're going straight to bed, my girl! We'll gossip tomorrow.'

She showed me to a spacious bedroom with a four foot wide tropical divan and mosquito net. A door led off to a bathroom shared by both bedrooms. I had to remember to snib the door into the other bedroom and be sure to unsnib it on leaving the bathroom.

Pete's last words were that he'd see me at four o'clock the next afternoon. The men worked from 6.30 a.m. until 11.30 and from 1 p.m. till 4, making the most of the cool hours.

'You just settle in and rest and I'll take you to the Club tomorrow night.'

Chapter 3

'Tanjong Seria Tepi Laut'

Settling and resting didn't sound like me! I was dying to get out and start seeing Brunei. In my previous travels I'd never wasted a minute. But Pete had said four o'clock so I curbed my impatience and sat around, talking to Audrey and writing letters.

When Pete arrived he took me for a tour of the field in his truck. What I saw confirmed what I'd seen from the air. It was still a rough and ready oilfield with no frills.

Pete explained. 'During the war the Japs occupied the field and in '45 when the Aussies were liberating Borneo, the Japs set fire to all the wells. There were thirty-five of them burning at one stage but the Australian Army engineers extinguished them one by one. Did a tremendous job and lots of 'em were offered jobs later by Shell.'

The young engineers who arrived to take the place of the Army had to get the oilfield operational again. Building was of prime importance – a new power station, pump station, staff quarters, commissariat, hospital; everything necessary for an oilfield to function efficiently. Speed was essential and there was plenty of local wood as well as palm trees, so some buildings were made of wood while *kajang* and *attap* were used for housing, even for the General Manager. The larger constructions used concrete and Pete was Construction Engineer in charge of building the new power station.

What surprised me most during the drive was that there were no forests of oil derricks as one sees in photographs of Texas. When a well went into production the drilling derrick, one hundred and twenty feet high, was removed leaving only a 'Christmas Tree', an intricate arrangement of valves and gauges to control the flow of gas and oil from the well into pipes leading to collecting stations.

The work force on the field seemed to be multinational. The drivers and operators of mechanical equipment were Malays, Indians were office clerks and formed the drilling crews, Chinese were tradesmen and clerks, and Dyaks were labourers and worked with the seismic and survey teams in the jungle.

I was intrigued by my first sight of the legendary Dyaks. Small and muscular in build, they wore only a loincloth, although when working on the oilrigs they sported shorts and shirts and either battered straw hats or pith helmets like the *tuan*, the white boss. Without these unnatural clothes they were singularly beautiful and had a most startling appearance. Their sleekly-oiled hair was cut in a pudding-basin fringe in front, the back hair hanging to the waist or tied in a knot on the nape of the neck. Their eyebrows were plucked in a delicate arch and their necks and shoulders were tattooed in a manner that increased their choked, surprised look. Their backs, arms and legs were also tattooed, and strapped around their waists were *parangs*, sword-like jungle knives hilted with human bone and tufted with human hair and carried in a sheath of woven rattan. Their earlobes, slit and weighted in childhood, swung in long loops down to their shoulders, although with the impact of American films, many were seeking surgery to cut off their lobes and restore their ears to match those of the film stars they saw. Some had their front teeth capped with gold by Chinese dentists, often with red or green inserts of hearts, diamonds, clubs and spades. Pete told me they were happy child-like people, easily provoked to laughter and extremely curious.

'Sometimes I'll be in my house and I'll look up and see a couple of Dyaks standing at the door, arms around each other, just staring at me. They'll wander in and perhaps squat on the floor, watching every movement. Some *mems* find it very unnerving! They'll look at pictures, peer into rooms, pick up ornaments, sometimes quite openly taking something pretty, but then they believe in common ownership and share everything.'

These Dyaks were not indigenous to Brunei but had migrated north from Sarawak in search of work, leaving their womenfolk behind.

We reached the Club. Like the bungalows it was made of round poles, *kajang* and *attap* and provided a large airy space for sitting, drinking and dancing with a dais in one corner for a band. There was a library, a restaurant, two bars, billiard tables and a barber's shop. Though not luxurious, the Club was the centre of oilfield life. When the men finished work, life began – swimming, tennis, golf, football (oh, the ludicrous long shorts the pommie soccer players wore!), hockey, softball, rowing and sailing during the daylight hours and dancing, parties or films at night.

Seria was essentially a young people's community. When Pete first arrived at the beginning of 1946 there were no white women although a few senior wives arrived soon afterwards. By the time I came in 1949 there was a lively community of young marrieds, mostly under thirty-five. I was surprised to see that the heads of departments were all fairly young men who held very responsible positions. Nearly all of the wives were either pregnant or had young babies. Conditions were ideal for having children as there were *amahs* to wash the nappies and baby-sit and cooks to provide the meals.

Audrey's Chinese cook was very handsome, clean and neat and an inspired cook. All Chinese cooks, I was to learn, had an outstanding virtue. They could rustle up a meal from nothing and no matter how late the *tuan* came back from the Club, the food would be piping hot and unspoiled. The meal could also be miraculously stretched to feed two or three extra mouths.

'*Lagi dua orang*, cookie! *Boleh-kah?*' (Two more people . . . can do?)

'*Boleh!*' (Can!)

Audrey's cook made superb dishes from whatever he found in the refrigerator and used his imagination in the way he served them. He also baked beautifully and we had fresh warm cakes for afternoon tea every day. It was from him that I learned the easy and decorative way of peeling a pineapple. The seeds on the outside of the pineapple are arranged in downward sloping diagonals, so if you cut them out in sloping rows, you're left with an attractive fruit with spiral grooves. Cookie would then cut the pineapple into rings and reassemble it to stand on a plate. And what pineapples! Even the cores were tender and sweet.

The Chinese *amah*, whose name I never knew, was plump and comfortable-looking with a broad smiling Buddha face. Her eyes disappeared into slits and her generous smile showed lots of gold teeth. (The Chinese way of putting money away for their burial.) Her thick black hair was coiled into a large bun at the back of her head. Unlike the traditional Chinese *amahs* who wear black wide-legged trousers of mid-calf length and a starched white jacket, this one was a Straits Chinese and influenced by Malay fashions. She wore a black *sarong* and a colourful floral *kebaya* or jacket. The night I arrived I dumped some dirty clothes onto the floor intending to wash them in the morning, but while I was having breakfast she slipped into my room, folded the mosquito net, tidied the havoc of my scattered cases and removed my soiled clothes and shoes to be cleaned. This happened every morning so I had to be careful and ration my laundry so as not to give her too much work, but the heat was so great that I had to change frequently. Underwear became wet through with perspiration very quickly. (It was essential to wear only cotton next to the skin as synthetic materials induced an irritating rash of prickly heat wherever garments fitted closely. My scanties made from panels of nylon parachutes were unwearable.) I thought of doing the washing myself but Audrey said that would result in great loss of face for Amah. Obviously if I did it, it meant that I didn't consider her washing good enough.

It was a joy to watch Amah. Just walking through the room carrying a bucket of warm water for the baby's bath, she was the epitome of grace. Barefooted, she walked regally, one arm extended at her side for balance. She was about fifty and had six children but Asian women never lose their superb carriage.

The oilfield staff bungalows were simply built, mostly to the same pattern. One entered by steps from the garden into a large lounge, open on two sides – a large verandah really, with bamboo 'chicks' to raise or lower against the weather. A raised section at the back of this served as a dining room with the bedrooms off it. There were no windows, only hinged flaps opening outwards, propped open with poles. Nearly every house had its walls decorated with Dyak hats – large, conical hats of woven palmleaf with geometrical patterns in red, black and natural straw-coloured leaves. A variation on this was the hat from Bintulu which was more interesting with tiny pearl buttons sewn on it.

Down some steps at the back were the kitchen and the servants' quarters. Everything was provided by 'Joe Shell' – furniture, refrigerator, gas stove, cutlery, crockery, glassware – as there was no way of buying household requirements locally. Gas and electricity were provided free as were oil and petrol, but there were no private cars, only Company vehicles. Buses, telephones, cinema shows and medical attention were all free but salaries were barely sufficient to pay for an inexpensive furlough every two or three years.

It was a great life though, especially for those who liked sport, and the majority of the young men renewed their contracts over and over again. They were mostly Australians with some British and a sprinkling of Dutch. There was an interesting difference in attitude between the Dutch and the Australians. Because of the economic situation in Holland, a job with Royal Dutch Shell was the height of the Dutchmen's ambition. Their first loyalty was to the job. They worked hard and took great care not to fall foul of the bosses or in any way to jeopardize the renewal of their contracts. The Australians worked hard too but viewed their work with a much more independent eye. Loyalty to their families came first. They would not tolerate any injustice or malpractice and if their contracts were not renewed as a result of their attitude, there would be plenty more jobs at home.

• • •

The King's Birthday was one of the main celebrations apart from Christmas and New Year. The others were Australia Day and Queen Wilhelmina's Birthday. The 'pommies' turned on an English Fair with sideshows and stalls, fish and chips, pies and coffee. There were several excellent cabaret items and dancing till dawn. The Seria Swingsters provided the music – Pete on clarinet and trombone, Ken Brockfield on drums, Reg Sung on saxophone and excellent guitar from Roy Clarke. I played piano. Vocals were by Filipino Reggie Azcona who accompanied himself on the guitar. It was wonderful for me to play jazz with Pete again. We had been closely involved with the revival of Dixieland Jazz in the early '40s and Pete had played trombone with Graeme Bell, the leading name in Australian jazz. When the Bell band was going abroad to play at the Prague Youth Festival, Pete had to decide what his career would be, music or engineering. He chose engineering and went to Borneo with Shell. The last time we had played together was when I came home from Darwin to play in the 2nd Australian Jazz Convention in Melbourne in December 1947. When I sat down to play in Seria, the intervening time was as nothing. Pete and I knew each other's music so intimately that we just slipped back into our accustomed parts.

The next day was a holiday and there was a regatta and sports meeting at Kuala Belait, the town at the mouth of the Belait river eight miles away. 'Squalor blight', Seria folk called it, and it wasn't a very exciting town but I went walking around the *kedai*, taking in hundreds of new sights and smells and buying my first *sarong*, an exquisite piece of turquoise cloth with tiger lilies and butterflies in coral. It was terribly hard to choose from all the beautiful lengths of cloth hung so temptingly over the footpath. There were expensive *batiks* but I found their colours drab. There were the ceremonial men's *sarongs* with silver-thread work on purple or emerald or cerise and there were the everyday ones with every shade of colour and variation of design one could imagine. No two were the same and the flowers, birds and butterflies which patterned the colourful cloth were not representational but imaginative fantasy creations, birds with long curling tail feathers, fairy-tale flowers and exotic butterflies. Their patterns were so distinctively oriental that I was shocked to see printed along the selvedge of one piece of cloth 'Made in Manchester'!

Sarongs consisted of a two-yard length of wide material which was then sewn up into a tube. There were various methods of tying them. Malay women in the *kampongs* merely knotted them across their breasts. In the towns they were overlapped and knotted around the waist or folded to make an inverted pleat before knotting, and a bodice and the delicate voile jacket were worn over the top of the body. An alternative to knotting was rolling the upper edge over a couple of times. (This was the method favoured by Pete and other oilmen who slept in *sarongs*. Few men who have been to Malaya will ever sleep in pyjamas again.)

Malay women will sometimes wear a second *sarong* over the head as a protection against the sun, using it also as a carrying cloth for a baby on the back. Nowadays the svelte *sarongs* worn by young women in Malaysia are tailored and zipped to fit neatly on the hips and around the waist as, I suspect, was Dorothy Lamour's but village life was still unsophisticated in 1949.

In the *kedai* I was also tempted by the Brunei silver on display. Superb belts of silver links with ornate engraved buckles, bracelets, earrings and brooches, liqueur jiggers, circular cigarette tins (to take a Players tin of fifty) and flat cigarette boxes were chased with intricate designs and all very beautiful. Not so the gold jewellery which looked very yellow and brassy to me. I didn't know then that

Chinese gold is pure and without the alloy which makes European jewellery more durable and gives it the 'old gold' colour which we prefer.

That night Pete threw a big party for me. Guests were invited to *makan kechil* (pronounced kitchee), meaning literally 'small food' as opposed to a banquet or *makan besar*. I learnt not to let that word 'kechil' deceive me. We started by eating dozens of *satay*, the vendor squatting by his brazier out on the lawn, followed by dim sims,* interesting savouries, sausages, prawn crackers, crisps and peanuts, washed down by an endless supply of beer, wines and spirits.

Pete was obviously concerned to keep me occupied during the time he was at work and he announced that he had arranged for me to take lessons from the golf professional.

'Me? Golf?'

I'd always associated golf with croquet. It was something elderly people played, hitting a small ball into the distance and then walking sedately to look for it.

'Yes, it's a wonderful game. Time you learned to play.'

I was shaken but next day he took me to Panaga Golf Course, a nine-hole course with smooth greens surrounded by graceful casuarinas and shade trees. He introduced me to the professional, Yin Fatt, a sturdy middle-aged Chinese with a brush haircut and very muscled calves. He possessed one golf club, a No. 4 iron, but could beat all comers with it.

Pete had borrowed some lady's clubs for me and whistled up a *budak* (little boy). Dozens of attractive Malay urchins besieged each player as he arrived, begging to be caddy. My *budak* was a smiling eager lad called Pe. He shouldered the bag and led the way to the first tee. Yin Fatt showed me how to stand and how to drive off. I did it a couple of times till he was satisfied and we walked off to find the ball. Pe was already standing guard over it, having retrieved the unsuccessful balls, some from the hazardous *sungei*

---

* the Australian term for *siumai*, minced pork dumplings.

which crossed the course in places, and proffered me a club as I approached. Like western golf caddies he was an expert and always knew which club was needed for a particular shot. I took it and addressed the ball.

'Don' dlop de sole!' yelled Yin Fatt. 'Keep da lie on the fee!'

I stared at him, uncomprehending.

'Glip the crub and f'low floo! So!'

He hit the ball cleanly and it soared into the air and came down two hundred yards ahead.

'See? Keep da lie on the fee!'

These inexplicable lessons continued for several weeks. I never did find out what 'dlop de sole' meant or what a 'lie' was and why I should keep it on the 'fee' but I did manage to get around the course fairly well. Some of Pete's friends even asked me to play a round with them, probably at his urging. Very soon I was won over and in no time was joining in the interminable post-mortem discussions over cold drinks. I have never known a game which could be

discussed afterwards in such detail, each player recounting in turn the hole by hole progress of his game that afternoon, and yet no one ever seemed bored.

In the mornings I swam or went with Audrey to coffee parties at other *mems'* houses, sometimes as early as nine o'clock. I had never heard of coffee parties. Tea parties in the afternoon, yes, but coffee parties in the morning! It was a strange experience for me. In Australia I earned my living and had no social contact with women. Anyway, married women there spent the morning doing their housework or shopping. It wasn't the time for entertaining. So I found it odd to sit around for hours talking to a group of wives. They were pleasant young women but as a single girl it was hard for me to join in their conversation about husbands, babies and servants.

By noon it was very hot and after going back to Audrey's for lunch, we slept till four when the men returned for afternoon tea. After that I went to Panaga for golf then back for dinner at eight or to a party or a film. Films were shown on the *padang* or sports field in a rather hilarious atmosphere. On one side of a large screen the Europeans sat in chairs. On the other side the Eurasian white-collar workers sat in chairs, while the Asiatic work force sat on the grass. The temperature of the air was the same as one's skin, neither hot nor cold. Every now and then there would be a groan from the audience as the film ignited and the projector stopped. There were other interruptions as reels were changed but no one seemed to mind.

On Saturday nights we played music for dancing at the Club. Our signature tune was 'Sarawaki', the song written by Harry Roy for his wife, Princess Pearl of Sarawak, followed by 'Back to Borneo'. We also played 'Hawaii calls', changing the words to 'Seria calls with a message of *selamat*' (peace) and later in the evening all the dancing couples would join in singing:

'*Tanjong Seria, tepi laut,*   (At Seria by the sea,
Jikalau suka, boleh ikut . . .'   If you wish to, follow me . . .)

Most of the time we played Dixieland jazz, slow waltzes and tangos, and when we rested there were records. I heard once more the lovely 'Reflections on the water' which I'd danced to in Singapore and a haunting rumba called 'Nightingale'. Inevitably the pommies would start singing. I heard songs that I'd never heard before, Cockney songs like 'I've got a luvverly bunch o' cokernuts', 'Knock 'em in the Old Kent Road' and 'My old man said follow the van'. Not to be outdone, the Scots would reply with 'Roamin' in the gloamin'', 'Wee Deoch an' Doruis' and 'I belong to Glasgie' or, if the hour were late and the singing unbridled, 'The Ball of Kirriemuir'. I can still see dear Haggis, a tall, rawboned Scot, bellowing the songs in his broad accent. He was drowned some months later in the river at Miri.

On Sundays there was always curry tiffin, *de rigueur* for Sunday lunch throughout South-East Asia, and I shall always remember my initiation into this elaborate ritual. I heaped a mound of steaming rice onto my plate then ladled on the curry – it might be beef, chicken, fish or prawn – and then added portions of up to two dozen *sambals* or side dishes. These included assorted fruits such as *papaya*, mango, banana, pineapple, shredded fresh coconut and sultanas; savoury or piquant dishes such as '100 year old' eggs, dried prawns, 'stinky' fish, Bombay duck (a kind of dried salted fish), peanuts whole and crumbled, crisp-fried curly onions (the small red *bawang merah*) and oddments like fried bread cubes. By this time the mound on my plate resembled the Great Pyramid so, finishing off with dobs of mango chutney, I retired to a corner and devoured it. A second helping was expected and after that I slid down in my chair and became rather somnolent.

There was still dessert to come. The traditional pudding to follow curry and the perfect antidote for a fiery mouth is *gula malacca* or Malaccan sugar. Each guest has an individual ice-cold moulded shape of sago. Over this was ladled melted Malaccan sugar (something like golden syrup but much more interesting, with a flavour of rich toasted sugar) and thick coconut cream. This is not what we call coconut 'milk', the water inside a coconut, but a thick cream obtained by infusing grated coconut in boiling water and then squeezing it until the white cream runs out. The combination of bland, innocuous cold sago and the rich sauces was quite heavenly.

Sometimes I was invited to *nasi goreng* or *mee goreng* instead of curry. As at curry tiffin we all sat around talking, the men drinking beer, the women with gin tonics or 'stengahs' (half pegs of whisky) until about three o'clock at which time, when we had almost despaired of being fed, we were summoned to the table and the cookie came in with a large oval meat dish heaped high with a mound of fried rice or fried noodles. It was a most impressive dish, not only because of its size but because of the rich variety of ingredients visible in it. On top were liberal garnishings of strips of omelette, chopped spring onion and coriander and sometimes fried eggs. Around the edge of the dish were tinder-crisp *kropak* or prawn crackers.

After these gargantuan repasts many people went home and collapsed on their beds. I found this was useless as I woke at about seven in the evening feeling dreadful. It was much better to go off and swim or play tennis or golf before finally succumbing in the evening.

In July I moved to the *kajang* of another Australian couple, Ernie and Muriel Martin. Ernie was tall and benign with receding hair and spectacles and was the engineer in charge of the Seria Pump Station. Muriel was a small sedate woman who had been a nursing sister in Australia. Her house was impeccably tidy and her manner precise. Childless, they spoiled me. Muriel decided I was too thin and made me drink an eggnog every breakfast, two eggs whipped up with sugar and vanilla. I began to gain weight and no longer did Ken Brockfield address me as 'Slim', although Pete still kept up the 'pale and wan' nonsense.

When we weren't going out to coffee parties, I worked hard at my Malay. I found it a fascinating language, full of delightful portman-

teau words. For example, *'mata'* is an eye. *'Mata hari'*, the name of
the famous woman spy in World War I, means the eye of the day –
the sun. *'Mata-mata'*, two eyes watching, means a policeman and
'mata-mata gelap', two eyes in the dark, is a detective. Bazaar Malay
was simplicity itself with very little grammar and no changes in
verbs. I go, you go, he goes, we go, they go . . . the word 'go' is
always *'pergi'*, pronounced piggy. *'Pergi mana?'* (where are you going?) was the standard conversational gambit after the greeting
'Apa khabar?' (what news?) *'Khabar baik'* (good news) one re-
sponded, then *'makan angin'* (I'm eating the wind . . . going for a
walk). Plurals were simply formed by repeating the word and to
save time writing it twice, one merely added the digit 2 to the word.
For instance, *anak* is a child, *anak*^{2} signifies children. The most important word was *'tid'apa'* – it doesn't matter or never mind; something like *mañana* but without the same sense of urgency. Most hot
countries seem to have a word like this, which always sums up a
philosophical unhurried attitude to life.

I bought a charming book of Malayan Nursery Rhymes by 'Haji'
Hamilton, an Englishman living in Malaya. All our English nursery
rhymes were translated into Malay, not only the words but the
settings. For example, 'The sheep's in the meadow, the cow's in the
corn', was translated as *'Kambing masok padang, lembu makan padi'*.
(The sheep's in the field, the cow's eating the rice.) The illustrations
similarly depicted Malay versions of the characters shown in our
nursery rhymes. 'Lucy Locket' was a demure little Malay girl in
sarong kebaya, carrying her green bamboo sunshade, and the old
woman who lived in a shoe was shown chasing her urchins, in
sarongs and *songkoks*, while in the background was her shoe, a heel-
less Asian slipper. 'Here we go round the mulberry bush' became a
frolic around a banana tree. Every page was a delight and I sent off
a copy to my doctor friend in Perth who had so enjoyed learning
the language.

Although my vocabulary was increasing rapidly, I lacked sufficient practice. I'd work out in advance a sentence to deliver to

cookie but his reply would be so rapid and unintelligible that I despaired of ever being able to conduct a conversation.

Muriel told me in her factual, non-excitable manner of her difficulties when first learning the language.

'I was in the kitchen one day and saw a stream of ants coming from behind the stove. "Quick, cookie!" I shouted in Malay. "Come and throw water behind the stove!" Unfortunately I didn't know that *buang ayer*, literally "throw water", is the term for "urinate". Cookie stared at me in utter disbelief as I told him to urinate behind the stove!'

•   •   •

Swimming at the beach was enjoyable but not very exciting. The water was usually calm and the sand was good but at four degrees from the Equator you don't lie on it to sunbathe. There was a small belt of undergrowth between the sand and the Vs of houses with some lofty casuarinas providing the only shade. Although seabathing is more invigorating than freshwater bathing, I always miss having something to dive off and a goal to swim to. It's all very well striking off in the general direction of Singapore but after a while you have to turn back. I prefer to swim between river banks or the sides of a swimming bath.

In August a sand pump started operating on the beach. It was like a giant vacuum cleaner, sucking up the sand and taking it inland to fill swampy areas for building sites. It gradually created a large circular pit into which the sea flowed. Voilà! We had a swimming pool. This was infinitely more satisfactory than the South China Sea and we started planning a Swimming Carnival for the first week in September.

•   •   •

Muriel and I shared a birthday in August. It was my twenty-third and the most enjoyable one I'd had for years. Ernie and Muriel threw a party that night and later in the week Pete entertained twelve of us to a Chinese banquet at a restaurant. Whenever we ate at the *kedai* we called for a basin of boiling water and stood our chopsticks in it. A simple hygienic precaution but I wondered if it offended the Chinese restaurant owner.

We had a splendid meal of eight courses: dim sims, chicken rolls, mushroom soup, shark's fin soup, sliced cuttlefish (most succulent and tasting like turkey), roast duck (completely filleted and then the meat replaced so it still looked like a duck), *nasi goreng* and finally, a huge baked fish lying on a dish, its glassy eyes staring sightlessly at us, its skin crisp and seasoned with delicious sauces. I have since enjoyed many Chinese banquets of even more courses but that was my first and I remember it well.

Saturday morning at the Club was *satay* time. Pete held the oil-field record for eating over ninety of them at one sitting. We never understood where he put them. Thin as a lath and quick in his movements (the Malays nicknamed him *Tuan Tikus*, Mr Mouse), oilfield life seemed to agree with him.

He shared a *kajang* on the beach with another bachelor. They were looked after by a splendid 'boy' called Chee Fong, a quiet middle-aged man. This term 'boy' is an affectionate rather than a patronising form of address. It is derived from the Indian word 'bhai' meaning younger brother and is used throughout the Far East.

Always a heavy sleeper, Pete found it hard to be roused at 5.30 a.m. each morning. Chee Fong would open the mosquito net, place a cup of tea on the bedside table and say respectfully:

'*Tuan! Pukul lima satengah, tuan!*' (Half past-five!)

A grunt from Pete.

A little later the silent wraith at his bedside would shake him again.

'*Tuan! Pukul lima empat-puloh minit, tuan!*' (Five-forty!)

A slight movement under the sheet.

'*Tuan! Pukul lima empat-puloh lima minit . . . pukul lima lima-puloh minit . . .*'

Through the ebbing waves of sleep Pete would struggle to rise, his drowsy brain striving to translate the interminable droning of Malay. It wasn't until the succinct words '*Pukul enam, tuan!*' (Six o'clock!) that he would leap out in a panic and rush to dress.

One of Pete's friends, Stan, was showing interest in me, but alas, I was not attracted. As usual, the handsome ones I fancied didn't look in my direction. Stan was in his late twenties with thick black hair and face sunburned to a dark mahogany shade. He had a strong northern England accent and couldn't have been more pleasant. He just had no romantic interest for me. He offered to take me on a boat trip up the Baram river. I was longing to go up-river to see some long-houses and natives untouched by civilization. The Dyaks one saw about the oilfield in their dirty shorts and singlets could hardly be considered Borneo's noble savage. I yearned to see them in their natural habitat so I accepted Stan's invitation and one Saturday morning we drove south to the Baram river. There was no village at the mouth of this great river, just a small Chinese shop stocking staple food, beer and soft drinks. The English are called a nation of shopkeepers but they can't hold a candle to the Chinese. Wherever a cluster of houses is built or a ferry crosses a river, there an enterprising Chinese will be sure to set up a stall.

As eager as a schoolboy, Stan led me down to the jetty where a *perahu* was moored. Misgivings assailed me as I saw it. He had furnished it like a boat at the Henley Regatta. Up in the prow, away from the boatman handling the outboard engine, were rugs and soft cushions arranged enticingly. I was alarmed. Stan might have his idea of a river trip but it wasn't the same as mine! Oh dear, it would have to be the Love of the Great Outdoors routine again . . . keeping up a lively interest in everything I saw, darting from one side of the boat to the other, bird-watching . . . anything but reclining on those cushions.

'No, I'm not a bit tired, thanks!'

Inevitably the atmosphere became rather fraught as Stan saw his chances disappearing. He was a surveyor and we stopped now and then so that he could go ashore and inspect a *rentas*, a path which had been driven into the jungle. These had to be kept open for his work force and guarded against the perpetual encroachment of the jungle. When we set off again I busied myself sketching our helmsman crouched in the stern. He was a Dyak and although he was wearing an old shirt and shorts, the elaborate tattooing on his thigh was visible just beneath the edge of his shorts. His ear lobes were pierced but his hair was cut short, a concession to western custom.

After about three hours travelling up-river with nothing to see but the jungle crowding along each bank and an occasional Chinese shop at a crossing, we rounded yet another bend and this time saw a ramshackle wooden jetty.

'Here we are!' shouted Stan, as a motley assortment of mangy dogs set up a vociferous welcome from the bank. 'This is Rasau.'

Extending about two hundred yards along the bank was a Dyak longhouse in which forty or more families lived. A number of children came shrieking down to the river to greet us, tumbling into the water and pushing our *perahu* into the bank. The *tuai rumah*, the headman of the longhouse, sedately descended the notched log which served as steps. Women peeped shyly around the corners of the windows.

These people were Ibans or Sea-Dyaks, a term which seems a misnomer so far up river but originates in their ancestors' piratical custom of setting off in huge longboats and fearlessly chasing trading ships out to sea.

We were ushered inside with much ceremony and offered drinks. Stan was given *arak*, the native rice wine, but I managed to refuse without causing offence and accepted some bottled fizz. Stan carried on an unintelligible conversation in Malay with the men while I made quick sketches of some of the residents of the house. I

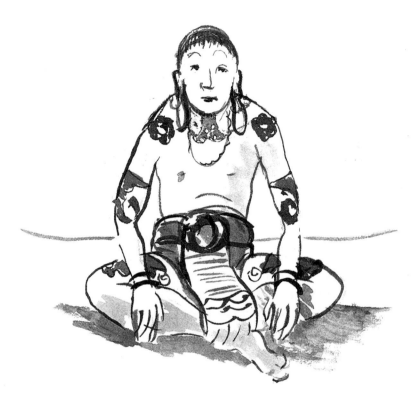

was fascinated by the tattoos which ornamented the men's bodies, the large rosettes which covered each shoulder, the heavy decoration of the throat which extended right up to the lower jaw and down to the salt cellars of the neck ending in a swallow-tail, the elaborate patterns on arm and thigh. The length of the ear lobes varied from a small loop into which one could fit a thimble, to shoulder-length ones on some men in their twenties or thirties, to those of an elderly man which swung halfway down his torso. The backs of his hands and the joints of his fingers were covered with tattoos indicating the number of heads he had taken in battle. The White Rajahs of Sarawak suppressed head-hunting but during the war there was a bounty on Japanese heads and the Dyaks needed little encouragement to go hunting again.

Only one or two women emerged to see the strangers and they had hurriedly covered their breasts. We were after all only three hours from civilization. The Dyaks further up-river are not so inhibited. I wished I could talk to the women but my Malay was not good enough so I had to content myself with smiling and looking friendly.

We were sitting on the floor of the broad corridor which ran the length of the longhouse. Rooms opened off it all the way along, each one occupied by a family. The corridor was the communal meeting place and sitting room, shared also by dozens of mangy, flea-bitten pi-dogs. Underneath the house pigs grunted and cockerels crowed which, together with the yelping of dogs as they were kicked out of the way and the crying of babies, filled the air with perpetual noise. Up among the rafters hung clusters of skulls, prestigious proof of successful battle. In the days before the White Rajahs brought peace and prosperity to the territory, before a man could take a wife he had to take a head. Consequently there was a brisk trade. The severed heads were boiled up to remove hair (used to tuft the *parang*) and skin and then the lower jaw of each skull was removed and the cranium enclosed in a lattice of rattan from which dark eyeless caverns looked out. Sometimes mirrors were placed in the eye sockets, which was rather ghoulish.

I had been told that it was better not to spend the night in a longhouse or, if one had to, to try and get to sleep before the attentions of the bedbugs in the sleeping mats became too persistent. It seemed a pity not to put it to the test but we were expected back in Seria that evening. All the inhabitants turned out to push us off and wave until we disappeared around the bend.

•　　•　　•

The lotus-eating existence in Seria was working a change in me. No longer my active self, I was becoming torpid, my mind lazy. The humidity was very high and the temperature usually in the eighties. I felt enervated and slept for long periods of the day. When Pete came to see me he'd now ask: 'Where's Wen? Sleeping?' Although I swam and played golf daily, the mental lassitude began to worry me. Life in Seria, though enjoyable, didn't stimulate me. I felt I was becoming a lump. But what was I to do? Should I leave? Should I go home to Melbourne? Or somewhere else? My money was dwindling rapidly. I didn't have the cost of a fare to Melbourne. Pete would of course lend it to me but it would take me years and years to repay him. Anyway, I didn't particularly want to go back to Australia. I was hooked on the Far East. But I couldn't stay in Seria for ever and Shell wouldn't employ European secretaries. What *was* I to do? Every night I lay in bed and worried about it but the next day would come and go without any decision being made. I felt incapable of ever making a decision. If only someone would do it for me!

Then Pete came in one afternoon and said he was taking me to Brunei Town for a few days. Lovely! My first visit had been all too brief and it would be pleasant to return.

'Where shall I stay? At the Rest House?'

'No, I've arranged for you to stay with a *mem* there. She's the wife of the manager of Harrisons and Crosfield – a big trading firm.'

I didn't ask where he and two bachelor friends were going to stay. I suspected they were going to spend the weekend in different pastures.

On Saturday morning we boarded the jeep and drove to Brunei Town, whizzing along the hard sand of the beach till we reached the Danau Ferry, drifting across the river then bumping along the unmade road until we reached the town in the late afternoon.

I was wearing navy shorts and a pale blue blouse, my feet in battered strap sandals. My legs were spattered with mud and sand, my blouse was sticking to my back and my hair was lank and dripping with perspiration. We came to a halt at the gate of a trim bungalow set in a neat garden. Pete and I climbed stiffly out of the jeep and walked up the path.

The front door opened and an elegant English woman stood at the top of the flight of steps leading down into the garden. She was wearing an immaculately laundered linen dress and her pale blonde hair was braided around her head like a coronet. I felt scruffy, sweaty and dishevelled.

Pete introduced us. 'This is Peggy Prentice. This is my sister Wendy.'

My initial sense of inferiority was banished when Peggy began to talk and make me welcome. Newly married in North Borneo, she and her husband had been transferred to Brunei and she was desperately lonely. Before long she was sitting next to me on the sofa and showing me the pictures of her wedding.

'That's the Church in Jesselton. There's a flight of about fifty steps up to it. That's my Tom and that's Tom Mitchell and that's Sandy . . .'

It had been a Highland wedding and the men in the bridal party had all worn kilts, velvet jackets and lace jabots despite the heat. Peggy waxed eloquent about Jesselton.

'It's wonderful up there! There are loads of bachelors and there are parties and dances every night. Not like this dump . . . it's as quiet as a grave here. You ought to go to Jesselton . . . you'd have a wonderful time!'

It certainly looked more attractive than Seria. There appeared to be a beautiful beach fringed with casuarinas, lush wooded hills and even a magnificent mountain of about 14,000 feet – Mount Kinabalu, revered by the natives. I was intrigued.

Peg's husband Tom came in. A handsome dark Scot with a neatly-clipped military moustache, he had lost no time in pursuing the attractive Peggy who had come out from England to stay with her planter uncle on a rubber estate down the railway line from Jesselton. Single girls were few in Jesselton, so on her infrequent visits to the town she had been rushed by the bachelors. Now that she was married and posted to the one-horse town of Brunei, she was missing the excitement.

She talked to me about Jesselton all that evening and while she took me sightseeing and shopping over the next few days continued to advise me.

'Go to Jesselton! You'll never regret it! It's wonderful there!'

I was thoughtful all the long way back to Seria. Peggy had opened up a completely new dimension. There were other places, exciting places. I needn't go back to Melbourne. I could try and get a job in the Far East.

The next day I wrote off to Singapore, Kuala Lumpur in Malaya, Kuching in Sarawak and Labuan, Jesselton and Sandakan in North Borneo. I wrote to the Chamber of Commerce in each town offering my services as a secretary. Gradually the answers trickled in.

'With reference to your letter, we regret . . .'

'If you could come to Kuala Lumpur we should be glad to interview you.'

'Unfortunately we have no vacancies . . .'

My depression deepened. What should I do! My money was just about gone. I felt incapable of making any further effort to shape my future.

Then a cable arrived from Jesselton.

'CAN OFFER YOU POSITION $400 A MONTH NO ACCOM-MODATION TRANSPORT OR MEDICAL STOP IF INTER-ESTED BOARD SS KAJANG MIRI SEPTEMBER 3 . . . STEEL BROS.'

My reaction was confused. It was great to be offered a job and in Jesselton (Steel Brothers was apparently a well-known firm) but it was rather discouraging. No accommodation or transport provided and no medical expenses. I felt rather scared at the prospect of leaving the security of Seria with my brother and friends for the unknown Jesselton where nothing was to be provided. It was rather a 'come if you dare' cable. Anyway, our swimming gala was on the 3rd of September. That settled it. I wouldn't be able to go. I had gone with a Seria team to the opening of the new Miri Club the month before and we had walloped the Miri swimmers. Now they were returning the visit. I had to be there.

Muriel in her calm dispassionate way put me right.

'Weren't you saying the other day that you wished someone would make the decision for you, that someone would say 'Do this!' or 'Do that!' or 'Go there!'? Well, it's all laid on the line for you. Catch the *Kajang* on Saturday and go to Jesselton!'

'But today's Monday! I'll never do it in time!'

'Of course you will! You could pack in a morning. Cable them and say you'll come!'

Of course she was right and I cabled my acceptance. Once it was settled, my excitement grew. Far horizons beckoned and wanderlust stirred in my sluggish veins. There was a rush to get my clothes washed and packed, there were goodbyes to be said, letters to be written to tell my family of my new address.

Then another cable arrived.

'ACCOMMODATION ARRANGED REST HOUSE . . . FIENNES CDC.'

I was mystified. What did it mean? What was Fiennes? What was CDC? I checked with the telegraph office to see if there were a misprint. Was Fiennes meant to be Finance? Was CDC an abbreviation for something? If so, what? No one could enlighten me.

On Saturday I made my last-minute goodbyes and Pete drove me south to Miri, the oilfield's port. My sadness at driving along the dusty road through the jungle for the last time was mixed with excitement at the journey ahead. Another ship, another voyage! We reached Miri and I looked eagerly for the *Kajang*. The only visible ship was a small unpretentious cargo ship lying offshore. My heart sank.

Pete helped me onto a launch with my luggage and we puttered out to the ship. It looked no better at close quarters. The Malay quartermaster at the top of the gangway showed me to my cabin. I pushed open the door and went in. Pete tried to follow but there was no room. The cabin measured about eight feet by six. A double bunk occupied one wall, a dressing table another, a very narrow wardrobe was alongside the door. I subsided on the lower bunk and burst out laughing.

'Well, it's not the *Queen Mary*, but I suppose it'll do.'

With me sitting on the bunk Pete was able to bring in my cases.

'It's only for three days. Will you be all right?'

'Of course, I'll just unpack a few things and shove my cases under the bunk. What's that dreadful smell?'

An overpowering, cloying smell pervaded the whole ship.

'It's copra,' said Pete. 'With rubber, it's the coastal steamers' main cargo. They go around the ports picking up copra and rubber and take it to Singapore.'

Now that I knew it was copra, I could identify the penetrating smell as coconut. Rancid coconut oil. It was sickening. I opened my small porthole and all the ventilators I could find but the air remained stationary and oppressive.

We were about to sail. Pete looked at me apprehensively and asked again if I'd be all right.

'Of course I will,' I said, giving him a last hug. 'You'd better go ashore.'

I saw him down the gangway and then went to my tiny cabin to unpack.

Loud shouts rang out. A bell clanged. There was the sound of naked feet running on the deck. An anchor chain rattled and the steady throb of engines told me that we were moving. I looked out of the porthole, waving to my brother on the receding launch then, as we headed out to the open sea, turned my attention to my cases.

There was a light tap at the door. I opened it and saw a very tall, owlish young man blinking behind horn-rimmed spectacles. I guessed he was in his early thirties, rather old.

'Miss Law? I'm Fiennes!'

He pronounced it 'Fines' so I didn't connect it with the strange word on my cable.

'Yes?' I said uncomprehending.

'You're going to work for me in Jesselton.'

'Oh, you're from Steel Brothers?'

'No, I'm from C.D.C.'

I felt totally unintelligent and weakly waved him into the cabin.

'I'm afraid I'm rather confused. I thought I was to work for Steel Brothers. What is C.D.C.?'

'Colonial Development Corporation. We develop Colonies but I don't know what we'll actually be doing in Jesselton.'

He laughed boyishly, self-deprecatingly. He didn't seem at all like a boss. I was relieved. My venture into the unknown should not be the ordeal I had imagined. He told me he had only just arrived from London and had caught the *Kajang* in Singapore. Steel Brothers had secured my services for him. Together we would open the new office in Jesselton. It sounded fun.

He was frightfully English, or what we Australians imagine to be English. He punctuated each sentence with 'actually' and roars of laughter. But he seemed shy and very nice. He invited me up to the deck for a drink before dinner. We were apparently the only passengers.

When I had bathed and changed I found my way up to the tiny square of deck where there were a few cane chairs. It was the only place to sit, there being no lounge or smoking room. We were shortly joined by the Mate, Monty Wright, an extremely handsome young man with dark hair and beard and a lively wit and intelligence. Things were looking up!

When the bell went for dinner I was escorted down to the dining saloon . . . another hurdle crossed. I had been rather nervous about entering shipboard life by myself. We sat at one table with the Captain at the head. Captain Cole was pleasant and kept the conversation bubbling. He had a perverse pride in his ancient ship and told us that the *Kajang* had been on the Borneo run since before World War I. Monty had said he was rather a gourmet and that the meals were excellent. They proved to be so. I had put on one and a half stone since leaving home and could see no chance of dieting while on the ship.

I woke next morning feeling very tired. It had been terribly hot in the poky little cabin and I didn't feel rested at all. Shortly after breakfast we berthed at Labuan, the hatch covers were removed, the derricks started grinding and offloading cargo from the hold. We stayed there all day and another night. There was no air in the cabin. Nothing moved. The heavy sickening smell of copra penetrated everywhere.

Monday afternoon we weighed anchor. Next stop Jesselton! It was the capital of the British Crown Colony of North Borneo. Two-thirds of the large island of Borneo had belonged to the Dutch and was now in the process of being transferred to Indonesia. The remaining third consisted of the two British Colonies, Sarawak and North Borneo, separated by the tiny independent Sultanate of Brunei. I had visited two of these territories. Now for the third.

Early on Tuesday morning I rose and looked out of the porthole. In the distance I could see land on the horizon, hilly land. In the background a large, unevenly-edged blue shadow stood out against the sky. Kinabalu! It was superb! I dressed quickly and went up on deck to watch our approach.

The air was fresh and light, the sea calm with an oily silkiness that I have seen only in the tropics. We were passing a string of islands. Opalescent water blended with egg-shell blue sky except for the emerald land that was so near now. Details began to emerge. There was an L-shaped pier with a ramshackle Customs shed and *godown* (warehouse) alongside. Along the shore I could see buildings of a nondescript kind, all made of *kajang* and *attap*, and a *kampong ayer*. Dotting the green hills which ran behind the town were a few houses and standing out prominently on the hill was a white clocktower. It could not have been more different from the flat aridity of Seria. *'Singgah Mata'* is the old native name for Jesselton. . . 'Where the eye lingers'. I couldn't wait to go ashore.

Chapter 4

Singgah Mata

My few belongings were already packed. I said goodbye to Captain Cole and Mr Wright and went ashore with David Fiennes. Into the shed we went to get our passports stamped by Immigration and then to be interviewed by the Customs Officer. He was dressed in olive-green shorts and safari jacket, his curly brown hair was receding and he had a strong northern England accent.

'Is this all your *barang*?'

'My what?'

'*Barang* . . . baggage.'

'Yes, just the cases and the typewriter.'

He showed interest in my ancient Corona typewriter which I'd bought secondhand before leaving home. It was so old-fashioned that it had not one shift key but two, each hammer bearing three characters on it.

'I'm afraid I'll have to charge you duty on your typewriter.'

'Duty!'

'Yes, it's a foreign make.'

'But it's an old wreck and anyway I haven't any money till I start work.'

He looked a bit shaken but relented.

'Oh well, I suppose it is a pretty old one.' He pronounced 'one' to rhyme with 'don'.

He chalked our cases and we went out into a sun which was already fiercer than it had been ten minutes before. The shrilling of cicadas filled the air.

I looked around me with interest. There were a couple of European women, dowdy, middle-aged, in faded cotton dresses. They were carrying shopping baskets and had come to try and buy some food from the ship. I suddenly felt a stranger again. In Seria everyone was young.

David had found a taxi and we climbed in. The driver was an amiable Chinese called Chin and we learned later that his was the only reliable taxi in Jesselton. He was reputed to run it on water, or petrol mixed with water. His English was fairly good and when it didn't suffice David smoothly switched to Malay. He had lived in Singapore previously and sounded very fluent.

After about a mile we reached the *kedai*. There were only two streets of shops, running parallel to the sea. Here and there were flattened blocks, the result of wartime bombing by the Australians when they liberated North Borneo from the Japanese. The local name for Jesselton is *Api Api*, meaning 'place of fires'; this dates not from World War II but supposedly from an episode when a rebel called Mat Salleh attacked and burnt down an early settlement on the offshore island of Gaya in 1896.* In 1899 a new settlement was built on the mainland and named after Sir Charles Jessel, a director of the Chartered Company which had been set up to run North Borneo in 1881, rather on the lines of a Colony. It wasn't until 1946, however, that North Borneo actually became a Crown Colony.

All the shops were made of wood and *attap* and so were the few offices. David asked Mr Chin to slow down and we located C.D.C.'s new office next door to Steel Brothers with Peat, Marwick and

---

* Despite this popular belief, there is in the State Museum a Dutch map of Borneo and the Celebes dated 1657 in which the settlement where Jesselton was to stand is clearly labelled *Api Api*. It may have some connection with the seaside tree with breathing roots that bears the same name.

Mitchell, Chartered Accountants, on the other side. A little further on was the North Borneo Trading Company, the Borneo Company and the Hongkong and Shanghai Bank. The shops were mainly Chinese shop-houses with the occasional Indian silk merchant's premises, open to the street and overflowing with merchandise, with accommodation above. Awnings jutted out from each shop over the footpath to provide shelter from sun and rain. In front of the shops ran a deep storm drain large enough to carry away monsoon rain. Down the centre of the street was a strip of green grass planted with spreading poinciana trees.

We turned left and came to a crossroads, in the centre of which stood a little *mata mata* on point duty. We crossed over and on our right saw the beautiful *padang* ringed with poincianas, with banks sloping up to the Sports Club, the Club for Europeans. On our left was the Recreation Club for Asiatics, or Asians as people were beginning to call them.

The road now began to ascend a gentle hill, made a tight hairpin bend and then curved past the white wooden clocktower I had seen from the ship. We had arrived at the Rest House, the only accommodation available for Europeans.

David paid off the taxi and we climbed a few steps onto a large square verandah from which we had a breathtaking view of part of the town, the harbour, a cluster of offshore islands, the *kampong ayer* and a long line of casuarinas on the western horizon.

The manageress came out to meet us. She was a middle-aged New Zealander whose son worked for Harrisons and Crosfield. It seemed that a lot of people had relatives here. Women frequently came to Borneo to visit a relative, as I myself had done, then stayed to work or marry. Mrs Whitton booked us in and directed a servant to take our bags to the Annexe. The main building contained a sitting area and bar as well as the verandah, the dining room and kitchen and half a dozen bedrooms upstairs. The Annexe was situated down the steps where the road from the town curved past the clocktower. It was extremely basic with a central corridor dividing two rows of small rooms. At one end of the corridor were two lavatories and two bathrooms.

Wah Kim, our stocky Chinese room boy, showed us to two adjoining rooms. My bedroom measured about eight feet by ten and like the corridor had a concrete floor. There was the usual four foot wide tropical divan with a mosquito net, a wardrobe, a dressing table cum desk and chair, and a door leading onto a small verandah. It was simple but adequate and I had that wonderful view of the town and harbour and islands. Up from the *kedai* floated the constant sound of Chinese songs, amplified so that it filled the town. The clock chimed the hours. These sights and sounds framed my world for the next year.

By lunchtime I had settled in and went up to the main building. Outside the Annexe, parked in the shade thrown by some large trees, was a caravan and from it came the perpetual staccato of Morse Code. It was a temporary Telecoms office. A young, handsome Filipino with liquid brown eyes was working there and looked me up and down as I passed.

All the other residents had returned from their offices for lunch and were on the verandah reclining in *kerusi malas*, those comfortable rattan *chaises longues* with leg rests and holes for glasses in the armrests. The men wore open-necked, short-sleeved shirts and those long, voluminous shorts irreverently known as 'Bombay bloomers'. It seemed to be the accepted daytime uniform, cool and comfortable, but David Fiennes, probably because of his height, only ever wore long white trousers to the office, never shorts. The women wore cotton dresses or blouses and skirts in crisp Horrocks cotton or Liberty lawn.

I was delighted to find two other Australian girls there, Diana and Dorothy. Diana came from Perth and was of Scottish descent. Small and dark-haired with blue eyes and a sharp nose, she was vivacious and sophisticated, sipping her drink and smoking as she chatted. She laughed a lot and then her eyes narrowed and almost disappeared. She had come to Borneo to visit her married sister and now had a job with Harrisons and Crosfield.

Dorothy was quieter and had fair straight hair, soft brown eyes and a rather nervous laugh. She smoked compulsively. Being from Melbourne herself she quickly made me feel welcome. She had come up from Australia with Diana and now worked for Steel Brothers.

We met the others on the verandah, an Australian Major Wikner (nicknamed 'Wik'), who was the Railways Engineer, the Accountant of the Chartered Bank and his wife who wore a hat and neat white gloves everywhere, a quiet Anglo-Burman who worked for the Railways and Douglas McDonald the dentist, who came from the Orkneys, his pretty half-Greek wife Marie and their baby son. Then up the road on his bike pedalled the Commissioner of Customs. He ran up the steps and was introduced as Roy Knowles. Removed from his office he proved very friendly and seemed to have forgotten the episode of the typewriter. The Manager of Cable and Wireless joined us, a tall, imposing man with the benignity of a bishop, snowy of hair and large of stomach. Known by everyone as 'Body' Barnes, the nickname was not due to his girth but to the fact that some years previously he had been a lay preacher in Suez and had buried many bodies during an outbreak of cholera. He played the organ at All Saints Church but neverthless had an astonishing collection of rude limericks to suit any occasion. Despite his awe-inspiring appearance, he was great fun, and Diana told me that one of the sights of the Rest House was Body leaving his room to bathe, a tiny Rest House towel insecurely wrapped around his middle, a long-handled brush and sponge-bag in his hand. He had a specially strengthened bed to bear his weight and was the only man I have ever met who could rest his drink on his *embonpoint* without spilling a drop.

There was also another Cable and Wireless man, a mechanician called George Pope. He was a short, squat version of Oliver Hardy, not fat but muscular, with the same square head and short tooth-

brush moustache. George had a lovely dry wit and seemed to be squiring the health visitor, Sister Bridget Colquhoun.

Over lunch of water-buffalo meat and salad, cold caramel custard and fruit (little *pisang mas* and green oranges), I was rapidly given background knowledge of Jesselton by Di and Dot.

'There's a lot going on. We have a Club Dance once a month and others on the slightest provocation. Last week there was a Race Meeting with a dance at night and next weekend cricket and hockey teams are coming up from Seria. That should be hectic. Then the Saturday after that there's a Treasure Hunt in cars and there's always a launch trip to the islands on Sunday mornings. When the Navy comes in it's very busy too – we staff a canteen and entertain them. We've just had the *Amethyst*.'

'Are you the only single girls?'

'No, there's Nancy Farrell – another Australian – but she lives with her sister Nell at Tanjong Aru. And there are two other girls who live in a *kajang* at the beach, and "Pete" and "Ginge" are the nursing sisters at the hospital.'

'There's a fleapit of a cinema in town. The rattan chairs have cane bugs in them and the films are always terribly old. They had *Nanook of the North* recently. We sometimes have films at the Club if there's anyone around who can work the projector.'

Roy Knowles butted in.

'The other diversion of note is the Governmental game of snakes and ladders,' he said wryly. 'This consists of a series of tricky pitfalls and stepping stones, the negotiation of which determines one's status in the Colony. The most deadly snakes are – failing to sign the Governor's Book on arrival in town and on other specified occasions. You must sign it today! Then there's treading on the Governor's wife's frock while dancing, failing to play tennis and so on. Ladders are the converse of these and a few more, like playing chess with the Governor and paying strict attention to all the correct social conventions.'

'Who is the Governor?' I asked in dismay.

'Well, there's just an O.A.G. at the moment, an Officer Administering the Government. He's known as "I, Claudius", but a new Governor is coming in a few months' time. You don't have to worry anyway, you're a commercial! It's only poor Government servants like me who have to be careful.'

David Fiennes smiled gently. 'We're neither fish nor fowl actually. We're Government but have to make a commercial success of what we do.'

'Like you did with the Groundnut Scheme in East Africa?' joked Roy.

'Ah . . . well, come along Miss Law! Let's go and look at our office.'

Outside the Rest House the heat hit us. It was like walking into a wall. We walked down to the town by a short, steep flight of steps alongside the clocktower. After stepping across the railway line, a short walk brought us to the line of commercial offices – 'Merchant Princes' Avenue' Body Barnes had called it, and he had told us how the last Governor, Sir Edward Twining, used to meet the Merchant Princes, the Managers of these establishments, on Saturday mornings at the Hongkong Bank to discuss business, refreshing themselves with brandy and ginger ale poured from a teapot. This Twining had apparently been quite a showman and stories about him were legion. When he was in Tanganyika, he used to go on tour with a brass band in attendance. Body Barnes had told us of his first meeting with this colourful character. There was a knock at his office door one morning and he had looked up to see a man, in shirt and shorts and carrying the stout stick with which he had hammered on the door.

'Good morning, I'm the Gov.!' Twining said, and stepped inside.

The second last office in the row bore a bright new notice reading 'Colonial Development Corporation (Far East) Ltd.' David produced a key and opened the door. We took possession together.

Inside was a single room about twenty feet by eighteen. There were desks and chairs in two opposite corners and a filing cabinet against a wall. That was all.

'Yes, well . . . I suppose that's all we need. You go out and buy some stationery. Charge it! I'll unpack my papers.'

I went to explore the *kedai*. Ignoring the usual fascination of *sarongs* and silks, stinky fish and sandals, I found the Chinese stationer. 'Tim & Ed' said a notice above the door. It stood for Timothy and Edwina. Fortunately Tim spoke English and filled my order for reams of typing paper, thick and thin, carbon paper, pencils, notebooks, pens, rubbers and envelopes. Under the envelope flaps were strips of greaseproof paper to stop them sticking in the humidity.

He said he'd deliver everything so I ambled back along the street absorbing all the sights, sounds and smells of this fascinating market.

I came to the establishment of Kishen Singh, a Sikh silk merchant. His shop, open to the street like all the others, was crammed with bolts of cloth, crisp bright cottons, heavy silks and satins, exquisite *saris* and *sarongs*. The sickly scent of patchouli drenched the air. A beautiful little Indian girl of about ten looked at me solemnly from behind the counter. She had a perfectly oval face framed by the thin gauze scarf she wore. Her eyebrows were smudged arcs above eyes like two coals. Her mouth was very full and shapely and parted to reveal white even teeth.

'Good afternoon!' she said carefully, in impeccable English.

'Hullo!' I said.

'What is your name?' she asked.

I told her. 'And what is yours?'

'Suwindar.'

She plied me with questions until she had elicited all the relevant facts about me and then asked me to be her friend. The curtain at the back of the shop was drawn aside and the proprietor came into the shop. Tall, black-bearded with a snowy turban, Kishen Singh was an imposing if intimidating sight. He greeted me politely though somewhat frostily and spoke sharply to the little girl.

'Come and see me again!' she begged as she ran out of the shop.

I murmured some excuse for not buying anything and went on my way.

Back at the office, David had spread his papers across his desk and tacked up a large map of North Borneo on the wall. It bore a startling resemblance to a pig's head. He was interviewing a young Malay lad who wanted to be our office boy. After an intensive crossfire of Malay, David looked at me.

'I think he'll do. We'll try him for a week. His name's Kipli.'

Kipli bin Mantalia was his full name. He was a clean round-faced lad of about fifteen with large feet which were obviously unaccustomed to shoes. He had come from his *kampong* in the country to earn some money. I discovered this was a common procedure. The country people grew enough rice to feed themselves and a little rubber to sell and were fairly self-sufficient and content. If they wanted to buy a bicycle or perhaps a *kerbau*, then they came into town to look for work. Kipli had no English at all. I realized I must bring my Malay books down to the office and improve my grip of the language.

At four o'clock David cleared his desk, locked his drawers and stood up.

'Home time!'

Kipli closed the shutters and we left the office.

'I've just realized . . . there's no light in there.'

'Good, we can't do any overtime! The power supply here is pretty bad. They're always having power failures. The power station just can't cope with the load.'

The power supply was indeed one of the bones of contention amongst residents. Power was supplied to half the town each night, the other half having to make do with oil lamps. On alternate nights, Wah Kim brought a battered hurricane lamp to the door of each bedroom at dusk. Trying to apply lipstick while holding the lamp up to the small wall mirror in my room was quite an art. On 'light' nights the supply was turned off at 11 p.m., just like a boarding school, so we had to keep candles ready in our rooms.

Another problem was that there were no long mirrors. I saw only the upper half of me for twelve months and never had any idea what I looked like when setting out for a party or dance in evening dress.

●   ●   ●

Pete had advanced me Straits $75 to tide me over till my first pay cheque. (I hadn't been strictly truthful with Roy Knowles!) If I were to repay him something each month, my $400 *gaji* would have to be carefully rationed. I decided I would have only breakfast and lunch at the Rest House and do without dinner. I took fruit from the lunch table to stave off pangs of hunger in the evening. Dot and Di had all their meals including afternoon tea, they ran up a not inconsiderable bar bill with drinks and cigarettes and they shared a wash *amah*. I didn't smoke and rarely drank and did all my own laundry. I washed my clothes after bathing each night and hung them over the verandah rail where they dried in half an hour. I ironed once a week. The iron was a charcoal one, a large heavy brass affair with a lid held in place by a hook. Wah Kim prepared it and when the charcoal inside was glowing nicely, he called me. If it cooled during ironing, I swung it backwards and forwards to make the coals flare up and produce more heat. My pampered life in Seria seemed a long way away, I thought ruefully as I perspired over the ironing board. Still, if I were very careful I should be able to make my money last. I soon settled into the daily routine of life at the Rest House and work at C.D.C.

At half past ten each morning, David pushed his papers away and said: 'Let's have some coffee!'

We walked across the street to the coffee shop opposite. Chinese coffee shops are the same throughout the Far East. Open to the street, there are bare, scrubbed marble tables and chairs where one can sit and observe the world going by. Most business is transacted in coffee shops, even by Europeans.

'*Towkay*!' David gestured with the Malay version of a beckon. Whereas Europeans use the hand with the palm facing and a finger pulling, Asians use the hand with the back facing and the fingers describe a pushing movement. It was understood and the waiter approached our table. He wore a white singlet outside his shorts.

'*Kopi-oh, dua*!' David ordered.

The waiter yelled '*Kopi-oh, dua*!' to the back of the shop and wiped down the tabletop with a damp cloth before shuffling off into the kitchen. He emerged some time later with two cups slopping coffee into their saucers. Coffee always came slopped into the saucers. Spoons were standing in the cups. White coffee always contained sweetened condensed milk so we drank ours black.

I learned a lot from David. As we sipped our coffee he pointed out passers-by and retailed snippets of information or gossip about them. He opened my eyes to the political state of Asia. Sleepy North Borneo, he said, was like the still centre of a typhoon of unrest. All around us was dissent and the growth of nationalism – Malaya, Indo-China, Korea, the Philippines, Indonesia – and further north the great sleeping dragon of China was stirring and flexing its limbs. How long would it be till the Borneo territories sought their independence?

I knew there was talk of subversive activities in the Chinese Middle School and something called the Special Branch, to be headed by George Chettle, was being set up, but I was still puzzled.

'But they like the British, don't they?' I asked.

'They'd rather have us than the Japs! I think they were genuinely delighted to have us back. But it won't last. It can't!'

To my naïve mind it seemed incredible that the sun should ever set on the Empire but I had been out of touch with world events for three years and new nations were emerging all over the globe. David started me thinking.

Sometimes he called a Chinese businessman to our table and sounded him out about some matter which concerned him. In the coffee shop he kept his finger on the pulse of commerce. On returning to the office he made cryptic jottings on pieces of paper or dictated a letter to catch the Friday plane. There was only one plane a week at first but that was soon increased to two. Whereas the week was previously fairly leisurely with an increase of activity on Friday to catch the mail, now two days a week were busy. Eventually there was a plane every day and then life in the offices became much like that in London or New York or Melbourne. The *dahulus*, people who had been in Borneo before the war, spoke regretfully about the days before the aeroplane when months would elapse between sending letters and receiving replies from England by ship.

At lunch time we all stretched out in long chairs on the Rest House verandah and played liar dice. We drank *ayer limau* at that hour, a refreshing drink of fresh squeezed lime juice and water which would not put us to sleep all afternoon. After lunch, consisting of scrawny water buffalo, stringy chicken or scraggy pork in strict rotation, followed by the eternal caramel custard or fresh fruit salad, there would be time for a quick nap before David tapped on my door and we walked down the steps to the office together.

I began to learn about C.D.C. David's job was to research any possible scheme, agricultural or industrial, which in his opinion might prove viable given a sufficient injection of funds. He then prepared a report presenting his case and sent it to London for approval or rejection. It never ceased to amaze me how competent he was, whether discussing the cubic capacity of timber in a forest of trees or a particular strain of rice with high yields or the likelihood of disease in a crop of ramie – a nettle-like plant producing a fine, strong fibre. A pile of pages covered with his spidery scrawl would thump down on my desk.

'See if you can make head or tail of that while I'm away,' he'd say as he was about to go on tour of a remote hill area to investigate timber or to Bandau to see if rice would grow there.

I usually finished typing his report in a day or two and then time dragged. I decided to teach Kipli English. He was quick to learn and had a retentive memory. As he learned English, so my Malay improved. I began to practise on Wah Kim my room boy who was also a *tukang ayer* or water carrier.

'Boy!'

'*Misi?*'

'*Ayer panas mandi!*' (Hot water for bathing.)

'*Baik, misi.*'

A little later he would totter down the steps from the main house with a galvanised bucket of hot water and place it in the bathroom.

'*Ayer panas siap, misi.*' (Ready!)

At mealtimes it was even easier. The word *ada*, with the accent on the first syllable, means 'Is there any?' or 'Have you got?'

'Boy! Marmite *ada*? *Pisang* (banana) *ada*?'

'*Ada!*' (accent on the second syllable) was the affirmative reply.

There was no Vegemite in Jesselton, that essential part of any Australian's diet, but Marmite was the next best thing and I ate pots of it. I think it supplied my daily requirement of salt as I never suffered from heat exhaustion or had to take salt pills. 'Marmite *ada*?' became a catchphrase amongst the Rest House residents.

Salt and iron were the two main nutritional requirements and a daily dose of Paludrine was essential as there was still a lot of malaria in the country. Paludrine had recently replaced Atebrin, the war-time anti-malaria drug. It was infinitely preferable as it didn't turn the skin a ghastly yellow as Atebrin did. Apart from these precautions we didn't worry about disease and remained remarkably healthy considering the varied quality of the food available.

Chinese-baked bread was sweet and light like raisin loaf, pure white and completely devoid of nourishment. Eggs were tiny and frequently bad and milk was evaporated, condensed or powdered. We became used to evaporated milk in our tea and coffee or poured neat over fruit salad as cream. Butter came in tins as did cheese. But vegetables were plentiful and varied: *pak choy*, a sort of spinach, *wong ah pak*, sometimes called Chinese leaves by Europeans, okra (lady's fingers) and cabbage. Tomatoes, cucumber and lettuce were available but as human manure was used to fertilize crops, any uncooked salad vegetables had to be sterilized by soaking in a solution of permanganate of potash or Condy's crystals for an hour. Fruits there were in plenty: *papaya*, mango, *durian belanda*, ordinary *durian*, jackfruit, pineapple, mangosteen, green bananas or tiny, sweet *pisang mas*, *chiku*, pomelo and green oranges. Tropical fruits were wonderful but how I longed for a crisp Australian Jonathan apple or some strawberries and cream!

The monotony of the meat was varied occasionally by the substitution of excellent fish. *Ikan merah*, the red snapper, and *ikan tenggiri*, the Spanish mackerel, were particularly delicious. The *udang*, prawns, were always superb, especially the King prawns. We never had these at the Rest House but down at Fatty's, the sole eating house in the *kedai*, we ate them in dozens. Large and fleshy they were, dipped in batter and fried to crisp perfection. Sometimes a group of us from the Rest House would decide to eat out and Fatty would welcome us to his rather sleazy restaurant. A round-faced Chinese with a prominent gold tooth and black hair slicked back, he would beam at us as we demolished a huge heap of *nasi goreng* piled high on a large oval platter. We were all adept at using chopsticks or if there were a newcomer amongst us he would be speedily taught by the experts. A game we played in order to practise our skill with chopsticks was to pass a slippery lemon pip in mid-air from person to person. It was quite difficult.

One night, as we all sat back replete, Fatty told us we could keep our chopsticks. Dougie McDonald, the swarthy little Orcadian dentist, was sitting next to me.

'Bring yours round to the surgery tomorrow,' he said, 'and I'll engrave them for you.'

Next morning I climbed the steps of the Sandakan Dispensary to the small room he rented on the first floor. It was at the front of the building and through the large window floated the sounds of the street. Dougie had no patient so he took my chopsticks and seizing his dental drill he pedalled hard. The cable began to whirr and he deftly carved out the legend 'Fatty's, Jesselton, Oct. '49' on each one.

'There you are! Something to remember that wonderful meal.'

While I was there I asked him to check my teeth. I hadn't been to a dentist since leaving home and my teeth, like those of most Australians, were lamentably prone to decay. Keeping an eye on the primitive, foot-operated drill, I settled into the chair and opened my mouth. To my astonishment he gave me a clean bill.

'Wait a minute . . . what have we here? A bonny wee *gigi*!'

It was a new wisdom tooth which had erupted without my knowledge. I left the surgery with a light step. Some months later, when Dougie and Marie went to Singapore, the only available dentist was, would you believe it, a Mr Chew, a qualified dresser from Kuching Hospital but an unqualified dentist. However everyone went to him, even the Governor's wife. His surgery was in the *kampong ayer* and one walked over a bridge to it. He was gentle, fastidiously clean and couldn't bear the thought of hurting anyone. Like Dougie, he had only a pedal-operated drill. I was amused at the way he would proffer a selection of porcelain before filling a tooth so one could approve the right colour to match the tooth. If a tooth had to be extracted, it was tossed out of the window into the water. After a year or so a Government dentist arrived. By then Jesselton Power Station was functioning efficiently and he was able to use an electric drill.

•   •   •

Letters from home kept me supplied with odd snippets of news. My brother Phil who was Director of the Antarctic Division of the Department of External Affairs had led an expedition to Heard Island and in 1950 would go as an observer with the Norwegian-British-Swedish Expedition to Dronning Maud Land. A penguin had been named after me. My sister Noël had married a British actor from the Old Vic Company which, with Laurence Olivier and Vivien Leigh, had been touring Australia. It all seemed very remote. Borneo was a different world and I had never been so happy. I was so glad I hadn't gone back to Australia.

The Rest House was home to all the single men in Jesselton with the exception of the Harrisons and Crosfield and Government bachelors who lived in *kajangs* at Tanjong Aru, the entrancing beach four miles away. *Tanjong* is a point of land and *aru* is a casuarina tree. The whole coastline of Borneo is fringed with these graceful, shady trees as the cones fall into the sea and are washed ashore again, to take root and grow. There were three H. and C. *kajangs* and one belonging to Steel Brothers along the point. They faced the South China Sea and from them one had a front row seat for the nightly entertainment, the superb blazing sunset. From their verandahs one could hear the eternal susurration of the sea and the soughing of the wind in the *arus*.

By now I had broken off my engagement. With only a few single girls and lots of bachelors, I was enjoying the social life in Jesselton. Dorothy, Diana and I would sometimes be invited down to the beach by the H. and C. bachelors, especially after a dance at the Club. We would walk along the shining sand under a brilliant full moon and a sky flashing with stars, or swim in the sea where every movement splashed water dripping with phosphorescence, each droplet a spark of fire. Kinabalu was a dark threatening shape on the velvet sky. I would play Chopin on Ken Summers' grand piano while the others sat dreamily on the verandah listening to the sea as it broke creamily on the beach, running smoothly up the sand before draining silently away. There never was such a romantic place as Borneo!

When the lights went out we stirred ourselves and Tom Mitchell, the only driver, would have to take us back to the Rest House.

The lack of transport was a perpetual problem for us girls. It was expensive to order Mr Chin's taxi to take us to the beach for a swim and to have him return later to collect us. There was no possibility of any of us ever buying a car, even a second-hand one, and it was not done for Europeans to use the ramshackle local buses.

Then one day Nancy Farrell rushed in to my office. She was an attractive blonde from Sydney, very lively and with a flirtatious eye. She worked at the Secretariat and lived with her sister Nell Wookey who was married to an Englishman. Nell had one of the few pianos in the Colony and I sometimes went to her *kajang* to play it. Nancy was bubbling with excitement because she'd heard that Harrisons and Crosfield had in their *godown* six Corgi motorscooters. Originally designed to be dropped with paratroopers, they'd been gathering dust for years. Harrisons couldn't sell them because the local Chinese thought it *infra dig* to ride them. So the price had been brought down and down, from $500 to $225.

'It's a wonderful bargain,' said Nancy, 'And think of all the money we'd save on taxis! Come and see!'

I went with her to H. and C.'s and Ken Summers showed us a Corgi. It was a funny little thing, very low with a wheel diameter of about twelve inches, but he told us they could do thirty to forty miles an hour and about 130 miles to the gallon. They had no gears, yet could fly up any hill.

'How do they work, then?'

'Dead simple! You've only got a clutch, an accelerator and a brake. Can't go wrong!'

Nancy was sold. She put down $25 deposit immediately and arranged to pay the rest off monthly. I would have loved one but told myself sternly that I just couldn't afford it.

A week later Diana won $100 on the Melbourne Cup sweep and ran in to tell me she was buying a Corgi too. After work she and Nan drove up to the Rest House in high glee to demonstrate their new acquisitions. Residents having afternoon tea on the verandah enjoyed themselves watching Di's attempt to start hers. She would run beside it down the hill, engage the clutch and it would stall, whereupon she would push it up to the top again.

I was deeply envious. What fun the three of us could have, roaring around the country! Just to be independent, to be able to go for a swim every afternoon or on trips to the surrounding villages or to parties without the expense of taxis. But how could I afford it? I immersed myself in interminable calculations of monthly budgets and repayments to Pete and tried to see how I could do it. Dougie McDonald, the astute Scot, said I wouldn't lose money on it. I could always sell it, probably for more than I'd paid for it.

When one of the bachelors began to talk about buying one, I was afraid that H. and C. might put up the price again with so much interest being shown. So next morning I went straight to their office. The clerk passed a weary hand across his brow and muttered:

'Don't tell me . . . another Corgi!'

I paid my deposit and arranged to pay $50 a month off the balance. In addition I had to pay $5 for registration, $4.50 for a horn and $27 for insurance. I also arranged for a shopping basket to be fixed to the handlebars. In the afternoon I went back to collect it. It was a smart little machine, the petrol tank painted a bright red with a picture of a Corgi dog on it. A squeeze-bulb horn and basket were now attached to the handlebars.

I wheeled it onto the road and tried to start it. It was quite difficult. Every time I engaged the clutch the engine sputtered and stalled. It was very discouraging. I was annoyed too because I'd been given a stupid little soprano horn which couldn't make itself heard above the engine. Then I stumbled on a fool-proof way of starting. I ran the bike along the road and leapt sideways onto the saddle in full flight, at the same time engaging the clutch. The engine roared into life and, after a couple of circuits of the Post Office, I drove home in a state of exhilaration.

At half past four there was still no sign of Diana so I rode out to look for her. I saw her outside the Railway Station pushing her Corgi. Scarlet and perspiring, she'd obviously pushed it all the way from Harrisons without managing to start it. As I came nearer, a bus, a bike and a car approached from different directions and rattled me completely. I screamed loudly and so startled everyone that all three vehicles stopped and I sailed through the *mêlée* unscathed.

Diana discovered after pushing her bike all the way up the hill to the Rest House that someone had turned off her petrol. She was furious but the people on the verandah roared with laughter and we became the daily butt of their jokes.

While we were still inexperienced, we found it very difficult to slow down, let alone stop and idle the engine. It usually stalled and we had to go through the weary routine of running to start it again, so we developed the practice of zooming down the Rest House hill, approaching the crossroads whilst blowing our horns and yelling at the top of our voices. The little *mata mata* would quickly stop oncoming traffic from all directions and allow us to sail across the intersection.

Jesselton thought it a terrific joke. Jimmy Mitchell, the Manager of Harrisons and Crosfield, beamed fondly at us every time he passed us in his sleek black limousine, and for the first painful week our shaky progress through the streets was followed by hoots of laughter and pointed fingers from the locals, looks of incredulity

and shouts of encouragement from Europeans in their cars, and backfiring and clouds of smoke from the exhausts of our machines. The three of us sped through the streets in triple formation, giving extravagant hand signals, nonchalantly passing long lines of cars and trucks delayed at rail crossings or bottlenecks and hooting our little horns imperiously as we flew past the Vice-Regal Daimler. Clarrie Hawke, the Chief Police Officer, called us the North Borneo Corgi Lancers and solemnly saluted us as we passed. I liked to follow Jimmy Mitchell into a petrol station.

'Sixteen gallons!' he'd command while I'd meekly ask for half a gallon.

Head-scarves became essential as protection against wind and rain (no helmets in those days), and New Look skirts which reached the ankle were hardly the thing for riding motorscooters. I used to take my seat after the flying start, then fold one half of my voluminous skirt into my lap, then the other, but petrol oozed from the filler cap on the tank between my knees and my skirt hems were always stained with oil. It became commonplace for our handbags to spill out spanners and spark plugs when we went shopping. We began to talk knowledgeably about sludge. Faults could usually be traced to the carburettor or the spark plugs which we learned to examine and to remove the tiny ball of carbon which sometimes accumulated between the points. But there were still many teething problems. Chains fell off or broke, magneto coils burned out, spark plugs didn't spark, stranglers didn't strangle and hardly a day passed without one of the machines being carried ignominiously in the boot of a car to be fixed by Roy Newman at Borneo Motors. Nevertheless, they brought a measure of freedom and independence to us that was invaluable. Gradually the machines assumed their own distinct personalities and with great hilarity we chose names for them. Diana's was Haggis; Nancy with complete *sangfroid* called hers Sodomangomorrah and I, after dallying with Sennacherib and Pegasus, decided on Bess, being short and snappy and an atrocious pun on Corgi/Porgy.

•　•　•

David's car, a dark green Morris Oxford, had arrived on the last ship and when he was away on tour and there was not much work, Len Shing, his *syce*, took me out for driving lessons. Our only means of communication was Malay so I did not acquire the finer points of driving nor an understanding of what was under the bonnet. After learning the gear positions I set off slowly and drove all the way to Tanjong Aru. On the way back we turned right along the Tuaran road, over a rough detour bridge then up a hill road. Dozens of Hakka coolie women in their picturesque black-fringed hats were working along it. The road was only wide enough for one car at any time and to make matters worse, the coolies had dug a deep ditch along one side and I was terrified I should put David's car into it. Then we came down the hill into the town again with only a few worrying moments when goats, dogs and occasionally children wandered into my path.

Next day I met Mr Chin. His round face split into a wide grin and he adjured me to relax whilst driving.

'You look so worried! Remember, calm features engender a tranquil disposition!'

He always spoke like a Chinese proverb. I laughed hollowly. I did not feel tranquil.

After a few weeks I applied for a driving test and Clarrie Hawke took me out. He failed me on my three-point turn which he asked me to make in a narrow cul-de-sac by Mr Mitchell's garage. I practised it assiduously all the following week and passed my next test.

•   •   •

In October a bombshell burst. The ordinary and registered airmail was stolen under the noses, or maybe with the connivance, of four armed policemen. When I went out driving with Len Shing we saw about a hundred *mata mata* diving in the *sungei* under the so-called 'Sydney' bridge, dragging it for the missing mail bags. On the Penampang Road we passed Clarrie Hawke and Bob Gay and dozens of *mata mata*, rifles on their shoulders, marching single file into a house. Such excitement! To complicate matters further, a taxi driver had disappeared and there were many theories being discussed.

1.   The taxi driver was the thief.
2.   He was an accomplice.

3. He'd been done away with by the thieves.
4. He'd been done away with by the spirits.

In support of the last unlikely hypothesis, I was told the story of a young girl who disappeared from the Carmelite Convent before the war. The oracle was consulted and she was found wandering trance-like through the swamp eating clay. On further consultation, the oracle advised the slaying of a young goat without blemish and the administration of the blood to the girl. She ate it, recovered and was now married and living happily in Tuaran!

The most amazing rumours were flying about. One day we heard that the taxi-driver had been found, trussed up and gagged under a tree on the Tuaran road. Later, no . . . no body. We heard that one of the mail bags had been found in the Likas swamp and then, later, that it was an old one that the Post Office had thrown away. The mail robbery was the main topic of conversation at each meal.

'Any more news?'

'What is your theory about . . . '

The police were looking tight-lipped and grim. The mother of the taxi-driver was nearly out of her mind.

Several weeks later the police, working quietly and persistently despite the contemptuous remarks of the townsfolk, arrested two Malay men. A third one turned King's Evidence and testified against the others. Apparently they'd calmly walked into the Post Office at night, past the customary guard of four policemen, had lifted the key off a hook and walked out with all the mail. They'd hired the taxi to make their getaway. Once out of town they'd tried to get the driver to join them but he wouldn't. So they bashed him on the head, drove his car backwards and forwards over him till he was dead then threw his body into Likas swamp where crocodiles or tidal water disposed of it. So no body! The men were brought to trial and one was sentenced to death by hanging. Dr Ozimek and a distraught Chip Plunkett, the Deputy Commandant of Police, had to witness the execution some days later.

All in all, October was a month of murder and mayhem. There was the shocking assassination of Governor Stewart of Sarawak. He had been only three weeks in that Colony when he was stabbed by anti-Cessionists, quite a strong faction who wanted the White Rajahs back. Then the *kedai* at Seria burned down and two days later two Mosquito aircraft collided and crashed on the beach there, with all lives lost.

·   ·   ·

David Fiennes was house hunting. A quiet-living man who loved his books and classical records, the Rest House was not for him. I had heard that there was a vacant house in Racecourse Road owned by a Eurasian, Mr Daniels. I rode out to inspect it on his behalf, past the *kampong ayer* and the lone cinema, along the road bordered with heavenly Pride of India trees with their trusses of mauve flowers, and on past the Batu Tiga (third milestone). The house was situated just past the police station there on the main road to the beach.

It was a delightful Malay house built up high on piles, clean as a new pin and panelled inside with a lovely dark wood. It had a large garden and space underneath for a car. I thought David would love it. However, by the time he had returned from a trip to Kudat, the house had been snapped up by the Chartered Bank for their employee, Welsh Gwyn Roberts. David found instead an attractive house in the *kampong ayer* and soon he and Kipli and I were involved in moving his possessions into it. He bought some bright cotton material and asked me to run up some curtains for him. Once they were hung and he had arranged his books and hung his pictures, it made a comfortable home. The sound of the sea slopping around under the house was soporific and I wondered what he would do if a high tide destroyed the bridge which was his only access. I sometimes went to listen to his classical records (he introduced me to César Franck) and my great delight was to recline in his Kudat chair. This was a most astonishing piece of furniture, native to Borneo, looking like an outsize highbacked deckchair but full of moving parts. Seated in it, one had only to stretch one's legs and the whole contraption flattened out till it was almost level, like a bed. One could arrest the movement at any stage, so that the chair could be used upright or partly reclining or fully reclining. I have since seen some modern approximations of the design but nothing as good.

David frequently went on tour in order to investigate some region, crop or industry which might be boosted and his continual worry was to keep me occupied in his absence. On one occasion he put a pile of paper with roughly written notes on my desk. It was the *magnum opus* of a Catholic priest in Penampang who had spent most of his life with the Dusun people and had studied their language and written a monumental dictionary and account of its grammar. Interested as I was in languages, I welcomed the task of typing out the grammar but after a dozen pages decided I didn't want to learn Dusun. It was the most fiendishly complicated language with prefixes, suffixes and exceptions.

Occasionally David would give me articles he had written for the C.D.C. magazine. One was a broadminded dissertation on 'Asians and Europatics' (how strange that word 'Asian' sounded!), stressing the similarities between races, not the differences. We all have eyes, noses, mouths, ten fingers and ten toes. Why should colour matter?

Another day he gave me one with an impish smile. 'I don't suppose they'll publish it,' he said, 'but it may amuse them.'

It was headed, 'The Door to Promotion – A Colonial Anecdote'.

A certain Colonial Governor was doing what even Colonial governors usually do after breakfast. He omitted to lock the door.

Being an Englishman, and this one thing Englishmen have in common with Chinese, he had need of paper.

Contemporaneously a certain Colonial Corporal of Police was doing his duty, as Colonial Corporals of Police usually do. Being neither an Englishman nor a Chinese, the exact purpose of this duty was to him a mystery. He knew only that the carton must not be empty or heavens would fall.

Now Colonial Corporals of Police are taught in a strict school. They do not deviate. They are tough. If they come upon Colonial Governors squatting behind unlocked doors they salute and carry on. They see the rank before the man. They regard the person before the pose. Every parrot has his perch, they reason, so to every excellency his throne.

So now our hero. And having done his duty, in silence as Colonial Corporals of Police are taught to do, he took two paces to the rear with a click of heels, saluted with his right hand (the empty carton was in his left), turned about and retired. He did not forget to close the door.

Never before had that Colonial Governor been so silent for so long. Never before has a Corporal been so soon promoted to Sergeant.

But the most absorbing task was when David gave me a wad of letters on another occasion.

'See if you can read these and make me two copies. I want to send one to the *Sarawak Gazette* for its centenary.'

David came from a very old Oxfordshire family. He actually had a three-barrelled surname, Twisleton-Wykeham-Fiennes, but sensibly used only the last name. The letters he gave me were written by his father, Gerard, who as a young graduate had been appointed tutor to the young Vyner Brooke, the Rajah Muda of Sarawak, later the third White Rajah. I spent a fascinating week transcribing these letters. They were written in 1897 during a voyage to Sarawak with the Ranee and her children and several months spent in Kuching.

Passing through Singapore they had been entertained by the Sultan of Johore.

He is like a portly comfortable old British farmer to look at and talks his own language execrably, but he is awfully kind and hospitable. He wore about twelve magnificent diamond rings on his hands, but otherwise was dressed exactly like a European, in swallow-tail coat . . .

On reaching Kuching, the capital of Sarawak, Gerard Fiennes met the second White Rajah.

The Rajah and I have got on capitally so far . . . he is extremely nice and kind, but a fearful Radical. The country is glowing with life, animal and vegetable . . . The outlook over the Astana (palace) gardens is quite lovely – splendid shades of light green, mixed with flowers in the foreground, gradually shading off into the dark green of the jungle, so that one hardly knows whether all is garden or all jungle; behind this looms a high wedge-shaped hill of about 1,900 feet, blue with distance.

No mad dog or stereotype Englishman, Gerard Fiennes exercised between 6 and 8 a.m. and between 5 and 7.30 p.m., wearing a strip of flannel tied around his waist to prevent chills, and never went out between eight o'clock in the morning and five o'clock at night without a sun hat and umbrella.

One doesn't wear much clothing of course – just a jersey and a suit of white cotton stuff, with white canvas shoes.

Fever (malaria) is almost unknown as a strong tide up the river and a daily heavy shower of rain wash away all impurities and keep the town far sweeter than most English towns.

He spoke admiringly of the Dyaks who formed the redoubtable Sarawak Rangers.

They are admirable artillerymen – very quick with their guns, though as they never get any ball practice, I don't know whether they would ever hit anything. They are armed with sniders and sword bayonets and in the daytime wear a white uniform with black frogging, black belts and black forage caps with a monogram in silver. At night they wear blue-faced red with white belts and a red fez. Their chief delight is presenting arms, which they do to every European with great gusto, but when they took to presenting to the Rajah's groom the practice was somewhat discountenanced.

It is most amusing to walk through the Malay quarter of the town with the boys [i.e. the young Vyner and his two younger brothers]. The natives turn out in swarms to see the Rajah Muda and we generally have a crowd of urchins, mostly in Nature's garb, following at a respectful distance and in wholesome awe. Vyner can't make it out at all. The last thing which occurs to his mind is that he is the object of their attention, and he has to be continually prodded to make him return their salutes. He always thinks they're salaaming me! It is very nice in him to be so entirely unconscious and free from conceit.

Just as I had discovered in Seria, Gerard Fiennes found the native Dyak tremendously curious. He tells of a performance of *Cox and Box*. As 'open house' was the rule in Sarawak and any native who liked could stroll in, about forty came in to see the play.

I prompted, with half a dozen Dyak soldiers, stripped to the waist and oily to the last extremity, peeping through every conceivable crevice. The scene was weird and original but odoriferous. They are very good fellows, and it is very odd that the more piratical and head-hunting they were originally, the more friendly they are now. It is rather an ordeal to meet about ten of these chaps as every one insists on shaking hands with you.

During morning service in the Kuching cathedral there would be prayers for Queen Victoria and Charles the Rajah.

The Rajah gave a great dinner party in honour of the Queen's Diamond Jubilee. All the native chiefs came in afterwards. The Ranee, finding the amusement flagging a little, set her second boy to turn head over heels down the drawing room for their amusement. It was a brilliant inspiration for the old fellows laughed until they nearly fell off their chairs, and then made their grandchildren try and do the same – which they utterly failed to do.

Chapter 5

Suka Hati

P eggy Prentice had been right. It was wonderful in Jesselton. We seemed to be insulated from the harsher aspects of life. Faint rumours of a war in Korea trickled through into our cocoon but I knew little about what was happening in the rest of the world. With no radio or newspapers, how could I? Of poverty and old age there was no sign. Old people there must have been but were they kept indoors? They were not on the streets and I never saw a funeral in Borneo. Nor did I ever see beggars as in other Asian countries. North Borneo was generous to its inhabitants. It provided fish, rice, fruit, vegetables, timber and rubber for very little effort and the living was easy.

As for the expatriates, they lived an unnatural life with little sickness and no old age or death. Apart from the occasional planter or Colonial Servant who chose to retire in the Colony, when a man reached retirement age he left the country. Everyone worked hard and played hard. The social life was exhausting. As in Seria I found that people got their work done by four o'clock, pushing it out of the way so as to start the real business of living. There was sport after work, tennis, badminton, cricket, football, hockey and swimming, and practically every night there was something happening at the Club or in private homes. *Sarong* and *satay* parties were popular. Dressed in native style we sat on the floor eating *satay*, talking and singing. Or we'd be asked to a 'Come as you are when invited' party, the more unexpected our attire the better. On other occasions there would be an urgent summons to someone's house.

'I think my *bunga rajah* is going to flower tonight. Can you come?'

This was the beautiful night-blooming cereus which flowered once a year for a few short hours only. A gathering would be quickly arranged to witness the unfolding of the creamy white petals, revealing hundreds of pale yellow stamens inside.

At the weekends there were excursions into the country or launch trips to the outlying islands.

Hywel George, known as 'Flywheel', the District Officer of Tuaran, was in the Rest House one Saturday night and offered to take us girls out to Tuaran for the Sunday morning market or *tamu*. It was a pleasant drive through the hinterland of Jesselton. At first we travelled through lush green valleys of *padi*, the young rice just sprouting above the water of the flooded fields (is anything greener than young rice?), overshadowed by blue mountains with Kinabalu looming behind them, perfectly visible in its jagged outline. Then the road ran through rubber estates, mysterious gloomy Disney forests with rows of dappled silver trunks. Each tree bore a chevron, an incision made by a skilled tapper who every alternate day removed a shred more bark so that sticky latex dripped from the wound into a cup attached to the trunk. Workers collected the latex from full cups and took it in buckets to coagulating tanks. It then passed through rollers to form soft white sheets of rubber which were hung out like washing on lines in the sun before being finally dried in the smokehouse. The resultant tough brown rubber was stacked and tied in 250-pound bales, stinking to heaven, before being taken to Jesselton ready for shipment to rubber-hungry markets in other countries. I wondered how the world had got on before the rubber seedling was introduced from Brazil in the nineteenth century and grown so successfully in south-east Asia. Imagine . . . no tennis shoes or Wellington boots, no bicycle tyres, no erasers or elastic! My mind boggled and I looked at the dark trees with respect. Later in the year, during the almost non-existent autumn, the rubber trees would be gay with orange and red leaves. I loved them but the planters who stayed at the Rest House laughed scornfully at me.

'You try living on an estate for months on end. You wouldn't think rubber was beautiful then. Horrid, depressing, dark trees!'

We left them behind as the road emerged once more into wide sunny *padi* fields mirroring the huge cloud castles, cloud piled on fluffy cloud, vast edifices reaching into space, and continued through open countryside to Tuaran. At the *tamu* ground there were great crowds milling around the vendors, the colours of their clothes forming a moving tapestry. Tiny Malay girls were dressed in their best and their faces were made-up with powder, rouge and lipstick like their mothers. At one place a quack medicine seller and a snake-charmer were the centre of attention. An unprepossessing fellow in baggy, patched clothes, the snake-charmer had magic in his fingers. Blowing softly into his gourd-shaped pipe he drew out the plangent music, weird minor notes from some unwritten scale, and a cobra rose from the basket at his feet. Hood extended, its head swaying from side to side, its beady eyes were fixed on the pipe. The onlookers too appeared hypnotised, the women gazing with fearful fascination at the snake, the children clinging to their mothers' *sarongs*, bodies turned away, heads turned to look over their shoulders, eyes large with horror. The song came to an end, the cobra wavered, the man took the lid and roughly slammed the snake down into the basket. The spell broken, the crowd dissipated as quickly as it had gathered.

There were various stalls selling *sarongs* and fabrics, woven straw and rattan ware. Nearby, women were sitting on the ground with bilious-looking cakes and colourful fruit spread out before them: *rambutan* (literally 'the hairy one'), a bright red fruit covered with pithy hairs and containing a delicious white 'grape'; large prickly jackfruit and *durian* which grew on tall trees and which when approaching maturity had to be covered with paper bags to protect them from depredation by bird or flying-fox; warm orange mangoes and *papaya*, rich purple mangosteens, little green oranges, and golden bananas.

By mid-morning most of the crowd had drifted to the *kedai*, moving constantly, greeting each other, buying goods, drinking in the coffee shops, eating *satay* from the stalls.

'*Apa khabar, tuan!*' they greeted Flywheel.

'*Khabar baik!*' he replied.

I watched with fascination a slinky Dusun woman dressed in her tight black short skirt and jacket, red cane hoops around her hips and hair dressed smoothly in a bun. She walked along in an undulating fashion casting dark glances up and down. I had never seen anything so provocative nor, I think, had many of the men but the seductive illusion was dispelled when she opened her mouth and displayed teeth reddened with betel-nut juice.

Dozens of mangy sore-ridden stray dogs were crawling around.

'Ugh! Why don't you get rid of them?'

'Can't,' said Flywheel. 'I used to have them shot but I'm not allowed to any more.'

'Why not?'

'Well, during my last dog hunt a woman who was sitting in a "little house" put her head out to see what was happening and a bullet grazed her forehead. I was most annoyed because she wrote a complaint about it. I told her she should change her laxative and not spend so much time in the privy!'

We came to a large crowd of people forming a ring. It was the weekly cockfight. Flywheel pushed his way through and found seats for us on the edge of the arena. In opposite corners were the antagonists, nursed and fondled by their owners. Bets were being placed by enthusiastic supporters. On a command, the owners carried their birds into the centre of the ring, placed them on the ground to face their opponent squarely and then ducked out of the way.

The two cocks, proud in their coppery beauty, fixed each other with a challenging beady stare, heads low, then all hell was let

loose as they flew at each other, striking with their sharp beaks and daggered claws. The dust rose, feathers flew and the air was loud with excited barracking from the onlookers. Suddenly it was over, for no reason that I could detect. Each owner scooped up his bird and retired to his corner. He took a mouthful of water and sprayed it in a fine mist over the bird. He wiped away blood and cleaned its eyes and nostrils. He checked the sharp spurs fixed to its ankles. Then the match was resumed. It would go on until one bird turned and ran or was badly wounded. We did not wait.

It was now very hot. Flywheel took us to his house which was delightfully situated on a hill overlooking the wide, muddy river. We sat on his verandah sipping *ayer limau* and relaxing in the peace which surrounded us. Over my left shoulder was Kinabalu, as intriguing as ever, wreathed in wisps of cloud, its side gashed by silver where dozens of giant waterfalls tumbled down the granite walls.

How I longed to climb that mountain! But I would not have leave until I had worked for a year and it could not be done in less than eight days. Dickie Wyile, the lady doctor from the hospital, and Dorothy had just returned from an exhausting ascent of the mountain. They knew a woman had climbed it in the twenties, long skirts and all, and if she could do it, then they could. They had had to get to Ranau first, a remote village in the foothills of Kinabalu, then pony-trek to the base of the mountain. Two days climbing brought them to the Paka 'cave' – an overhanging shelf of rock which offered some shelter from the damp and the cold. There they slept, rising before dawn to go up to the summit (close on 14,000 feet high) for the sunrise, then descending to the cave before the swirling clouds again swathed the mountain. One more night was spent there before they started the homeward trek. They had reached Jesselton weary, dirty and covered with leech bites. Such a trip required a lot of organization. Equipment and food had to be bought, a guide and porters had to be arranged. Also, as the natives held the mountain sacred ('*Aki Nabalu*' – home of the spirits of the departed), they had to take along a priest to say prayers at specified places and times and to make a sacrifice at the summit. A chicken was supposed to be killed but, owing to the difficult of lugging a live chicken to the top, he usually made do with ceremoniously breaking an egg. It didn't look as though I should be able to climb the mountain this year, but . . .

•   •   •

Launch trips to the islands on Sunday mornings were fun. Obligatory equipment was a 'Beautiful Sun Hat' (a Chinese straw hat printed with gaudy flowers and with those words actually written on it) and a 'Good Morning' towel. This was a small hand-towel, probably intended for shaving, and was invaluable when anyone or anything needed mopping. A basket crammed with swimsuit, large towel, camera, cold drinks wrapped in wet paper and a packed breakfast completed the *barang* and we all clambered on the Customs launch at 8 a.m. and headed for Pulau Sapi. Pulau Gaya was much bigger but Sapi was our favourite. It would take about an hour to cross the intervening water and once clear of the fish-traps we'd pass the time aquaplaning on boards towed by the launch. Water skiing wasn't heard of then but aquaplaning needed the same skill. A tumble in the water wasn't serious. I don't think I ever heard of sharks in those waters. Towards the end of the year there were jellyfish, huge cyclamen clumps of tentacles like fantastic dahlias which each turquoise wave turned over like a wind shaking down blossoms. These were not harmful but the Portuguese Man o' War was. This creature tended to be found in the shallows trailing its long streamers and children were often the victims. Even 'dead' tentacles separated from the creature could inflict serious wounds, clinging to the flesh until dislodged by a handful of rough sand. I saw a child who had been lashed by these tentacles as though by a whip.

However, there was no danger at the islands. The water was the palest duck-egg blue and so clear that twenty feet looked like six. We dived off the launch and swam around the boat till we were tired, then had breakfast and cold drinks and perhaps a sleep on deck. A few energetic souls might walk around the island. Sapi was so small we could complete a circuit in an hour, clambering over great rounded boulders and swinging on vines. On one occasion we saw young turtles, newly hatched from their rubbery eggs, teetering unsteadily down the beach to the safety of the sea. By 11.30 or 12 we were on our way back to the mainland for curry tiffin.

Even during our launch picnics the Customs Department never relaxed its vigilance. One day Roy Knowles directed the *serang* to turn the boat and head for a large junk half a mile away on the starboard bow. As we approached the strange, ancient craft, I was fascinated by its prehistoric appearance. Ungainly, slow, built in a fashion totally foreign to western eyes, its sails made of patches of woven pandanus with patches over the patches where the sails had torn, it looked like a huge bat and wallowed helplessly becalmed like a stricken animal. Roy climbed aboard it as we came alongside and made a swift inspection of its hold before returning to the launch. He was on guard against the smuggling of narcotics. On the East Coast another Customs officer, Jim Tocker, had acquired a great reputation in his fight against smugglers. He had a fine Alsatian dog, Rufus, whom the locals credited with supernatural powers in his ability to sniff out drugs. Rufus must have been one of the first dogs able to detect them and when he appeared on the scene, culprits knew the game was up.

●   ●   ●

Life in the Rest House was never dull. Besides the hard core of permanent residents, there was an ever-changing crowd of transients – planters spending a weekend in town (two days a month was their leave allowance), chartered accountants doing the rounds of their clients, District Officers from the *ulu* or outback, geologists and seimologists prospecting for oil and minerals, and R.A.F. and R.A.A.F. aircrews from the Sunderland flying boats which called regularly. Travelling salesmen often set up their pitch on the verandah. The girls and I were perpetually in debt to the Chinese linen man who spread his wares to tempt us. The exquisitely embroidered tablecloths, table mats, guest towels and handkerchiefs were quite cheap so of course we succumbed. Another regular visitor was Simon Yew, Borneo's local Chinese artist who produced a prodigious number of attractive watercolours. Junks, *padi* fields with *kerbau*, native *kampongs* with bamboo and dozens of Kinabalus poured from his brush and into the houses of expatriates.

Sometimes round-trip tourists from Singapore or Seria appeared and one morning at breakfast I was astonished to see David Marshall who had come to represent a client in a lawsuit.

Borneo seemed to attract eccentric characters, people like 'Body' Barnes, Chip Plunkett, Irish Paddy Heaton and Scottish George

Hardie. George was the Government printer, a short, stocky man in his fifties with a thatch of grey hair, a beaky nose and piercing blue eyes. He hailed from Aberdeen and spoke in a high, squeaky voice with an accent as thick as porridge. Each morning he left the Rest House neatly dressed in a checked open-necked shirt, worn outside his Bombay bloomers, long stockings, and shoes, and walked down to the railway station below the Clock Tower, carrying his lunch box, a folding chair and a large striped golf umbrella. He alighted at Kapayan beyond Tanjong Aru where he was met by a retinue of attendants who carried the umbrella, the chair and the lunch box to the Printing Office.

At breakfast one morning, he turned to a woman of questionable reputation who was visiting Jesselton. In his penetrating voice he shrilled: 'You were snoring like a pig last night!' Secrets couldn't be kept long in the Rest House. Everyone knew George's room was next door to that of another man and many a giggle was suppressed by crunching cornflakes.

A planter whom we all liked was Australian 'Tux' Tuxford from Beaufort. He and his Dusun wife Dodie had a wonderful family of about ten children and Tux, devoted to his wife, gave her anything she wanted. In his weary sardonic voice he would tell us about their recent trip to Australia and Dodie would show us the opal-encrusted jewellery which graced her fingers, throat and wrist.

'Tommy' Thompson was a well-known character too. He would suddenly appear in Jesselton after an absence of some weeks, walking rapidly along the street with his short, brisk steps and his straight fair hair falling over his ears at a time when 'short back and sides' was the fashion. A chartered accountant, he travelled around the country seeing his clients, entertaining the inmates of whichever Rest House he stayed in with a wide range of improbable stories and retailing juicy bits of gossip he had gathered on his round of the towns and estates. It was amazing to watch him adding a long column of figures, his finger travelling smoothly down the lines of numbers, tossing some answer to a query over his

shoulder without pausing in his calculations. He had an encyclo-
paedic memory and could provide information on any subject re-
quested. When his next appointment was with a client in the *ulu*, he
would set off in his neat white shirt and shorts, long stockings and
shoes, carrying a bundle of files spilling papers, swinging his stick,
and walk there, no matter how far, probably indulging his passion
for birdwatching on the way.

However, everyone else was eclipsed by the legendary R.K.
Hardwick. His name was Richard but he was only ever called
Hardwick, or Mr Hardwick by Dot who did his typing. He was a
Visiting Agent which meant he was God to the rubber planters,
travelling up and down the line and round the coast, visiting and
reporting on the running of the estates. When he arrived at the Rest
House on his infrequent visits to Jesselton, he was treated with
great respect by the servants while the Europeans related stories
about him in reverent whispers.

An adventurous but impecunious young Englishman, he had
been sent by his family to Australia and landed up in the primitive
outback of Western Queensland in the early 1900s. After several
years we hear of him becoming buckjumping champion of Queensland. After this he was commissioned to take a thousand brumbies
or wild horses to Indonesia and on arrival there he made a highly
profitable deal to break them in. With the proceeds he gravitated
from Indonesia to North Borneo where he became a planter. An
issue of an early newspaper *circa* 1908 mentions that R.K.
Hardwick, 'armed only with a revolver' successfully overcame an
amok! (One who runs amuck in a frenzied thirst for blood.) He was
reputed to be the only *orang puteh* (white man) to become a blood
brother of the Dyaks, having been initiated into all the rites of
manhood and having himself taken a head. Dr Herbert Wyile told
me the circumstances in which Hardwick had taken the head. The
story involved another *amok* on board a fishing boat who pursued
Hardwick round and round the deck with a *parang*. Hardwick
snatched up a *parang* himself and by some devious strategy suc-

ceeded in cleaving his pursuer. In Herbert's words: 'the two halves of his bottom fell apart like the halves of a ripe peach.' When I first saw Hardwick he was old and grey and sedate. The stories about him were all the more incredible. I wonder if anyone will ever know all his adventures.

There were other Somerset Maugham characters too. One lunch time there was a solitary woman, dressed in a heavy black fur coat and hat, seated at a verandah table staring lugubriously into her glass. What brought her to this backwater? Nobody knew.

Geof Faulkner was a quietly-spoken man in his fifties who was full of surefire schemes for making money. He argued plausibly but never managed to persuade anyone, certainly not C.D.C., to back him.

George Angalet spent a few weeks with us. He was hunting a particular wasp which he hoped to introduce into Hawaii to combat a destructive fruit fly. Was his wasp ever named *Opius angaleti*?

A middle-aged couple arrived. He had been an engineer in Africa. His wife was a gentle Scottish woman, charming and eager to enter into all the Rest House activities. Some weeks later she asked Mrs Whitton for a single room in the Annexe. She said the main house was too noisy, too hot, but one night as I was going to bed I heard the sound of weeping. I went into her room and found her sitting on the concrete floor, propped against the wall, very drunk. She had, it transpired, found a letter in her husband's pocket from a woman with whom he had had an affair in Africa. Twin boys had been born to her. My friend dissolved into maudlin tears.

'To think how I've scrimped and saved! I've tried to be a good housekeeper. I've wondered where our money was going and all the time he's supporting this woman and TWINS!'

A little later he was posted to the East Coast and she went home to Glasgow.

Theirs was not the only marriage to founder on the rocks of isolation, idleness, heat and primitive conditions. There were other dangers too. When handsome dark-haired Dougie McDonald and his beautiful blonde wife Marie moved to Singapore, disaster came from an unexpected quarter. Marie was a Roman Catholic, Dougie a Presbyterian. While Dougie was out at work each day, the local priest visited Marie, pointing out to her that as she hadn't been married in the Catholic Church, she was living in mortal sin and her little son was therefore illegitimate. Day after day he badgered her until the poor girl, worn out with worry and guilt, took her little boy and ran to a convent, refusing to see or even talk to her distracted husband. We never heard the outcome of their personal tragedy.

A significant new addition to Jesselton's commercial life were the 'émigrés', European and Chinese, who streamed in from China and Hong Kong. With the establishment of the People's Republic of China on the 21st of September, businessmen were seeking new areas to operate in. We could tell these men by their brisk, go-getting manner and their high-pressure salesmanship. In particular, architects and builders came, rented offices and prepared to cash in on the bonanza of rebuilding Borneo.

One of the most engaging of these men was 'Honkee' Kwan. An architect from Hong Kong, he was a likeable scamp, generous and hospitable but unscrupulous in business.

'There's only one way to get on in this world, Wendy,' he said, 'Climb on your friend's back!'

Honkee's firm quickly acquired many contracts for building work, some of it for Cable and Wireless, but his normally astute brain would seem to experience a slight aberration when sending in his bill for work done. He would show his percentage as 5% when it should have been .5%. 'Body' Barnes would read through the invoice, snort and scrawl right across it: 'Think again, Honkee!' Quite unabashed, Honkee would alter the bill and submit it again.

Another new arrival was Monica Glyn-Jones. Recently graduated from Cambridge she was an anthropologist and had come to Borneo to study the native tribes. I helped her unpack her crates of field equipment, tent, mosquito net, wet and dry bulb thermometers, cooking utensils and so on. After spending a few weeks reconnoitring the immediate environs of Jesselton, she applied to her headquarters to study the Bajau, one of the more interesting indigenous Borneo peoples. Known as 'the cowboy of Asia', the Bajau is adept at riding the funny little Borneo ponies. In his turban-like head-dress and moustache he looks like a piratical desperado and it is not so very long since he was just that. The Bajau are *orang laut*, men of the sea, and before they settled on the land, growing *padi* and raising cattle, were savage pirates roaming the seas far and wide.

Monica was directed instead to devote her energies to researching the Dusun people.* The Dusuns (their name means 'the orchard people') are the largest indigenous group in the country. They are the cultivators of the land and their life revolves around the annual rice cycle of ploughing, planting and harvesting. They are short and stocky in build with a fairly light skin, probably due to intermarriage with Chinese over the years.

Monica made her home in the small village of Tomposik, a predominantly Dusun area just beyond Penampang, nine miles from Jesselton. She rented a small native house under which buffalo snorted and rolled and there she tried to busy herself in her work, her only recreation playing tunes on her tin whistle. Had she been deep in the interior the project might have been more successful but, only nine miles from the bright lights of town, she was tempted because of her loneliness to come to Jesselton every weekend. Friday afternoon saw her pedalling her pushbike furiously up the Rest House hill, her glasses glinting in the setting sun, her face scarlet with exertion. Sunday evening she returned to her *kampong*, exchanging her feminine dress for serviceable shorts or a *sarong*.

•   •   •

---

* Now called Kadazan.

On Guy Fawkes Day 1949 there was to be a grand opening of the new Club at Beaufort, sixty miles south down the railway line. Nancy, Diana, Monica and I caught the 1.15 p.m. rail car, a quaint vehicle nicknamed the 'matchbox'. It consisted of one small carriage with six comfortable seats screened from the hot sun or sudden rain. Sitting in the front seat was like riding on a switchback. Although the track was level, it was, said the jokers, the only railway in the world made up entirely of 'straights', so that at every bend in the track there was a sudden sideways jolt.

Once out of town we passed the airstrip and followed the coast south-west through mangrove swamps, their exposed roots like a tangle of old baskets, never far from the sea, and some time later crossed a river and stopped at the town of Papar. It looked charming. All around were emerald ricefields, the *padi* growing sturdy and lush with the November rains. *Kerbau* had cropped the surrounding grass till it resembled lawn. Dusun children played near the river or rode their *kerbau*. The rice harvest would not be gathered in until January and November was a time of relative leisure. There was no time to observe any more. The guard's whistle shrilled and we were off again, clickety-clacking down the line, passing picturesque *kampongs* built on stilts amongst clumps of coconut palms or bamboo and crossing rivers where women in colourful *sarongs* bathed or washed their clothes. Soon we were into dark plantations of rubber and I recognized the names of estates I had heard of from visiting planters . . . Kinarut, Kimanis, Membakut . . . and then we arrived in Beaufort. I saw a very green valley with pleasant hills surrounding it. The Rest House was built on one of these hills and we climbed up to it.

It was packed with visitors and we had to put up our camp beds in a narrow strip of corridor, erecting mosquito nets with all the ingenuity and safety pins we could find. Then we all bathed and got in each other's way trying to dress and do our make-up in front of one small mirror before making our way in the dark down to the new Club house.

Lots of planters had come from up and down the line, many of them unknown to me, and after the Club was officially opened dancing commenced. One man had been watching me across the room and after a while made his unsteady way towards me and asked for the dance. My heart sank. He was already drunk and his face though still young showed signs of dissipation. His conversation was objectionable.

At the end of the dance I rushed to Nancy and told her about him.

'Oh yes, him!' she said. 'He's the son of General Whatsit, you remember, in the war. He's obviously the black sheep of his family. He asked me if I was a virgin . . .'

'Gosh,' I breathed in awe, my innocence affronted, 'What did you say?'

'I said that he'd be the last person I'd tell if I were!'

Further confidences were interrupted by a disturbance at the end of the room. A barrow was wheeled in with an enormous Guy and dozens of bamboo rods with soaked rags bound around their tips. We all grabbed rods, lighted them and followed the Guy in a torch-light procession across the wet fields, chanting 'Lloyd George knew my father' loudly. An immense bonfire had been built and we heaved the Guy on top of it, kindled it with our torches and danced the Hokey Pokey* around it, to the great amazement of the natives to whom the doings of the *orang puteh* are incomprehensible indeed.

•   •   •

Christmas was approaching and Dot and I were going to carol rehearsals. The make-up of Jesselton society was such that in any group of people you would find young women and men, very junior in the social scale, rubbing shoulders with brass hats. The carollers included the Attorney-General, the Commandant and

---

* Known in England as the Hokey Cokey to avoid confusion with a confection.

Deputy Commandant of Police, the Assistant Commissioner of Customs, the Manager of Cable and Wireless, the lady Education Officer and assorted spouses, all under the indefatigable baton of Ted Cox, the Police Band Master, Fire Master and Quartermaster. I only met these people socially, rarely needing to go to their offices to see them with their official hats on and it always seemed like an elaborate charade to me, that they were only play-acting at being exalted personages, Pooh Bahs running the country.

'Right!' Ted said one night, 'Next one! "Angels from the realms of glory".'

Mike Saville, a tall fair Government officer, interjected flatly: '*Orang burong* squared *dari negeri.*'

The pedantic, literal translation of English into Malay was a constant source of amusement amongst the *orang puteh*. At the end of a drinking session someone would always call: '*Satu empat jalan!*' (One for the road!) This used the numeral 'four' instead of the preposition 'for'. The greeting '*Apa changkol, buah tua?*' (What-ho, old fruit?) made a pun on the word *changkol*, an agricultural hoe. Mike's translation involved no pun but was an inept schoolboy translation to do with bird-men.

Ted quelled him with a look and gave us our starting notes. As the evening progressed the carollers, well-oiled by frequent libations, were bellowing lustily. Inevitably we ended up singing 'Sing a song of sixpence' to the tune of 'Adeste Fidelis'.

> When down came a bloody great blackbird,
> When down came a bloody great blackbird,
> When down came a bloody great blackbird
> And pecked off her nose.'

Ted and his good-tempered, placid wife Gladys were popular characters. Ted had a whimsical sense of humour and an inexhaustible supply of jokes but there was no doubt about his musicianship.

When it was announced that the huge U.S.S. *St. Paul* was to pay us a visit, plans were made and Colonial protocol rehearsed. On stepping ashore, the visiting Admiral would be greeted by a 17-gun salute by the Police firing party on the hillside above the harbour. The Governor, in ceremonial white uniform and plumed hat, would welcome him. The neatly-uniformed *mata-matas* would be reviewed and then the Admiral would be whisked off to Government House for lunch.

The night before, Ted Cox was calming his nerves at the Rest House bar. He was responsible for the firing parties as well as the Band and it had been a heavy day of rehearsals.

'Everything ready for tomorrow?' asked someone.

'Yes,' replied Ted morosely into his beer. 'But I've got a surprise up my sleeve. We're going to shoot live and give the Yanks something to talk about!'

The morning dawned fine and hot with that breathless hush as the jungle awaits the onslaught of the sun. Even the cicadas seemed to hold their breath. There was tremendous excitement in the town. At 10.30 I locked the office and with Di set off on the long walk to the wharf. The Police Commandant's chauffeur-driven car overtook us and pulled to a stop. Commandant Atkinson cut an imposing figure. He was 6'2" tall and carried about eighteen stone. I had heard tales of how in the internment camp in Kuching, when other prisoners became emaciated through malnutrition, he had looked fairly presentable. Moreover, he had frequently taken the blame for minor misdemeanours in order to protect frailer inmates. Now Atkie, his face beaded with sweat, his tunic unbuttoned at the neck until the last minute, offered us a lift in his official car. An innately kind man, he didn't let the pomp and circumstance of the day affect him.

At the jetty lots of people had gathered, swarming up every vantage point that offered a better view. The great grey shape of the *St. Paul* lay offshore and soon there was a buzz of excitement as the word went around that the Admiral's launch had left the ship's side. The Governor stood with his A.D.C. and officials around him. Atkie nervously walked up and down looking at his watch while the neat ranks of policemen stood at ease and the brilliant sun blazed on the silver instruments of the band.

The fussy little launch made a creamy curve and came alongside the jetty. American sailors, impeccable in their crisp tropical whites, made fast and secured the gangway. Orders rang out. The parade came to attention. Now we could see the Admiral with his rows of medals and lashings of gold braid. He ran smartly up the gangway, set foot on the jetty and came to attention. His arm snapped up in a faultless salute.

At that precise moment one of the hillside batteries fired its first shot, followed shakily a few seconds later by one from the other gun. Hundreds of people stood breathlessly in the heavy heat, counting. Three, four, five. Unevenly spaced, the guns bellowed erratically from the hill. Six, seven, eight, nine, ten. The Admiral's smile was fixed and wooden, his arm tiring. Eleven, twelve, thirteen, fourteen, long pause, fifteen. Sweat was pouring down Atkie's jowled face. Sixteen, seventeen.

Relief! Nothing had gone wrong. The Admiral snapped his hand down and stepped out briskly, hand extended to meet the Governor.

BANG!

A last despairing boom came from the hill.

The Admiral froze in his tracks, clearly wondering if he'd miscounted, then with a shrug and a rueful smile continued on his way. The populace was delighted and Ted was fêted that night in the Club.

The *St. Paul* swamped our small colonial outpost with 1,800 sailors. We entertained a lot of them at a cocktail party and dance at the Club and the Americans brought ashore their own twelve-piece dance band, loud with brass, which was too big and overpowering for our small dance floor (a badminton court during the day) but made such a change from our normal corny records. The hit of the evening was a song the band sang called 'All right Louie, drop that gun!' which I'd never heard before nor have since, but by the end of the dance we all knew it and for months afterwards it was included in our repertoire of party songs. We danced non-stop from seven till one then headed to the beach for a swim, staggering back to the Rest House at 4 a.m. The ship sailed at 6 a.m. leaving Jesselton to face the new day with a bleary eye. Not much work was done in any office that day.

Royal Navy ships were always with us. The Survey Ship *Dampier* was working around the coast and called on us fortnightly and the Admiral of the Far East Fleet's flagship *Alert* was no stranger. Some months later H.M.S. *Jamaica* arrived. There were four days of non-stop sports fixtures, dinners, cocktail parties, canteen duties, dances and beach picnics as well as office work and a few hours of sleep to be crowded in if possible. Each day saw Jesselton a shade seedier, more listless and exhausted but how we adored the *Jamaica*! We adopted the officers' catchphrases: 'It's just *heaven*!' and 'Not to worry!' Great crowds jammed the wharf on Open Day to be shown over the ship. There was a wonderful pirates' party on board for the children and on the last night the ship's company repaid our hospitality with a splendid dance on deck, the ship's orchestra dressed as Hawaiians against a backdrop of palms. Delicious *makan kechil* was followed by an informal party and jam session in the wardroom and a late supper of bacon and eggs. Then the shore boats pulled away, the ship's rails lined with cheery hosts and the robust strains of 'Cigreets and whusky and wild wild women' floating across the water.

•   •   •

David Fiennes was working very hard preparing for a visit of a high-ranking Director from London and the Far East Director from Singapore. They were to appraise all the schemes David had been working on and were to go to the East Coast to inspect the *abaca*

(Manila hemp) estates. They were to sail on the coastal steamer to Tawau and back, stopping at all the North Borneo ports, Kudat, Sandakan and Lahad Datu. Tawau was practically on the Indonesian border and was my Ultima Thule.

I joked with the girls about *my* trip to Tawau and told David I was going to prove how efficient and indispensable I was to the Directors, persuading them that it would be much more satisfactory to take me with them and do all their reports and letters on the ship, rather than be snowed under when they returned.

David laughed. 'Who would look after the office?'

'Kipli.'

He didn't think this was a good idea and didn't take my suggestion seriously. Nevertheless I kept up my positive thinking and made sure I had a stock of clean clothes in my wardrobe. The thought of seeing all those Borneo towns was exciting. I hadn't stayed in the same place for so long for three years and was longing to travel.

The Directors, Mr Weekes from London and Mr Mott from Singapore, arrived on the Sunday plane and were to board the ship on Tuesday night. Monday morning saw me dancing attendance on them in the office, sparkling with clean, well-pressed clothes and efficiency.

'Cigarette, sir? Light?'

I sent cables for them and typed their letters with speed and accuracy but had no opportunity to mention the matter to them.

That night the girls asked: 'Well Wen, going to Tawau?'

'Well, er . . . not yet. That is, I'm laying the foundations. I'll speak to them tomorrow.'

They laughed at me.

Next morning Mr Weekes came in and gave me a letter.

I said banteringly: 'You know, I ought to go to Tawau with you. Think of the work you could do! All your reports and letters . . . '

'Yes, good idea, but someone must keep the Jesselton office open.'

They were busy with the Governor all afternoon. I waited for them to return and at six o'clock they came in and Mr Weekes dictated a long and involved letter which had to be done immediately. It was almost dark and there was no light in the office.

'You'd better come up to Government House with me,' said Mr Weekes. 'You can type in my sitting room.'

We picked up the typewriter, paper and carbons and I followed Mr Weeke's car on my Corgi up to the Government House Annexe. He settled me in his room and departed.

I ploughed through my shorthand outlines, typing doggedly. I was so tired! And so hungry! A storm broke and the lights went out. Everything seemed to conspire against my getting the job done.

The power was restored and I finished the letter at nine o'clock. It was now raining heavily and I spent ten minutes running my Corgi up and down the road in the deluge trying to start it. By the time the engine roared into life I was soaked. I flew down Government House hill and into the main road, bumping in and out of pot-holes, huge waves of water flying up over my legs and filling my shoes. The rain beat into my eyes and my hair stuck on my face. Visibility was practically nil.

Shivering and dripping, I reached the Rest House and yelled for Wah Kim. There was no sign of him. There was no sign of anybody, guests or staff. A wave of self-pity swept over me. All my friends were out enjoying themselves.

I fetched a bucket of hot water from the kitchen stove, bathed and washed my clothes. I wanted nothing but to get to bed but my room had not been touched since morning. The bed was unmade. I couldn't take my Paludrine because the tumbler was still dirty from tooth-cleaning and the water jug was empty. I was furious. When Wah Kim finally answered my calls, I let loose a stream of care-fully-prepared Malay about the bed, the glass, the water. He re-plied in much fuller and more extravagant Malay which I couldn't understand so I turned and left him.

I made the bed myself and had just turned out the light and was trying to forget the rumblings of my empty stomach when Wah Kim knocked at my door and said I was wanted on the phone. Muttering, I threw on a dressing gown and ran up to the main house.

A bright voice greeted me. 'Miss Law? Fiennes here. How would you like to go to Tawau?'

I shrieked disbelief.

'Mr Weekes has decided he'd like to do some work on the way. Right? Pick you up in half an hour.'

I rushed from the phone in near-hysteria, laughing and crying with surprise, shock and the frustration of having no one to tell. Down to my room I raced, emptied all my freshly-laundered clothes into a case, dressed, left notes for the girls, signed out of the Rest House for a week and was waiting, panting, when David arrived.

He had brought the typewriter from Government House but we went down to the office and with the aid of a torch collected typing paper, carbons, pencils, notebooks, rubber, maps, everything we might need, and then drove to the wharf.

I was still very light-headed, my fatigue miraculously gone. The three men had come from dinner at Government House and were wearing evening dress – white sharkskin jackets, black ties, cummerbunds and black trousers. Staggering up the gangway of the *Darvel* with our bundles we looked like a party of drunken revellers. A sleepy steward met us. David airily said that there was an extra person and did they have a cabin for me? They did and at half past midnight I found myself sitting on the edge of a bunk in a roomy double cabin pinching myself.

Once more I smelt all the wonderful exciting smells of a ship, the tarry, resiny, painty smells all overwhelmed by the inevitable cloying stench of copra. I crawled between the crisp, starched sheets on my bunk and the creaking of timber, the lap of the waves against the ship's sides, the hum of the generator deep down in the hull, subdued footsteps padding along the passageway and the constant splashing of water falling from the bilge soon lulled me to sleep. When I awoke we were far out to sea.

Chapter 6

Pelayaran Timor

After breakfast I presented myself to Mr Weekes with my note book and pencil, ready for work. He stretched lazily in his deckchair, looked through the rails at the shimmering sea and re-marked to David and Mr Mott:

'This is really most pleasant, isn't it! I think I'll read for a while. Come back at twelve, Miss Law!'

As I suspected, he rapidly succumbed to ship lassitude and we did very little work.

We sailed up the coast north of Jesselton and rounded the pig's ear, turning south into the vast expanse of Marudu Bay. Here, on a peninsula facing the bay was the small town of Kudat, neat and orderly with its wharf and *godowns*, two streets and a *padang*, its District Office and Police Station, with the Union Jack flying on the flagpole. Mr Weekes was to have discussions with the District Officer about David Fiennes's plan to develop a huge rice farm at Bandau, at the southern extremity of Marudu Bay, but Kudat's economy was firmly based on the coconut. Rows of coconut palms could be seen extending back from the sparkling beach and the wharf was cluttered with sacks of copra waiting to be loaded. Copra is merely the sun-dried flesh of the coconut and produces the pervasive sickening smell so noticeable on the coastal steamers. Kudat was full of it.

While the men were in conference with the D.O., I wandered through the *kedai* and tried to picture Kudat as the pirate haunt it used to be. All the North Borneo coast from Brunei Bay in the south-west right round to Tawau in the south-east was known for piracy as long ago as the mid-eighteenth century and Marudu Bay with its numerous creeks and rivers was ideally suited as a bolt-hole. Maritime charts of the coastline bore the cryptic word 'Pirates' and ships avoided the area. Villages along the coast were terrorized by pirates looting and burning. They often took prisoners and sold them as slaves in Brunei or Sulu. In 1845 the first White Rajah of Sarawak, James Brooke (a young English adventurer who had helped the Sultan of Brunei quell an uprising and been rewarded with a modest tract of land almost the size of England), was trying to extend his rule of peace and order northwards and sought the British Navy's aid in suppressing the pirates who were preventing the settlement and development of the Borneo territories. The Navy despatched a squadron of eight warships which pursued the pirates right to their hideout in Marudu Bay. There the chief pirate, Sherip Osman, and hundreds of his men were killed and many of their large war *perahus* were sunk. Notwithstanding, there were still sporadic attacks all along the coast and by the 1870s there were no villages closer to the coast than sixty miles up the rivers. Despite the peaceful rule of the Chartered Company which governed North Borneo from 1881 until the 2nd World War and the establishment of North Borneo as a Crown Colony of Great Britain in 1946, piracy was still known around the Borneo coast. Looking at sleepy little Kudat it all seemed unlikely in the twentieth century but the Union Jack was reassuring.

Our next stop was Sandakan on the East Coast. Originally called Elopura, the beautiful city, it was North Borneo's capital from 1883 till the 2nd World War (apart from short periods when the Governor resided in Jesselton) and I knew its name well from wartime news reports. It was from here that 2,400 prisoners of war, 1,800

Australians and 600 British, set out on the infamous Sandakan Death March which Australians see as the greatest tragedy in the Pacific War. Even more Australian P.O.W.s died in Borneo than on the Siamese Railway.

K.G. Tregonning in *North Borneo* paints a horrifying picture of the prisoners who in the closing days of the war were marched out of the Sandakan camp to Ranau, 150 miles away, 1,500 feet up in the mountainous interior of Borneo.

> These men, some hobbling on sticks, some with ulcers through to the bone, the 'walking wounded' of a three-year war with malnutrition, maltreatment, malaria, dysentry and beri-beri, men with distended stomachs and swollen limbs, men whose heads wobbled from side to side, left Sandakan in the belief that the war was over. It was only when they reached the main road and turned not left to the town but right to the road's end and the wall of jungle that they knew that this was a march not to freedom but to death.

They staggered through muddy swamps and clawed their way up and down unending chains of mountains. Those too weak to move were simply shot. Some of them actually reached Ranau but appalling conditions, cruel treatment and executions killed most of the men. Of the two and a half thousand prisoners, only six Australians survived.

During the bombing which accompanied the liberation of the Borneo territories, Sandakan was completed flattened and even four years later, when I saw it, it was still a town of *kajang* and *attap*, more so even than Jesselton. Situated in an idyllic setting with hills surrounding a beautiful bay, Sandakan's life centred on the busy wharf from which it derived its sustenance. Its lifeline was the sea and the ships which came weekly from Singapore or monthly from Hong Kong brought its imports and took away its timber and cutch (a product derived from mangrove bark used for dyeing and tanning). It had virtually no roads, its long rivers and the sea being all it needed.

I picked my way along the broken, uneven pavements, dodging the inevitable pi-dogs, until I reached familiar ground – the *kedai*, comfortingly the same in every town throughout Borneo. Here, in the makeshift shelters erected between the bombed ruins with their reinforcing iron sticking out grotesquely at crazy angles, beat the steady pulse of Chinese commerce. Here were the cheerful tailors, treadling their sewing machines in the shops opening straight onto the footpath, bales of cloth spilling into the dust; the Chinese herbalists with their neat jars of incredible, unlikely medicines; the market where women were carrying off their purchases – live crabs or chickens encircled by a loop of rattan or neat packages wrapped in banana leaves. It could have been Jesselton so I turned away and climbed to the ridge of the hills. At the top I found the ruins of the Anglican Church and sat there to rest from the heat. I was feeling lonely and full of a gentle melancholy. I didn't know where my life was going nor quite what I was looking for. I sat in the shattered church and hoped for some kind of answer. It was quiet but it was an empty shell. There was no answer there.

I turned back to the ship but on my way through the town ran into Ted Cox's married daughter Joan who promptly carried me off to her house. She and her husband Mike were having a party that night and wouldn't hear of my not being there. As usual single women were in short supply, with bachelors from Harrisons, the Banks and other merchant firms to be partnered. It was a good party – Joan and Mike Wade were a popular young couple – and they returned me to the ship just before it sailed.

A couple of days steaming brought us to Lahad Datu on the East Coast. Here C.D.C. was interested in an *abaca* estate. While the men had discussions with the District Officer and local business men I went for my usual ramble through the town, interested in the different sort of native people. Lahad Datu and Tawau are on the

Celebes Sea. They look to the Celebes and the Philippines, not Malaya, and so are more likely to be the target of motorized pirates from the Sulu Archipelago. Speedy *perahus* land at any of the coastal settlements, shoot up the town, loot the shops and depart as quickly as they arrive, back across the Sulu Sea to any of a thousand island hideaways. I felt a vicarious thrill of danger at the thought.* In Tawau the next day I saw hordes of picturesque, colourfully painted craft which had sailed across from the Celebes, smuggling copra for which they could get a better price in Borneo. The crews spent their profits on new flamboyantly coloured *sarongs* and strutted around like peacocks, unrolling and rerolling them in the sheer joy of possession.

Tawau was a very small town deriving its livelihood from coconuts and *abaca*. The visit of the weekly ship was always welcome and the passengers from the *Darvel* were invited ashore for dinner with the District Officer, Rex Blow, and his wife Diana. Rex was an Australian and had become something of a legend for his war exploits. Dick Horton in his book *Ring of Fire* describes the activities of the Australian guerrillas against the Japanese, some operating in night raids against shipping in Singapore harbour, others parachuting into the Borneo jungle to organize resistance by the native tribes, to gather intelligence and to harass the Japanese. Rex Blow had been a District Officer before the war. Like the other civilians he was interned by the Japanese but was one of the few to escape from Berhala Island prison camp. He made his way to the Philippines where he operated successfully as a guerilla leader, earning the D.S.O. and Bar and the American Silver Star. From there he was recruited by the Services Reconnaissance Department whose headquarters were in Melbourne and who masterminded the guerilla

---

* In March 1954, several motorized *kumpits* came into Semporna, a small settlement south of Lahad Datu, and tied up at the jetty where a newly-arrived young European Forestry Officer was fishing. When a Customs clerk came to check their papers, firing broke out. Police arrived and in the shoot-out, the European and five Asians were killed. The shops in the town were then ransacked and the marauders left.

operations in Borneo. He took part in Operations *Agas* and *Semut* and was present with another famous Borneo character, Tom Harrisson, when the last pocket of Japanese surrendered in the interior on the 30th of October 1945. It was not till thirty-five years later that I learned the details of his war exploits (internees and guerillas rarely mentioned their experiences), nor did I know that Egerton Mott, my Singapore Director, had been the first head of the organization in Melbourne which later became the Services Reconnaissance Department. Even after his return to London in 1943 Mott was responsible for choosing Harrisson and Blow for their guerrilla missions.

However, there was no mention at dinner of their shared experience although conversation did turn to the double-handed Japanese sword hanging on the wall, perhaps the very sword surrendered by the Japanese commander to Harrisson and Blow. Kidman Cox, an Agricultural Officer travelling on the *Darvel*, was persuaded to do his party trick with the sword and asked me to be his victim. I declined out of concern for my evening dress, so Rex lay down on the woven grass mat and a banana was placed on his diaphragm. Kidman grasped the ornate sword, raised it aloft and with a delicate flick of his wrists brought it down swiftly to slice the banana neatly in two, leaving Rex unscathed.

Kidman Cox was a much-travelled man. During the return trip to Jesselton he talked to me at length about his time in West Africa and gave me his recipes for Groundnut Palm Oil Chop and Kitcheri Jhallfrezi, his favourite African dishes.

Kidman Cox is credited with the introduction of cocoa into North Borneo where it has become a profitable crop on the East Coast. Ted Ellison, the Development Secretary, told me of the time he was leaving Accra in the Gold Coast. As he waited at the airport, Kidman Cox arrived breathlessly, clutching two trays of special disease-free cocoa beans. They flew to Cairo together but on landing Kidman was arrested for some reason and placed under detention in a room at the airport. There was a small heater in a corner of the room and he was able to keep the beans warm. After several hours spent demanding his freedom, they let him go just as a plane was about to leave. As the boarding steps were being wheeled away, Kidman sprinted across the tarmac still clutching his precious trays of cocoa beans, boarded the plane and eventually brought his cargo to Jesselton.

An accomplished artist, Kidman had an eye for beauty and one day we argued hotly about the relative merits of the Malay women's costume and that of the Dusuns. I held that the Dusuns were dull beside the butterfly colours of their Malay sisters.

'Fancy wearing black in the tropics!' I protested, 'With all the colours of nature surrounding them!'

'But what elegance! Those trim, form-fitting black sheaths they wear, piped with gold, the scarlet hoops around their hips and silver or gold jewellery to set it off!'

I was unconvinced at the time but remembered his words later.

And so we returned to Jesselton. How glad I was to see the clocktower! How happy to come back to my little room and to my friends. The well-worn Chinese recording of 'Rose Rose I love you' floated up from the *kedai*. I was home.

Nan came up after work to see me. Apparently she had rung the day after the men had sailed to commiserate with me on not going to Tawau, only to be told that I had gone.

'You see!' I said triumphantly, 'Positive thinking!'

Chapter 7

Terang Bulan

My return coincided with the arrival of several new permanent residents in the Rest House and Mrs Whitton's removal to hospital for the treatment of severe tropical ulcers on her legs. Diana was asked if she would manage the Rest House and after comparing the salary and benefits, she agreed. We decided to throw a party to celebrate the opening of 'Di's Dive'. It was the week before Christmas and festivities were in order. We sent out invitations and, tongue in cheek, I did lots of silly drawings and posters to put on the walls, advertising the non-existent services and the dubious attractions of the establishment.

Gil Brown the architect, generally known as Tuan Broon fra' Troon, studied one of the posters.

'"Running water in each room!" I'll say . . . when it rains! "Efficient *tukang ayer* service"? You must be joking!'

There were drawings of the North Borneo Corgi Lancers and one which I particularly liked. It showed a rear view of a group of men propped at the bar. It was simply titled 'When I was in Africa . . .' One of the men was wearing green corduroy trousers and was meant to be Dr Pasqual. I think he liked the picture too as it disappeared from the wall the morning after the party.

A couple of residents manned the bar and a plentiful supply of *makan kechil* soon disappeared. We pushed the dining chairs and tables aside and danced on the rough concrete floors. Rawicz and

114

Landauer, the piano duettists, were very popular at that time and we loved their rendition of 'Samba Sud' and 'Cavaquinho'. Sambas were less tiring than foxtrots and you didn't have to slide your feet. Men who said they didn't dance could always manage a samba. We samba'd till we were exhausted, then formed a long Conga line and danced through the kitchen and back along the corridor to the verandah. Di's party was a tremendous success.

The rest of Christmas week was even more exhausting. The carollers were much in demand. We sang to the patients at the hospital and then went to Government House where H.E. and his wife had invited guests to hear us. After running through our repertoire we were offered food and drink and then departed, going on to another house with assembled guests. The same procedure completed, we went to another house and then another. By the fourth house the singing was ragged but exuberant. Everyone joined in the choruses, even 'Down came a blackbird'.

Next day there was the children's Christmas party at the Sports Club. There were not many European children in Jesselton, half a dozen babies perhaps and a handful of children under eleven. There was no Government provision for teaching them, the greater need being for schools for the local children, but one of the wives taught a small group of primary children at the Club. Instruction in the Anglican and Catholic church schools was in English but most European parents sent their children home to be educated at ten or eleven years. (One often heard the rueful comment that a man stood to lose either his wife or his children and sometimes both if the wife pined for her children and went home to look after them.)

Several of them had come back from boarding school for the Christmas holidays and, gathered on the Club hill, their excitement mounted until Santa was perceived whizzing down the Rest House road on the pillion of a motorbike driven by Chip Plunkett, whose handlebar moustache did its best to resemble the antlers of a reindeer. (Santa was later revealed to be Robin Black, the Chief Secretary. At New Year, a week later, he proved his versatility by coming to the Fancy Dress Ball as the St. Trinian's Games Mistress beset by a horde of gym-slipped, hockey stick-brandishing fiends. Shortly afterwards he was sent to Hong Kong as Colonial Secretary and later became Governor there, but I shall always think of him, not in his gubernatorial trappings but as the persecuted Games Mistress.)

Christmas Eve at the Club was festive and joyous with carols and dancing interrupted by dashes across to the Lucky Bar for *durian* icecream. Christmas Day dawned like any other day of the year. Instead of a hush broken only by church bells, there was the usual cacophony of raucous Chinese songs, bicycle bells and lorry horns as the town went about its normal business. I was thankful for that as after breakfast I was given presents by Dorothy, Diana and several other Rest House residents, some of whom I had over-looked. As all the shops were open I was able to run down quickly and buy some extra gifts from Ban Mui, Huat Lee or Tong Hing, the three shops which catered for European tastes.

On Christmas Night there was a big party at Mitchells'. The head of Harrisons and Crosfield lived in a beautiful and luxurious home, so different from our spartan accommodation at the Rest House. All of the single girls had been invited to partner the H. and C. bachelors and our eyes opened wide at the sumptuous furnishings. Everyone received a present. Mine was a flame-red chiffon square and a Brunei silver brooch in the shape of a *keris*. After we'd had drinks food was served . . . a full Christmas dinner with all the trimmings, turkey and stuffing, bacon rolls, chipolata sausages, baked ham and pineapple, Christmas pudding and brandy sauce, all washed down with every variety of drink one wished. Then we sat around, replete, and sang carols. As many of the trained carol-lers were there, we were able to sing in parts and again I revelled in this aspect of Christmas which was not common in Australia. We sang all the party songs next – 'Foggy, foggy dew', 'Lloyd George knew my father', 'Bluebells are bluebells' with all its variants, 'Far far away in a small town in Germany' which went on for ages and

had everyone imitating a musical instrument. Then we got on to
'*Rasa Sayang*' and the Malay translations of 'Ten green bottles' and
'One man went to mow'. The more outlandish the translations, the
greater the fun. Nan, who was now going out with Ken Summers,
considered herself almost an H. and C. *mem* and flirted gaily with
Mr Mitchell. It was the best Christmas I had ever had.

When I returned to the Rest House, I took the gardenia out of my
hair and put it in a tumbler of water. At the end of the week the
stalk had sprouted hair-like roots. I told Mrs Whitton who knew all
about gardening.

'Oh, it's struck! You must plant it!'

She told me how to press it down firmly in the earth and water it
in. To my great joy it grew and at the end of a year was a large bush.
This was the beginning of a life-long interest in flowers and gardens. I planted lots of balsam outside my balcony and enjoyed the
bright display of pink, purple, white and cyclamen spikes of flowers. The cheeky little Java sparrows with their red beaks (they were
actually a sort of finch) hopped in and out of the balsam looking for
seeds.

I made a garden outside the office, planting vivid cannas against
the wall and a low border of a plant we called Java violet. It had
dark green leaves and clusters of purple bells but I have never
discovered its botanical name. My garden was the only patch of
colour in the main street.

•   •   •

On the 10th of January Major-General Sir Ralph Hone, our new
Governor, arrived in the Colony. We were all invited to his Instal-
lation in the morning and a Garden Party at Government House at
five o'clock, and there was consternation amongst the ladies who
had to find two outfits to wear. I managed to borrow some stockings and gloves and wore a linen dress and small white crocheted
beret in the morning. The late afternoon party was more difficult. I

planned to wear my tomato-red ballerina which was the dressiest short frock I had, but what to wear on my head? My red dress was really a cocktail frock and didn't need a hat. Then I had a bright idea. Under their conical hats the Chinese coolies wear an annular cane shape. I swathed one of these in my new flame-coloured chiffon scarf and achieved a smart little cocktail hat.

The lawns at Government House were thronged with people of different races, many wearing national dress. Malay servants padded around with trays of drinks and plates of *makan kechil*. The Police Band played light music. The new Governor had an erect, military bearing, silver hair and clipped moustache and startlingly blue eyes. His wife was very tall, younger than he but prematurely white-haired. Like many young women with white hair, she was exceedingly handsome with a fresh complexion. Their young son Richard was brought out by his Nanny and enjoyed himself making the rounds of the guests.

Suddenly there was a drum roll. Chatter ceased as the heart-breakingly lovely sound of 'Sunset' drifted across the lawn. People turned to watch the Union Jack as it slowly, so slowly, started its journey down the flagpole. Oh, the sad clear trumpet notes and the haunting minor harmonies! A lump rose in my throat and as I watched the still crowds splashed with the colours of national costumes and brave uniforms, the lowering sun picking out the vibrant stripes of the flag, I thought that if the Empire were indeed on its way out, it was making a splendid exit.

•   •   •

Before we could draw breath Chinese New Year was on us. Four days of deafening noise, staccato explosions of firecrackers, raucous music floating up from the town, the mind-thudding tattoo of wood blocks and the nasal whine of Chinese opera from a large marquee. Four days of dragon dancing, grotesque head and bulbous eyes wobbling, lamplight flickering on scintillating scales, long body gyrating and undulating with neat pairs of snowy tennis shoes on brown legs capering underneath; crashing cymbals and pounding drums; masked attendants with fans taunting the monster. Crowds at the market place where the Chinese went to gamble, play fan-tan, buy raffle tickets and try their luck at darts or the lucky spinning wheel. Four days without shops, four days without servants, *mems* with cut or burnt fingers due to unwonted work in the kitchen, offices closed except for hurried visits to collect and read incoming mail. At the Rest House we made our beds and cleaned our rooms and somehow Diana managed to feed us, leaving drinks in the refrigerator for people to help themselves.

And then on the fifth day, the relative quiet of the trucks honking, cars hooting and bicycle bells ringing as the town got back to the business of making money. The relief of *mems* being brought their early morning tea in bed, of *tuans* having their starched white clothes laid out for them and their shoes shining with polish, the appreciation of appetizing meals served on time and being able to get up and leave the devastated table without a backward glance at the washing up! For these four days each year expatriate households got a frightening glimpse of Life Back Home, only to blot it out and sink back once more into the lotus-eating existence they were used to.

•　•　•

An interesting new couple had arrived in the Colony. Harry Gatford was to be General Manager of the North Borneo Railway, that modest little line with 116 miles of track which ran from Jesselton south through Papar and Beaufort, then through Tenom to Melalap in the interior, with a spur line to Weston on Brunei Bay. Harry was short and slight in stature with receding pure white hair, a red complexion and bright blue eyes. He looked like a beardless Father Christmas. He had spent twenty-five years in India managing thousands of miles of railway in one of the Indian regions, so this was a gentle sort of retirement job for him. His meagre rolling stock included steam and diesel locomotives, a few carriages, four six-seater diesel railcars (the 'matchboxes') and two 52-seater railcars open at the sides, known as 'toastracks'. The Railways Engineer, Major Wikner, used a jeep with its tyres removed which bowled merrily along the rails, warning yellow flags fixed to the front wings.

Harry's wife Mabel, a large jolly woman rather reminiscent of actress Margaret Rutherford, had been awarded the Silver Beaver for her many years' work for the Guide Movement in India. She and Lady Hone got their heads together and decided it was time that Guiding was started in North Borneo.

Mrs Gatford called a meeting of interested young women over eighteen and formed a Company of Rangers whom she trained and enrolled as Guides before commissioning them as officers to run Guide Companies. I had never had the chance to be a Guide in my youth and as I was adventurous and loved outdoor activities, it appealed to me. Every Thursday at half past four, a multi-national group of young women assembled at Mrs Gatford's wood and *attap* bungalow overlooking the Likas plain with Kinabalu rising high in the east. There were Eurasians Vicky and Rosie Perkins and Agnes Stephens; Kathy Ferdinands who had just arrived from Burma; Pushpam from India; Chinese Elsie Chung, Wong Ling Ling, Margaret Yong, Poh Lan and Judith Thien, Monica and myself. Our Lieutenant was Sister 'Pete' Peters from the hospital and Mrs Gatford was Captain. We learned our Laws and knots, tracking signs and stalking, Morse Code and Semaphore, First Aid and Home Nursing, played nerve-wracking hunting games in the jungle and learned games and songs for campfires. We were a congenial company and I enjoyed my first real contact with the young women whose home was Borneo. Apart from little Suwindar I had never met any local girls.

Mrs Gatford asked me to draw the North Borneo Coat of Arms so that enamelled and embroidered badges could be made in Hong

Kong for the Guide uniforms. The upper third of a shield featured a lion and in the lower section there was Kinabalu in the background and a trading schooner in the foreground. On the mainsail of the sailing ship was the letter 'T' commemorating the liberation of North Borneo from Japanese occupation by the 9th Australian Division. The 'T' represented the shoulder badge of that Division and stood for Tobruk, where the 9th Division won an historic victory over the Germans. I thought the schooner was dull and substituted a Chinese junk but took great pride in drawing the letter 'T' on its mainsail. When the badges were made and worn by the Guides, I was taken severely to task by a senior Government official for having changed the official Coat of Arms granted to the Colony by a warrant of King George. He may have even thought I had some ulterior political motive depicting a Chinese junk instead of a European schooner.

I used to ride my Corgi to Mrs Gatford's after work on Thursdays and join her and Harry for afternoon tea before the Ranger meeting began. She always had sardine sandwiches and a Dundee cake with nuts on top and encouraged me to eat, knowing I would have no dinner. We became very close and I was able to confide in Mabel to an extent that was impossible with Dorothy and Diana. She became a surrogate mother to me and helped me through some unhappy romances.

It was now April 1950. Life continued to be gay and exciting. Away from my large family in Melbourne and separated from the girl with whom I had cycled around Australia, I was maturing and becoming a person in my own right. I was able to please myself what I did and choose the company I wished. In Melbourne I had been too influenced by family opinion and it was impossible to please everyone. I now felt independent and able to make my own life. I was branching out and doing things I'd never done before, choral singing, Guiding, sports and even acting. The Jesselton Players had been formed, at first with the aim of reading plays but then it was decided to stage a production in order to give us an incentive. Charles Taylor of Harrisons and Crosfield had had experience in directing and sent me the script of a play to read. It was a modest little comedy called *Jane Steps Out* by Kenneth Horne. Charles asked me if I would play the part of Beatrice, Jane's sophisticated elder sister. Audrey Pretious, a woman in her thirties, who had had a lot of acting experience, was to play the lead part of the young Jane. As I was then twenty-three, it seemed strange casting. When it was discovered that Audrey was pregnant, it was decided that she and I should change parts although I was nervous about taking the lead. Rehearsals became a weekly occurrence and I learned my lines when David was away on tour.

Despite all these interesting activities, I felt bothered. As in Seria, I wondered what to do next. Where was my life going? I adored North Borneo but was I going to stay there for ever? If not, where should I go? My father was due to retire in December, leaving the Melbourne Teachers' College where he had been Principal for fifteen years. He and my mother were planning their long-awaited trip to England, or Home as Australians still called it. She was writing me agitated letters. What should she do with all my belongings, my books, my clothes, my junk? More from necessity than desire I decided I should go home and so I booked my passage on a ship from Jesselton to Singapore in September, after the play had finished. I could always come back if I didn't want to stay in Melbourne.

In the meantime, Diana was to be married to Sandy Sandford, a surveyor who was one of the permanents in the Rest House. It was an up and down romance and I felt it wasn't solidly enough based to be successful. I think Diana did too as she used to confide her misgivings to Dorothy and me, but she had accepted Sandy who had then gone off on tour to the East Coast. Wedding plans were progressing. I think Di felt trapped by her promise and couldn't bring herself to stop the proceedings. Sandy sent her a sizing kit for her finger so he could order her ring from Singapore. Another irrevocable step? Poor Di! Perhaps if Sandy had been with her during these weeks she might have had the courage to break off the engagement. As it was, she let things ride.

The date was fixed for the 4th of June. Dorothy and I were to be bridesmaids, Sandy's surveyor friend Peter Ellis would be Best Man and Peter Burbrook groomsman. 'Body' Barnes was to give her away. Her mother was coming up from Perth for the wedding. Dresses were ordered, Diana's from an expensive salon in Singapore, the bridesmaids' from Mary Pang, the Chinese dressmaker. The ceremony and reception were planned. There was no turning back.

On the 3rd of May I was zooming up the Rest House hill after work when I passed 'Body' Barnes's car coming down. Next to him sat a young man and I remembered that a new Cable and Wireless chap was arriving that day.

'I wonder if I'll marry him,' I thought idly as I revved up the hill.

New blood in the Rest House was welcome. We had a very amicable hard core of young folk but there was no one to whom I was attracted in a romantic way. The last man I'd been interested in had gone on tour. It had been an unsatisfactory affair as I cared for him more than he did for me. I had gone into a decline – nowadays I suppose it would be diagnosed as anorexia nervosa – and had difficulty in eating. I had lost a great deal of weight.

That evening 'Body' introduced the young man to us. His name was Brian Suart. Yes, Suart. I ran to check it in the Register. How odd! He was quiet but nice. Already suntanned, unlike most newly-arrived pallid Poms, he was tall and slim and seemed to radiate calmness and tranquillity. 'Robbie' Robinson, an architect, had also arrived on the plane.

Nancy, who by now had come to live in the Rest House, had a women's magazine with one of those quizzes which have multiple choice answers. Depending on which answer he picked, one allocated a score and ascertained the personality of the young man being questioned. We had been analysing all the men in the Rest House with much hilarity.

'Let's do Brian!' said Nancy.

I felt rather apprehensive. He didn't seem to be the sort of man who would like baring his soul to a lot of strangers.

Nancy fired off questions at him. He answered them simply. Then she said:

'Is love the most important thing in your life?'

I shrank inside myself with embarrassment. Most people would duck such an intimate probing into their life. What would he say?

'Yes,' he answered, quite unabashed.

I've forgotten the outcome of that stupid quiz but I have never forgotten his honesty. Brian had no guile. I was impressed.

The next morning he came to breakfast unshaven.

'Forgive my stubble, I'm growing a beard,' he said.

He was friendly, but not over-friendly, and uncomplicated. He said what he thought and I didn't have to think first about what I was going to say. My previous inamorata blew hot and cold, one day warm and affectionate, the next cold and offended. Meal times had become a time of stress. Hence my anorexia. When Brian came to the Rest House I started to eat.

H.M.S. *Dampier* came into port. Coming along Gaya Street on my Corgi after work, my attention was distracted by a group of sailors and I failed to notice a stationary truck in front of me. Just in time I swerved to avoid it and went into the deep storm drain. Chinese shopkeepers helped me out and then fished out Bess. The bike appeared to be undamaged but I was grazed and shaken. Robbie came along in a Land Rover and took me and Bess on board and drove us home. That evening I was too tired and sore to go to the Club with the girls so I sat on the verandah and chatted with Robbie and Brian. They were both English and were to stay in Borneo for a three-year tour. Robbie was to work as an architect with the Public Works Department and Brian was to be Engineer of Cable and Wireless's new Jesselton Branch. I knew 'Body' Barnes and George Pope went to Tanjong Aru each day but I didn't know what they did there. Brian invited us down next day to see.

Robbie and I joined him in a brief inspection of the Cable and Wireless property. There were sites for a large office block, workshop, instrument room, engine room and living quarters for Europeans and Asians, all on the drawing board. He would have plenty of work to keep him occupied for three years.

We went for a swim. Asians were rarely seen at Tanjong Aru and never swam there. Several hundred yards offshore were a couple of arrow-shaped fish traps and occasionally some fishermen in a *perahu* would paddle by and collect the accumulated fish. Once I saw two old Dusun women, their faces wrinkled like old apples, dragging long poles through the wet sand at the water's edge in an attempt to catch small mud crabs, but usually the glorious sandy beach, miles long, was deserted.

Debating who could stay under water longest, we all took a deep breath and went under. I came up fairly soon and after a while

Robbie surfaced. We stood waiting for Brian but he was still spreadeagled in the water.

'Let's leave him!' said Robbie conspiratorially, so holding hands we left the water and tiptoed in melodramatic fashion towards the belt of casuarinas, expecting him to surface and see us making for the woods. He still didn't surface and we hid behind the trees. When he finally came up, the South China Sea and the long, long beach were quite empty.

I was finding Brian increasingly compatible. He had a beautiful English voice (much admired by Australians), a delicious wit and above all, a gentleness and tolerance which I thought quite un-usual. He had no interest in team sports but liked badminton. We arranged to play one day after work.

I raced home from the office and changed into my white clothes and tennis shoes. There was no sign of Brian. At half past four . . . still no sign. At five o'clock I was feeling sick. Surely he wasn't like my previous boyfriend who would make arrangements and not turn up. I was moping around the bar when at 5.15 he came rushing up the steps, two at a time.

'Won't be a minute . . . just change my clothes . . .' he panted.

No apology. When he returned I said I was beginning to think he wasn't coming.

'But I don't finish work till five!'

Joy! I didn't know that Cable and Wireless kept to British hours of work whereas everyone else finished at four o'clock. I was flat-tered that he had come bounding up the steps so eagerly. Perhaps he enjoyed being with me?

He played a devastating game of badminton, depending more on deft movements of the wrist and skilful placement than rushing around the court. He beat me hands down!

We began to go for long walks every evening. If we climbed Atkinson Road up to the ridge of the hill which lay behind Jesselton, we could descend by the Tuaran Road, returning past the *kampong ayer*. Or perhaps we would follow a rough track which led from the Rest House along the hill to a point overlooking the harbour. It was always very quiet there and we could watch the reflections of lights in the water and the dark masses of Gaya and Sapi islands offshore.

Sometimes we would even walk down to the pier to watch the moonlight on the water. One night we were sitting close together on the pier, swinging our legs over the edge. Brian put his arm around me and leant comfortably against a bollard. The Customs launch *Langgisan*, was moored nearby and some Malay sailors were singing the hauntingly beautiful love song 'Terang Bulan'.

Brian brushed my cheek with his lips. 'I think I'm falling in love with you.'

He turned my face to his and kissed me gently on the mouth. We looked at each other in the moonlight and kissed again.

I felt I had come home.

•　　•　　•

Gradually I learned more about Brian's background. He came from the East End of London and was the younger of two sons. His older brother Mervyn was a well-known artist and, between him and Brian, their parents had tragically lost two infant daughters. He attended the excellent Leyton County High School for Boys and was evacuated with all the pupils to Brentwood in Essex, nicknamed 'Bomb Alley'. There they were able to watch German bombers flying over and the fields bore evidence of crashed planes, shot down by the R.A.F. So much for children's safety!

After joining Cable and Wireless, he spent a couple of years at its training school in London, doing stints of fire-watching at night during the blitz. His starting salary was £39 per annum, of which five shillings a week was withheld by the Company to buy his overseas kit. He was one of the first group of four men to be dual-trained in both cable and wireless engineering techniques before going abroad and as soon as his training was completed, he and another young engineer, John Rippengal, sailed to West Africa. That was in January 1945 and the war in Europe was reaching its climax. Making a wide sweep around the North Atlantic because of the danger of German submarines, they landed at Takoradi and rode in the back of a truck to Accra, one hundred miles away. From there they travelled in the bomb bay of a Canadian Liberator with one mailbag and lots of blankets to Ascension Island, the highly strategic dot in the South Atlantic where Cable and Wireless have had a communications station since 1899.*

In addition to its normal function, its radio station along with two similar stations in Freetown and St. Helena formed a deadly triangle which on several occasions led to the destruction of German U-Boats, pinpointing their position accurately.

Brian's salary had now risen to the princely sum of £115 a year, to which was added a Foreign Service allowance of £60 a year while he was in Ascension.

He loved the island, the stark beauty of the volcanic areas with their twisted shapes and craters contrasting with Green Mountain rising to nearly 3,000 feet in the middle of the island. Up there lush tropical vegetation grew in abundance with flowers and fruits of every description. No ship called at Ascension with supplies during the war years but a Company farm on the mountain grew fruit and vegetables for the inhabitants. Protein was limited to such fish as could be caught. Sometimes large predatory fish would pursue swarms of fry in towards the beach and find themselves stranded. Great tuna, dorado and wahu proved a welcome addition to the cooking pot.

Also on the mountain were the large concreted catchment areas where moisture precipitated from the clouds and blown against the northern slopes was funnelled down pipes to Georgetown. Brian's

---

* Until 1964 when the Colonial Office appointed a full-time Administrator, Ascension was virtually a Cable and Wireless island, ruled by the Manager. His secondary function was that of a Magistrate with two policemen under his control and he was a lay preacher to boot.

daily water ration was only four gallons, two gallons of which were taken by the Mess for cooking and laundry. Sanitary arrangements were primitive. There were no flush toilets, only large buckets under the lavatory seats. A box of clinker was kept nearby and shovelfuls were put into the bucket after use. The buckets were emptied in the early hours of the morning by the 'frou frou' man.

Despite the basic living conditions, most people loved a tour of duty at Ascension. Gin cost two old pennies a tot, whisky and brandy three pence and a carton of two hundred cigarettes was only seven shillings. Living was relaxed and clothing casual (apart from the surprising formality of black tie and 'bumfreezer' jackets every night for dinner in the Mess). There were several beautiful beaches but the great Atlantic rollers coming in from South America made it dangerous to swim there. In fact it was forbidden. Ascension is only the peak of a mountain on the Mid-Atlantic Ridge rising from horrendous deeps and engineers were not expendable.

'What did you do for entertainment?' I asked Brian.

'There wasn't very much, apart from the 9-hole golf course made of clinker and stones (the "greens" were called "browns") or clinker crawling . . . climbing up the slithery volcanic slopes. I fell once, gouged a hole in my knee and must've passed out. When I came to, I was surrounded by a circle of giant land crabs clicking their pincers menacingly.

'But the most moving experience,' said Brian as he lit another cigarette, 'was to sit on the beach around midnight at full moon when the turtles were coming ashore to lay. The huge 500-pound females would make their way laboriously up the beach and then, if the sand were right – not too moist, not too dry – they'd start to excavate a large hollow with their front flippers, sighing from exhaustion – after all, they'd swum all the way from South America – and with great tears rolling down their faces. Then they'd start depositing scores of leathery eggs, looking just like ping pong balls, in the hollow, gently covering them with sand shovelled by their rear flippers before slowly making their way, all strength spent, back to the sea.'

After six months in Ascension, Brian and John were needed urgently in Colombo so instead of going by sea they hitched another ride with some bomb-happy Americans who were delivering a new Dakota DC3 to the Middle East. The crew of three appeared to be nervous wrecks before the take-off and so were John and Brian after seeing the navigator checking the internal extra fuel tanks with a dipstick, a cigarette drooping from his mouth.

'There were no seats in it at all except crew seats in the cockpit,' said Brian. 'They made me sit on an upturned kerosene tin in the tail during the ascent as they needed some weight in the back end of the plane. Across the Atlantic they steered on a radio station's transmission but hit Africa at Takoradi instead of Accra, a hundred miles off course. Having found Africa the captain wasn't going to lose it and we did the rest of the journey at near zero feet, following the beach to Accra. Once we'd landed, John and I hid. There was no way we were going to fly on to Cairo with that bunch of lunatics.'

Instead they found another plane and flew on to Cairo by way of the R.A.F. staging posts of Kano, Maiduguri, El Gemeina, El Fasher, Khartoum and Wadi Halfa. This was the established route for U.S. and Canadian-built planes being ferried to the Middle and Far East. By now the war in the Far East was in its last days. From Cairo they flew in a Sunderland flying boat to the Dead Sea, the Sea of Galilee, Lake Habbaniya near Baghdad, Basrah, Bahrain and Sharjah in the Persian Gulf, Gwadur and Karachi in Pakistan and from there to Bombay and Colombo. It had taken twenty-two days from Ascension to Colombo although only eight days of flying were involved.

In Colombo they started work, outfitting a Press ship which was to join Admiral Mountbatten's huge fleet setting out from Trincomalee to reoccupy Malaya. Code-named 'Operation Zipper', this fleet sailed across the Bay of Bengal to Malaya and, on approaching the island of Penang, they heard that the Japanese forces had capitulated. Instead of making a landing at Port Swettenham as planned, the fleet continued to Singapore and the little Press ship, which was to serve the war correspondents, was amongst the first to tie up in Singapore harbour.

The Japanese were still in charge of the Cable and Wireless office but the Commander surrendered his sword to Mr Mackie, Manager of the Press ship. The ship became operational immediately, sending telegrams and pictures back to Colombo. Brian and John worked twenty hours a day, sleeping on another ship nearby as the thumping engines bolted into the deck above their bunks precluded any rest.

In due course they moved their operations to the old Company office in Robinson Road and lived in the Mess above. They ate Chinese food as there was nothing else, but when they saw the newly-released P.O.W.s from Changi prison camp, walking skeletons who came begging for food, they felt abundantly supplied.

Brian and his colleagues were part of the Telcom organization which was established under an agreement between the War Office and Cable and Wireless. The effect of this was to make members of the Company's staff in certain overseas theatres of war members of a uniformed non-combatant force which accompanied troops to the forward areas. They bore the honorary rank of Lieutenant.

'It was great,' said Brian. 'We'd wear slouch hats and go to the NAAFI or free film shows and then put on peaked caps to go to the Officers' Club. The regular Army didn't know what to make of us. They'd salute us and then notice the strange insignia we wore.'

Other Telcom men were now arriving daily. They were all Cable and Wireless civilians, some from Britain, some from Australia and New Zealand. Their purpose was to re-establish civilian communication. None of the submarine cables was working, so to cope with the volume of traffic they took over some Japanese transmitters installed in a house and with the help of the Japanese N.C.O.s got them working. Cable ships arrived and restored the submarine cables. A radio transmitting station was developed at Jurong and a temporary receiving station at Katong. Finally a permanent receiving station was built at Trafalgar, an old rubber estate.

'I used to go to the Trafalgar Estate every day during the planning stage – I'd eat my lunch in the factory building there,' Brian told me. 'One day an office secretary came to me looking worried. Her boss had dictated a letter to Head Office in which he referred to a map of the estate and "a factory building which no longer exists". He had signed the typed letter and then gone away for a few days.

' "I thought that building was still there," she said to me.

' "Of course it's still there! I eat there every day. You must have misheard him."

' "Well, do you think I should alter it?" she asked.

' "Yes, it's wrong the way it stands."

'The secretary altered and despatched the letter to London. A few weeks later I was summoned to the boss's office.

' "What the hell do you mean by altering a letter over my signature?" he roared, his face livid with fury.

'I explained what had happened. "The factory *is* there, sir." I have never seen a man so angry but he couldn't deny the fact. After storming at me for a while, he let me go. But it's obvious he had intended selling the factory building and making a lot of money for himself. I had thrown a spanner in the works.

'There were all sorts of rackets. One engineer who had been in Singapore before the war arrived like all of us with one kitbag. A year later he left with thirty crates of stuff. He had a lot of stickers made with his name printed on them. When visiting any of the Company houses, if he saw a handsome piece of furniture, he'd surreptitiously slap a sticker underneath it and then say casually: "You know, that looks very like the table I had before the war." He'd upend the table. "Well, what do you know! There's my name on it!" '

He stubbed out his cigarette and laughed at the shocked look on my face. 'Bad eggs were very few though.

'And then there was the time when one of the chaps took me to a prayer meeting at a Mission. People were jumping up to testify to the power of prayer in their lives, but I remained seated. A few days later I was passing the Mission and stopped to read the noticeboard outside. There was a list headed "People for whom we should pray" and my name was on it!'

After a summer leave in England in 1949 Brian worked for four months at the Company station in Aden, a strange desert landscape perched on the edge of Southern Yemen. There were about forty men in the Mess and breakfast was served on the verandah at a long row of small tables, one for each man, each with one chair facing the same way so there was no need to converse with anyone first thing in the morning. Each table had a bookstand and if he needed mental stimulation he sat reading *Punch* or *Blackwood's*. The only alternative was silently staring at the back of his neighbour's head. By contrast, lunches and dinners were very convivial.

From Aden Brian went on to Singapore where he spent a month preparing equipment, a lot of it from the old Press ship, for the new station being built at Jesselton, before flying to North Borneo in May.

On top of all this travelling he had somehow found time to indulge a multitude of interests from flying and motorbikes to Beethoven and Bertrand Russell. He read omnivorously, history, philosophy, archaeology, mathematics and comparative religion all grist to his mill, but like me he also loved Thurber and Nancy Mitford. I found we had a lot in common. He was very knowledgeable about classical music (although he couldn't sing in tune) but alas, didn't like jazz or Gilbert and Sullivan. He was a linguist and shared my delight in words and word games. He had a delicious sense of fun and besides all this was very handsome!

His beard was growing well. Despite an invitation to Government House when he had eight days of stubble on his chin, he bravely refused to shave and presented himself to the Governor and his wife. It was a strange beard. It didn't grow on his cheeks but hung down in a fringe from his jawbone. His hair, brows and beard were dark brown but there was a plentiful sprinkling of grey in his hair although he was only twenty-five. His eyes, behind horn-rimmed glasses, were very large and of the deepest blue. He had a lovely smile with flawless teeth. When we went to the Club for dances, I thought how stunning he looked in his impeccable white sharkskin jacket, black cummerbund, black trousers and tie even though, in the course of the evening and much exertion, sharkskin jackets became increasingly sodden with perspiration and slimy with wet starch! Fortunately there was an efficient Chinese laundry in the *kedai* and the day after a dance there would be lines of men's sharkskin jackets freshly washed and ironed hanging in the shop.

There was a welcome new batch of records at the Club. Words had been put to Waldteufel's 'Dolores' waltz which now emerged as a romantic ballad called 'All my love'. Bing Crosby and the Andrews Sisters had an updated version of another nineteenth century song, 'Sweet Marie', and a lively rendition of 'Tombstone City', but Brian and I liked a song called 'If I loved you' which we later discovered came from a new musical show called *Carousel*. As we left the Club Dance one night, we walked across the *padang* and clambered up onto the Rest House road. The *kelip-kelip*, fireflies, were flitting around the trunks of the tall shade trees and in the deep gully alongside the road. We tried to catch them in our hands but as we made a grab their lights went out. The music from the Club floated clearly across to us so we danced all the way up the hill, laughing when we stubbed our toes or stumbled in holes in the bitumen. I liked Brian's lack of inhibitions and complete disregard for convention.

On the 4th of June Sandy and Diana were married. As she left the reception she whispered to me apprehensively, 'Wish me luck!' and they departed on the railcar to Weston, the terminus of the railway, sixteen miles south of Beaufort on Brunei Bay.

Dorothy bought 'Haggis' and Nancy took over the reins managing the Rest House. Brian, George Pope and 'Body' Barnes moved

out and with a new Cable and Wireless man took up residence in a
temporary Mess at Tanjong Aru. I was sad. It seemed strange not to
see Body and George around the house and I missed having breakfast with Brian. He didn't want to go. He said he'd miss our walks
and he didn't like walking by himself.

'You'll have to come down to the beach on your bike and see me
and I'll come and see you. I'm going to buy a motorbike. I must
have transport.'

So a new routine developed. When he was off-duty he came to
the Rest House and we walked around the hills. When he was on
shift, I'd ride down and wait for him to finish and then we'd sit on
the beach under the casuarinas. He always brought some of his
long woollen socks for me to pull on my legs (mosquitoes couldn't
penetrate wool though they loved nylon!) and we smeared our
faces and arms with mosquito repellent.

I always felt embarrassed returning to the Rest House after
midnight when Bess's engine announced to everyone that Wendy
was creeping in. Reputations had to be carefully guarded and nur-
tured like the *bunga rajah* as they could shrivel overnight in the
blast from slanderous tongues. Sometimes I'd cut the engine and
push the bike up the last few hundred yards or I'd see Nan's taxi
leaving Ken's bungalow and ride home beside it, creeping up the
Rest House hill behind it, my engine mingling with the noise of the
car.

Mrs Gatford had been observing my growing romance.

'What do you think of Brian Suart?' she asked one day.

'I like him very much,' I replied.

'Well, I think he is the most remarkable young man. I have never
known such a mature or responsible person. Harry thinks so too.'

I thought so too! In fact, Brian provided all the attributes which
I had on a mental list of the requirements for a perfect husband
(except that he smoked too much!). By now we were discussing marriage but I hesitated. My head had always ruled my
heart and I felt I must really be sure. My eldest brother had been

divorced when I was only ten and it had been a traumatic experience for the family. When I married it would have to be for keeps. I remembered Diana's doubts about her marriage to Sandy. How could I be sure of my feelings? I agonized to Mrs Gatford.

'Look at Nancy! She's starry-eyed about Ken! I don't feel like that. I don't want to shout it from the house-tops the way I'm supposed to.'

'But you're different from Nancy. People don't react the same way.'

I wasn't convinced. People had told me all my life that when you met the right man, you *knew*! All I knew was that I was very comfortable with Brian, we had a lot in common, there was nothing about him that I didn't like and he was fun to be with. But did that mean that I was in love?

He came to the Rest House to see me one evening. It was raining softly and as I kissed him I smelt the fresh rain on his skin and felt the damp springiness of his beard. He was wearing a Norfolk jacket in rough tweed and I suddenly saw him as he would be at home in England, wrapped up against the weather, strong and dependable yet gentle and comforting. He was really very attractive!

'How's the new Mess?' I asked.

'Pretty cramped for the four of us and terribly hot. Last night we'd all gone to bed . . . there was a bright moon and the bullfrogs were kicking up a devil of a row. Waaaaaak! Waaaaaak! Next thing we knew 'Body' had gone outside in his *sarong* and was striding up and down alongside the ditch spraying them with a Flit gun . . . "Bloody bullfrogs!" Flit! Flit! "Bloody bullfrogs" Flit! Flit! There'd be quiet when he'd sprayed until he'd moved on to the next bit, then they'd start up again behind him . . . Waaaaaak! Waaaaaak! It was wonderful!'

'Well, I've news for you. I'm afraid I must tell you there is Another Man. This letter came today.'

The letter, written in very poor English in red ink on a torn-off page of foolscap, read:

My Dear Miss Low, c/- Clonial Development,

I am very glad to send for you some litter because I see you very happy today and I hope don't you angry white me

I am very freaight to send to you some litters and I hope you
can reaply this litter to Day or Next Day and I hope you
dont smiled this my English because I Not much understand English and know I cannot tell you Who are me but I
am in Jesselton and if I see you my heart very Love for you
Miss Low. I cannot forged for you. Day and Night please
reaply so quickly. My Edris like this . . .

   To Mr. A.M._____, c/- _____, Jesselton.

I love you very much. I love you you Love me.

'Who is he?' asked Brian. 'Do you know?'

'I've no idea . . . unless it's that Telecoms chap in the caravan who
looks at me.'

We joked about it and would probably have forgotten all about
it had I not received a parcel two days later. Inside it were three
pairs of the new nylon stockings which had just appeared in the
shops, and six exquisitely embroidered Chinese handkerchiefs.
There was no indication of who had sent them. I showed Brian who
promptly said they must be from my admirer and they must be
returned.

'Oh dear, they're so lovely! I've never had any nylon stockings . . .
must I really return them?'

'Yes, of course. Enclose a short note saying that you can't accept
any presents or any more letters.'

I did so but shortly afterwards received another note.

My Dear Miss Low . . . I am very glad to reacived Your litter
from the last week and I say so very very thank about
your present for me but why you send for me the girls
shoke. I don't want the girls shoke. Know if you send me
again bitter you send the Man shoke. and another
Thing. Because know my big day want to come. My big day
is 17/7/50. Please send for me again thing. If you have
send for me some thing I dont write again For you Dont
worry. I hope you can send for me some thing. So quickly

Thank you very much I dont Write again But you must send for me some thing singlet or what. But dont you send singlet only you must plast Any thing please I waiting your sending and I hope I can reacived your Thing please send so quickly. I must stay in 10/7/50. I recived That day. that all your

sincerly

A. M——

please quickly I am Await

I was furious but Brian rolled about roaring with laughter.

'You can laugh! You made me return them to that chap and he didn't send them. I could have kept them!'

' "Why you send for me the girls shoke",' he mimicked. ' "I don't want the girls shoke".' He lay back on my bed and lapsed into further delighted hoots of laughter.

'We've got to get them back! You'll have to help me write a letter.'

With Brian's superior grasp of Malay and the aid of a dictionary, we composed a letter to Mr M——, pointing out that there had been a dreadful mistake and would he ever so sweetly return the girls' socks to me.

It didn't do me any good. No doubt he sold the loot or gave it to his mother and the correspondence ceased.

•   •   •

The play was staged on the 11th and 12th of August. It was well received on the first night but the second night was to be a gala affair. The new Governor of Sarawak, Tony Abell, and the Commissioner-General of Malaya, Malcolm MacDonald, were in Jesselton for a conference with our Governor and they were to be in the audience. I thought it would be a good idea to inject a topical note into the play. In the third act the rather stuffy hero, ably played by Jim Rutherford, is idly turning the pages of a novel. I got him to substitute the North Borneo Annual Report for the novel and when he said:

'H'm! Read it! Can't say I thought much of it either . . .,' there was a howl of mirth from the audience who had instantly recognized the cover.

At the final curtain I was presented with a be-ribboned sixteen-ounce jar of Marmite instead of flowers.

There was to be a dance and supper after the play and I deliberated over what to wear. Mary Pang had just made me a beautiful *cheongsaam*, the elegant high-necked sheath worn by Chinese ladies. It was in turquoise *moiré* taffeta and I was longing to wear it.

'Then wear it!' said Brian.

'But no one else will be wearing anything so dressy!'

'All the more reason for you to look stunning. The men will think you look marvellous and the women will eat their hearts out with jealousy!'

I wore the *cheongsaam* and, after the play, Brian and I sat on high stools at the bar, sipping sherry. He took his programme and wrote something at the bottom of the cast list. He pushed it along the bar to me and I read: 'And I will not let thee go. All my love, Brian.' Then he looked me straight in the eyes and said: 'Will you marry me?'

I felt the blood rushing to my cheeks and took a quick sip of sherry. What an ideal occasion to announce our engagement! I had had a great success in the play, the Club was full of friends in festive mood, but still I held back. I was afraid of a permanent commitment. I looked at him in distress.

'I don't know. I just don't know.' All my doubts and fears swept over me and my lip began to tremble.

'That's all right, darling. I don't want to rush you. Think about it.'

He didn't really understand but he wanted me to be sure. He was willing to wait.

A month later I left Jesselton for Australia. I despised myself for running away. It seemed I was always running away from marriage but I told myself that I had to go home to pack up my belongings and buy things for our new life together, should I decide to return. Brian didn't ever try to persuade me or beg me to return. When he said goodbye to me at the ship he merely said: 'I hope you'll come back soon.'

Chapter 8

Intermezzo

Diana was travelling as far as Perth with me. Married only three months, she was suspected of having T.B. and was going home for treatment. She was also pregnant and very depressed about the future of her marriage. Sandy's employers would not pay his wife's fare anywhere and they hadn't any money. His job in Borneo being finished, he would probably have to go to the United Kingdom soon and then to Africa. She would have to try and save her fare to join him. Sandy was pleased I was travelling with her.

'Try and cheer her up,' he said, 'and give her this on her birthday.'

He handed me a small gift-wrapped package and a letter.

We sailed at midnight and I wondered if I would ever see Brian again.

• • •

In Melbourne I found my parents in a state of confusion. We had lived at the Teachers' College for fifteen years and my mother was trying to sort out the belongings of six absent children. After their return from Europe she and Dad would be living in a small suburban bungalow so the contents of the house had to be halved.

The new Principal and his wife had come to see the accommodation and planned a complete redecoration and refurnishing. I couldn't bear to think of the changes they were going to make. The house was visited daily by interior decorators and workmen. My bedroom had already been stripped and I had to sleep in an empty student's bedroom in the College. Our carpets had been taken up and the corridors echoed dismally. My life was all confusion and upset. I, of all my brothers and sisters, had spent my formative years at the College. I had played in the superb seven-acre grounds and explored the ramifying cellars which spread labyrinth-like under the old Victorian building, I had built tree houses with Pete and camped on the lawns. During the long Christmas holiday when the students were gone, we had sunbathed and played in the spray of the water sprinklers. I had ridden my bicycle all around the University Grounds and knew every corner of them. My first romance had been with a College student and my social calendar was that of the students.

What was I to do now? Get a job in Melbourne and live in digs somewhere? Melbourne suddenly seemed provincial and uninteresting. Everyone's face was the same colour. I took to hovering outside Chinese restaurants just to see an Asian face. No, I couldn't see myself living a humdrum life in Melbourne for ever. My cycling friend Shirley was travelling around Europe, my brothers and sisters were scattered. The prospect seemed cheerless.

I looked at the photos of Brian. How I missed him! How nice he was! How reassuring! How loving!

I wrote to tell him that I was coming back to marry him.

• • •

I found a ship sailing from Melbourne to Singapore. It was the S.S. *Surriento* of the Italian Line Flotto Lauro. A girl I knew was also sailing on it and we decided to travel 3rd class and save money.

'If we're together it won't seem so bad. We can laugh about it.'

We sailed from Melbourne on Boxing Day. It was blazing hot and Mum and Dad waited hours on the quay for the ship to sail. Sad as all partings are, this one was worse for them. I was going away to marry an unknown man and who knew when I should return? It was a relief when the cables were finally slipped and we swung away down the river. My bridges were burned.

In the hold were eight crates of linen, crockery, cutlery and glass and in the cabin I shared with June was a large trunk of new clothes and a cardboard box containing my wedding dress. As a wedding present for Brian I was bringing a leather-bound volume of Shakespeare and a pair of gold cufflinks engraved with his initials, and in a tiny flat purse was my wedding ring. I had no engagement ring. What little money Brian and I had was better spent on making a home. Brian had never been one to save money. As a bachelor in Singapore he had spent every dollar on learning to fly. He now had his pilot's licence but no savings. I had paid off my debt to Pete and owned Bess but there was little money left.

Our cabin was meant for six passengers and so was fairly roomy. It had three lots of double bunks but June and I were the only occupants, apart from the cockroaches! I had never seen so many. They were black and armour-plated and evil. I don't mind snakes or mice or spiders but cockroaches revolt me . . . scuttling underfoot or regarding me with antennae quivering. Our cabin was a few doors away from the galley so I suppose they liked the warmth and the proximity of food.

The ladies' shower and toilet block was also just along the passage. It took all my willpower to go in there. There was an overpowering stench of excrement liberally laced with disinfectant. June and I would postpone the moment of entering this hellhole then dash in with scarves swathed around our noses. The shower and lavatory cubicles had saloon-type half-doors. Quite often, while we were ensconced on the toilet, the outside door would open and an Italian steward would come in. June was showering one day when this happened. She looked over the top of the half-door and waved him away.

'Go away! Go outside!' she commanded imperiously.

He approached the door to hear her better. 'Signora?'

Only the officers spoke English so communication was impossible.

Meal times reminded me of Oliver Twist in the workhouse. When a great gong boomed we third class passengers trooped into the dining saloon and sat at long refectory tables. At the head of each table stood a steward. Ours was very handsome in a dark operetta style with black curling moustache and flashing eyes. He stood proudly holding in the crook of his arm a large bowl of spaghetti. We passed our plates to him in turn. With a contemptuous curl of the lip he dolloped a pile of spaghetti onto each plate, his scornful gesture implying that we were lucky to receive any sustenance at all. On the table was a large bowl of oil-sodden salad and carafes of Chianti Rosso. I was not used to drinking wine and craved cold water. I longed for fresh fruit and vegetables. When we reached Sydney I rushed ashore and stocked up with fruit, sultanas, chocolate and all sorts of snacks. We were perpetually hungry and used to hover around the galley door, sucking in our cheeks to look under-nourished. The chef was a kindly man and gave us portions of chicken which we took back to our cabin to devour.

There was nowhere for us to sit in comfort so I decided on action. I went to the purser and explained to him that I was a professional pianist and needed to practise daily. Otherwise, on a three-week voyage my music would deteriorate, was it not so? Would it be allowed for me to use the piano in the 1st class lounge each morning.

'Of course, signorina, please!'

June and I therefore found our way each morning at eleven to the 1st class lounge, an elegant drawing room, comfortably furnished, with a beautiful grand piano. While I rambled through all my favourite songs, ('Bewitched, bothered and bewildered' and 'My foolish heart' were hits at the time and seemed peculiarly apt for my situation), she reclined nonchalantly on a sofa, sipping coffee and chatting to the passengers.

One morning the Captain came in. After listening a while he came to me and said: 'Good morning signorina! Do you perhaps know "The man I love"?'

'Of course, would you like me to play it?'

He sat back in his chair, his eyes closed, relaxed. When the song was finished he sat up again, nodded his thanks to me, squared his shoulders and strode off for another stint at the bridge. Thereafter whenever I saw him enter the lounge, I played Gershwin for him.

As we neared the tropics the heat became unbearable. There was no air-conditioning on the ship and the only access to swimming for the 3rd class passengers was a canvas tarpaulin slung on the deck and used by the crew.

Again I sought the purser.

'It is so very hot,' I said, 'and you will understand that my friend and I . . . it is not seemly . . . we are embarrassed to swim with the men on the deck. Would it be permitted to have a quick swim each day in the 1st class pool?'

He nodded understandingly. 'Of course, signorina, please!'

So we swam each morning in the beautiful tiled indoor pool with its marine murals, changing rooms and thick-piled towels.

I was amazed at these concessions, particularly as no money changed hands. Two young men whom we met when boarding the ship were not apparent on deck or at meal times. I thought they'd disembarked at Sydney until I met them one night going into their cabin on our passageway. It transpired that they had each given the purser ten pounds and spent every day in the 1st class section, eating superb meals and drinking fine wines, only creeping home, like Cinderella, after midnight.

At the ports where we called letters were awaiting me from Brian. Encouraging, reassuring, loving, they insured me against doubts and fears as the ship headed northwards. He related lots of news and anecdotes about our Jesselton friends. It all seemed a long way away.

George Pope had developed sore feet. He found it helpful to walk in the sea every evening until a fish bit him on the nipple. George was incensed and walks were discontinued. 'Body' Barnes had been posted to the war theatre in Korea and had been replaced by A.G. Hill, a small man. One night when the inmates of the Mess had gone to bed and the last light was turned out, a plaintive voice issued from Ag's room.

'I've bought it! I've had it! Body buggers off and leaves me with a book on sewage and another called "How to build a house".'

George laughed so much he cried himself to sleep.

Keith and Nell Wookey were going on leave and were asking if we'd mind their dog Jeep during their absence. He was a large, rough-haired terrier and with his mate, Juno, had produced most of the dogs in Jesselton's European community, Juno usually having twelve pups in a litter. Jeep was a good dog and Brian thought it might be pleasant to have him. What did I think?

The sea which had been steadily encroaching on Tanjong Aru for years had finally threatened the *kajang* of Tom Mitchell and Ken Summers and it had perforce been demolished. A lot of memories went with it.

Brian's letters were also full of news of our new home. He was of an age to marry, being over twenty-five. Government and commercial firms frowned on their foreign service bachelors marrying under that age and many an unfortunate couple marrying 'under the strength' was saddled with the crippling expense of setting up a home or travelling because their employers gave them no help. At one time, not so far distant, the age of marriage had been twenty-eight and many bachelors on attaining that age, rushed home on their next leave and speedily contracted marriages, often unsuitable ones. (Jesselton was still amused by the story of the accountant, quite a ladies' man, who went home on leave to marry his fiancée and returned married to the girl's mother.) But Brian was of age and therefore eligible for Company housing, furniture and various allowances. However, as Jesselton Station was still being built, there was no housing for us. Head Office decreed, therefore, that Suart should find some suitable accommodation to rent and the Company would meet the bill. (In this decision I detected the fine hand of Ted Mockett, Staff Manager *par excellence*, who had a reputation for sweet reason and consideration. He had written a treatise on Staff Management, Brian told me, which began with these words or something very like them: 'When a Company employs a man, it employs not only that man but his wife and family . . .' His decision certainly earned my loyalty.)

To my great surprise and delight, Brian wrote to tell me that Gwyn Roberts had been transferred and that Mr Daniels' delightful house, which I had inspected on David Fiennes's behalf, was now vacant. Gwyn, a sardonic wit, had christened the house 'Hemlock Cottage'. My excitement grew as letter after letter detailed its charms and the improvements which the Company had sanctioned. Mr Daniels was to install a septic tank, a flush lavatory and a hand basin in exchange for a higher rent. The Health Department had sprayed the house with DDT. Furniture was coming from Hong Kong, a refrigerator and kerosene stove and lamps would shortly appear and a vast mosquito net had been ordered, large enough to cover two tropical divans pushed together. It seemed there was no such thing as a double bed in Borneo.

Brian himself went to the Cottage every day, checking up on the work being done, sweeping and scrubbing the house from front to back, doing repairs and making things for our home. He was at present working on his wedding present for me, a teak jewel box with an inlaid 'W' on the lid and two trays inside, each compartment lined with green baize.

My letters told Brian that I had not been idle. I had bought all our household requirements, had had the wedding invitations printed and sent to Jesselton, had bought the material for the bridesmaid's dress and sent it to Nancy and had my own dress made in Melbourne.

Wedding plans were progressing well. The date had been fixed and the church booked. I was to stay with the Gatfords until the wedding. Pete was coming up from Seria to give me away. Poppa and Mrs Gatford were to have the reception at their lovely bungalow but I had asked Sister 'Pete' to tell Mrs Gatford gently that I didn't want a Guard of Honour formed by Guides and Rangers. Brian would have hated it. A Singapore businessman, a regular visitor to the Rest House, had offered to give me a wedding cake but I didn't want one. I thought them repulsive things, covered with rock-hard icing and twee dolls and symbols of fortune and fertility, so with great difficulty and tact I had to refuse his offer. *Kechil makan*, curry puffs and champagne were the only refreshments we were to have before departing for our honeymoon at Kota Belud, in the foothills of Kinabalu. It was all very exciting but the *Surriento* was dawdling its way to Singapore and would not be hurried.

There was a friendly group of young Australians on board, including some young Jews going to settle in Israel. They used to sit up on deck learning Hebrew and I would sit with them, sewing my trousseau on a portable sewing machine. It reminded me of my voyage to Singapore on the *Charon* eighteen months before. How my life had changed since then!

Our leisurely voyage took us up the vast Queensland coast, weaving through Torres Strait and the necklace of jewelled islands of Indonesia and on to Java. We spent a blistering but exciting day at Jakarta. I felt at home in an environment so like Borneo, speaking Malay and eating juicy *rambutan* and mangoes. I bought a set of silver *wayang* spoons as a present for Mrs Gatford and some cake forks for Nancy, who was to marry Ken in six months.

And so to Singapore. I longed to revisit my old haunts but Brian was expecting me the next day. I decided I didn't want our reunion to be at Jesselton airport watched by all and sundry, so I sent him a cable saying that I'd be arriving not the next day but the day after.

Brian received this just as he was about to drive to the airport in Mr Chin's taxi. Disappointed, he cancelled the taxi and went back to work. My plane came in soon afterwards and one of the Customs officers drove me to the Cable and Wireless office close by at Tanjong Aru. He went in and told Brian a package had arrived on the plane for him. Brian came out to the car where I was hiding. I love surprises!

He was just as I remembered him, sweet and loving and gentle. I was so glad I had come back to him.

Chapter 9

Baharu Kahwin

Our wedding day, the 27th of January 1951, dawned fresh and fragrant. The hanging coconut shells on the porch were smothered in orchids and the morning air was sweet. Mrs Gatford brought me my breakfast in bed and I luxuriated as the rest of the household bustled around making preparations. My beautiful dress made of crisp *broderie anglaise* patterned with daffodils was hanging from the mosquito net rail. I reached out a hand to finger the sweeping train in the skirt and left a Marmitey imprint on the hem. My sister's long tulle veil which I had painstakingly ironed the day before (it was like ironing cloud) hung beside it and the stiffened head-dress made in tatted lace by my mother was standing on the table.

I jumped out of bed and ran to the window. Likas plain lay before me in the valley, the stumps of an old coconut plantation protruding from the seawater which had flooded the land after the wartime bombing. There was Kinabalu etched clearly against the sky. It seemed a good omen. I was glad, it would be shrouded in cloud by noon.

My brother Pete had arrived the day before from Seria. Brian and I met him at the airport. Pete was rather stiff as I introduced him to Brian. He told me months later that he would have taken steps to stop the wedding had he disapproved of the match. I suppose my family were worried about the unknown bridegroom but Pete evidently approved and they got on well.

In the sitting room Freddie Dixon was busy making the bouquets. As it was to be a morning wedding and a garden reception, I wanted fresh, spiky flowers. Not for me heavy bridal satin and sophisticated bouquets. I had wanted white daisies with yellow centres but these, alas, were not to be found in Borneo.

'Leave it to me!' said Nan.

She roared out to the airstrip on her Corgi on Friday afternoon, met the plane from Singapore and begged the pilot to bring back some gardenias from Sandakan. On Saturday morning she repeated the trip, collected the flowers from the obliging pilot and took them to Freddie to arrange. Using a stalk of white agapanthus as the centre of the bouquet, she grouped around it starry Borneo crocus, fragrant gardenia and white yellow-centred moon orchids. Nancy had a bouquet of yellow allamanda to tone with her sunny dress of white georgette patterned with field flowers in yellow, blue and red. In her hair she wore exotic *gloriosa superba* in yellow and flame.

I kept out of the way, bathing and dressing slowly. Brian brought Nancy and Pete to the house but obeying the custom did not see me. Robbie Robinson had alarmed me the day before by saying that several of the Rest House bachelors were intending to descend on Brian as he slept and shave off half his beard so that he would have to remove it all for the ceremony. No one liked his beard. One chap even remarked that he looked like one of those men who let bees swarm on them! They all thought he would look much better without it. I was incensed and fiercely forbade them to do any such thing.

So there he was, beard intact, his hair beautifully cut (I had stood on the pavement outside the open-air shop to make sure the Chinese barber wasn't over-zealous) and wearing his grey suit and the grey wedding tie I had brought from Melbourne.

'See you in church!' I called through the window.

It was a rumbustious wedding. At 10.15 Nan and I joined Pete in Mr Chin's gleaming new black car with its white satin ribbons. As we drove off, Pete said cheerily: 'What about a song?'

He told me later he thought I might have been nervous. I wasn't nervous at all but we wound our way down the hill into the town singing at the top of our voices. 'Daisy Daisy', 'The bells are ringing', 'Come away with me, Lucille', 'Oh Joseph, Joseph', 'Abie my boy', every song about weddings we could think of. The back of Mr Chin's head was eloquent with disapproval. As we drew to a halt outside All Saints Church, Brian, standing tensely at the altar rail with his Best Man Robbie beside him, heard our noisy arrival. Like a band of carousing revellers we climbed the fifty steps to the porch of the church, giggling and joking in high spirits.

With 'Body' Barnes's departure to the Korean war front, I had been desolate at the thought of not having an organist for my wedding. Peggy Prentice had told me that she'd had to make do with an old gramophone playing 'Where e'er you walk'. However, we heard of a talented Indian musician and as he worked for the Railways Mr Gatford arranged for him to have the morning off to play at the ceremony.

The little wooden church was a mass of flowers and Father Rusted, a cherubic curly-headed young minister who had just arrived from Newfoundland to take charge of the Anglican Boys' School, officiated.

All I saw as I walked down the aisle was Brian turning to smile at me. Any doubts or indecision in my mind had long since disappeared. I blinked both eyes at him in affectionate greeting.

As we emerged from the vestry after signing the register, my long tulle veil snagged on the rough concrete floor and held me anchored. My first words as a married woman hissed through the little church:

'I'm caught!'

The reception at Gatfords' amongst our close friends was good-humoured and hilarious. No one remarked on the absence of a cake.

After changing to go away, I threw my bouquet from the top of the steps and Monica caught it. We dodged showers of rice and walked out to the Land Rover which made a weekly trip taking supplies to Kota Belud, forty miles to the north of Jesselton. In the back, alongside our suitcase, were two dozen cabbages.

'Ah,' cracked my brother, 'You're going to eat like rabbits too!' He was so right!

•   •   •

We had booked a room at Kota Belud Rest House for two days, all the time Brian was allowed for his honeymoon as the Cable and Wireless men were hard at work getting the permanent station ready. However at the reception, A.G. Hill, mellowed by champagne, expansively extended the time to three days. A confirmation of accommodation had come from the Rest House with a footnote reading: 'A crocodile has recently been seen in the pool. You are advised to make enquiries at the Rest House before swimming in the river.'

We drove out of Jesselton, cramped up with the driver in the front seat, while on the back a string of tins jangled and a notice in Jawi script announced to the natives that we were *'Baharu kahwin'*, newly married. ('Gosh, I'm not a *misi* any more. I'm a *mem*!') Our road led north, forking right at Tuaran through Tamparuli and Tenghilan and leaving the coastal plain behind. Now we began to climb, grinding up the steep spurs of the Crocker Range which follows the west coast southwards all the way from Marudu Bay nearly to the borders of Brunei. About thirty miles from Jesselton we reached the ridge of a mountain and pulled in to a tiny Rest House. The girls and I had been there once before. It was so idyllic, remote and peaceful that we called it Shangri-La. I had wanted to spend a night there but the Rest House wasn't functioning and there was only an old caretaker on the premises. However we paused there and opened a bottle of champagne which Robbie had given us. In all directions we had a magnificent, unlimited view, looking over endless valleys and jungled mountains to the south, a glimpse of sea to the north and Kinabalu to the east. The silence penetrated and the heat of the coastal plain had changed to a crisp, bracing air which made one want to climb mountains.

Eight miles further on we came to Kota Belud, beautiful in its emerald setting. The placid Tempasuk River looped around a plain backed by rolling hills culminating in lordly Kinabalu. Here there was no jungle crowding and the open vistas led one's eye away and up to the jagged crest of the mountain. Kinabalu was closer now and showed a different aspect. It was still unattainable. How could we climb it in three days?

The Rest House was charming. Built as usual of *kajang* and *attap* and shaped like a chevron, its airy sitting and dining room overlooked the river and the mountain while its wings went off at each side. We had a bedroom at the far end of one wing.

Kota Belud is Bajau country. There are a few Chinese and a plentiful sprinkling of Dusuns but the Bajau is on home ground. At the weekly *tamu* we saw them in scores coming in from their villages to the market, splashing across the river at a shallow ford. Many rode or led their *kerbau* and at the *tamu* ground there was a large parking area for their animals under the giant shade trees, but I liked to see Bajaus mounted on their small Borneo ponies, looking very piratical in their wound cloth headgear and moustaches, their tight wrinkled trousers and ornate jackets, sometimes carrying a lance or a gun in one hand. They are Moslems, unlike the Dusuns who are animist if they haven't been converted to Christianity.

At the *tamu* rows of women squatted in long rows, their produce spread out in front of them on cloths. There was Dusun tobacco, grown in the foothills of Kinabalu and carried in by natives on foot, *bongons* on their backs. An abundance of luscious fruit was displayed on clean banana leaves, ubiquitous and almost as useful as palm leaves, and used for so many purposes from wrapping purchases or holding over one's head as an umbrella to wrapping a steamed pudding for Europeans. Fresh seafood was brought from the coast by Land Rover and strange meats – some dried and black and quite delicious to chew, some coloured an artificial red and revolting to look at – gave off unusual smells. Live chickens were leg-roped together and baskets of tiny eggs crowded stocks of the inevitable betel-nut, saccharine sweetmeats and vivid pink and green jelly confections known as 'instant dysentery'. Next to them was a series of stalls selling native produce made from the third member of the trio without which life in the tropics would be unthinkable: palm trees, banana trees and rattan. Here were the beautiful woven mats, baskets and food covers, rope and balls of thin rattan twine (essential for stringing up purchases or looping around a live crab to carry it home). Then there were the food and coffee stalls and the inevitable noisy corner where the weekly cock fight was in progress.

Rex and Diana Blow, whom I had last seen in Tawau, were now occupying the District Office of Kota Belud and were glad to see us. Brian and I swam in the river – not a crocodile to be seen – and went for long walks around the valley, crossing the river on the swaying wire suspension bridge or the wavy *attap*-roofed bridge.

I picked up an old Chinese copper coin from the dust. It was a Ching dynasty coin over a hundred years old. It is known that as far back as the T'ang dynasty, about 1,200 years ago, the Chinese came to Borneo in large sailing junks and certainly traders have

been moving into South-East Asia for over six hundred years. Traces of their life in Borneo are frequently found. I kept my coin as a lucky talisman.

We called on old Mr. I.H.S. Evans, writer of many books on native customs, who lived in a *kajang* bungalow overlooking the river and had many wonderful stories to tell of his life with the Borneo people. Dressed in a *sarong*, he lazily surveyed the beautiful river valley from a comfortable long chair. A pleasant retirement!

It rained every afternoon, refreshing the land and the air. By late afternoon it was clear again and the nights were always crisp, fragrant and spangled with millions of stars.

As I lay with Brian under the vast mosquito net, it was as though I had always known him. All the years of unhappy uncertainty and searching fell away, all the dross of other romances with the wrong men was discarded. When I touched Brian, I felt as though his blood were flowing through my hand in an unbroken current. His flesh was mine. We were one person.

Chapter 10

Perkakas Rumah

We drove back to Jesselton, reaching Hemlock Cottage in the afternoon, and Brian carried me over the threshold of our first home.

Inside the door was a small alcove separated from a large living area by an arch. On the walls of the alcove were two horn trophies mounted on shields. The first was labelled 'Basutoland 1912', the second 'Swaziland 1913'. The previous tenant, Gwyn Roberts, had pinned up a brassière labelled 'Blackpool 1946' but it had since been removed. Off one side of the living room was a dining room, a rarity in Jesselton, everyone else having a combined lounge/dining area, and off the other side was our bedroom and a small bathroom. Here were the new hand-basin and lavatory installed by our landlord and a deep concrete trough fed by rainwater from the roof. A cloth-wrapped bung at the bottom enabled water to be drained and the trough cleaned. Bathing was done in the usual Borneo fashion by filling the basin with hot water (brought in a bucket from the kitchen stove), adding cold water from the trough, soaping oneself and rinsing off with a dipper of water. There were of course drain holes in the concrete floor.

Leading off the living area to the rear was a large farmhouse kitchen and off it a small storeroom and another tiny cubicle, only six feet by six, which was our only spare room. The storeroom was cool and dark and on the shelves were stacked our wedding

160

presents. Cracks of light between the floor boards gave one the impression of walking along a pier with the sea underneath. It smelled of secrets and fragrant wood and seemed a magical place to me.

There were windows everywhere, glassless with wooden shutters to open and shut against the weather and steps led down into the garden on three sides. The house being built on piles, there was a large airy space underneath suitable for parking a car, hanging washing on wet days, washing dogs and so on. There was also a large room for servants. We had no servants. I had hoped to get Wookeys' cook and amah but they were promised to Dr Ozimek.

There was scarcely any furniture in the house. The building contractor had lent us two beds as the Company furniture had not yet arrived and, so far as Cable and Wireless was concerned, we slept on the floor for three months. Nancy had lent us Rest House sheets, blankets and towels until my crates arrived by sea. The huge mosquito-net, the size of a small room, had been delivered and rigged up to enclose the eight-foot wide expanse of bed. A mosquito-net is another magical thing, hot and stuffy sometimes but a private snowy enclave which excludes the world like the hangings on an old four-poster bed.

Between the living room and the kitchen stood a gleaming new refrigerator which ran on kerosene. Mrs Gatford had lent us a kerosene-burning stove and the landlord had left some rickety tables and chairs. After four days some teak furniture for the kitchen arrived, one draining-board table with a surface of parallel bars, one food cupboard and a table which was much too nice for the kitchen so we transferred it to the entrance alcove. I put a vase of colourful croton foliage in the middle of it and stood back to admire the effect. Brian, however, wouldn't have symmetry at any price.

'No, dear, put it left of centre!'

'But it'll look lopsided!'

'Well, put a small ashtray on the right-hand corner to balance it.'

Brian always jolted me out of my comfortable way of thinking, turned me around and put me down facing a different direction. He had wonderful taste and taught me about good architecture and furniture, paintings and elegance in all things. But that came later.

Gatfords had given us a 92-piece dinner and tea set in beautiful Japanese china, produced and sold cheaply as part of a war reparation scheme. I had chosen the design while passing through Singapore, a traditional English pattern of flowers bordered with burgundy and gold, and the Chinese shopkeeper who had agreed to ship it to Jesselton for me exclaimed:

'Ah, Miss Law! You have Chinese name! Ten per cent discount!'

The only cutlery we had was a velvet-lined case of fruit knives from Tosh and two teaspoons and forks borrowed from Gatfords. Among our other wedding presents were an expensive silver condiment set given to us by 'Body' Barnes, a charcoal iron, a Pyrex casserole, a soda siphon, a kettle and a saucepan, the two last gifts from Monica, ever practical, who said:

'It's all very well having silver toast racks but you've got to have a kettle before you can make a cuppa!'

For the first two weeks when we were without furniture we ate in the kitchen, eating from the draining table with cutlery and cruet balanced precariously on the parallel bars. Thus, half way between poverty and opulence, we made do until my crates arrived and I was able to unpack cutlery, crockery, linen and kitchenware. With a tablecloth spread on the draining table, our cutlery no longer fell through the bars.

On the first night in Hemlock Cottage I suddenly realized that we would have to eat. No longer would meals come up at regular times as in the Rest House. I had to produce them. Brian went off to work next morning saying he would be back for his lunch at five past one. After making the beds and washing the dishes I sped into Jesselton on my Corgi and bought the makings of a salad at the market. I also bought bread, a tin of butter, a tin of salmon and some fruit. Back home I mixed up an evil brew of Condy's crystals and submerged the fresh young lettuce, cucumber and tomatoes in it. By the time Brian returned I had lunch of a sort laid out on the draining table, panting quietly as I greeted him. There was no tin opener so I had had to run across the swamp to Mr Falconer's house to borrow one.

As meal followed meal I was plunged further in gloom. Our food depended on a tin-opener and poor Brian was subjected to tinned sardines, tinned corned beef, tinned salmon and then sardines again. At night I would give him something hot like sweet corn and bananas on toast. He was beginning to look distinctly uneasy. Eggs were really the only things I could cook and I had to remember always to break them into a cup first as there was sure to be a bad one. Potatoes too were not very good and had it not been for my pressure cooker, they would never have been ready in time.

In desperation I rode into Jesselton and went to the Rest House to consult Nancy. She wasn't in so I left a note for her.

'What am I going to *feed* the brute!'

She came down on Sodomangomorrah later.

'Why don't you buy some meat?'

'What . . . buffalo? Or that stringy chicken? I wouldn't know what to do with it.'

'Why not Cold Storage meat?'

Singapore Cold Storage had opened a branch in Jesselton a few months earlier and at the Grand Opening everyone had been agog to see fresh strawberries, apples, peaches, oysters (sold by weight in the shell!) and every variety of imported meat but the prices were frightening.

'Surely that's too expensive!'

'No, not for two of you. Get two chops, put them in a Pyrex dish, chuck in some onions and carrots and a bit of water and bung it in the oven.'

Doubtfully I ventured into the world of meat and Brian began to lose his panicky look. I experimented with liver and bacon, chops, stuffed heart, kidney. We ate dozens of eggs and breakfasted on *papaya* and cornflakes.

The whole business of housekeeping was difficult and time-consuming, quite apart from the fact that I had absolutely no experience. The supply of water, for example, which people in most countries take for granted, occupied hours of my day. Our bath water in the trough was supposed to come from rainwater on the roof but there had been no rain for two weeks, so all washing water had to be carried up from a huge rainwater catchment tank under the house. The mains supply was turned on only twice a day at unpredictable times and the water was so filthy it could only be used for flushing the lavatory and house cleaning. Drinking water had to be filtered twice, first through a very porous dripstone like an inverted beehive. This was quite rapid and eradicated anything visible like twigs, leaves, little red worms and mosquito larvae. Then it passed through a very fine bacterial filter which took hours for the water to drip through, drop by precious drop. The resultant elixir had then to be boiled, cooled and poured into empty Gordon's gin bottles, standard practice in the Far East as the rectangular bottles stack neatly in the refrigerator. Consequently there was a tremendous demand for Gordon's gin, though I think the Royal Navy might have had something to do with it. But what a carry-on, just to get some water for cleaning teeth or to drink. Oh for sparkling Melbourne water straight from the tap!

Laundry was another problem. With no facilities for heating water in large quantities and with the frequent changes of clothing necessary in our hot and sticky climate, I made an arrangement with Nancy's *amah* at the Rest House and dropped a bag of soiled clothes off each day on my way to the market.

Mrs Gatford gave me useful advice. As a result of her life in India, where riots were a common occurrence, she always kept a well-stocked larder in case of emergency.

'I buy six tins of everything, ' she said, 'and replace each one as it's used so I always have six.'

I adopted this practice and in later years my 'typhoon store' was invaluable.

Brian suggested I keep housekeeping accounts, at least until we could see how our income was going to cope. An enlightened man, way ahead of his time, he did not restrict me to a housekeeping allowance. We shared a joint bank account and both signed cheques to pay the bills. I had had a careful upbringing and was not extravagant but we still needed to know where our money was going. I bought an exercise book and ruled it into columns – Food, Drink, Transport, Cleaning, Toiletries, Miscellaneous. Inevitably there was a discrepancy between what I had had to spend and what I had listed as spent so I ruefully added another column.

'What's this?' asked Brian, checking my figures. 'H.O.K. . . . 87 cents.'

'Heaven Only Knows. I've thought and thought and I can't remember what else I bought.'

• • •

One day, two weeks after our wedding, we had just finished lunch and Brian had gone back to work. I was already thinking ahead to dinner. Sausages perhaps? Followed by . . . yes, banana custard. I had never made custard but I had a tin of custard powder in the larder. I mixed some milk then fetched the tin and began reading the instructions on the label. 'From one pint of milk take two tablespoonsful and add to two tablespoons of custard powder, mixing carefully until well creamed . . .'

There was a knock at the door and in came Cookie, Wookeys' former cook, his wife, their *amah*, and a trail of children. He said he had come to work for us.

'But Cookie, you're supposed to be going to *tuan doktor*!'

'*Tidak mahu, mem.* I don't want to go to *tuan doktor*, I want to work for you.'

Hope leapt in my breast! The best cook in Jesselton working for us! But I was worried about Dr Ozimek. It was the cardinal sin to steal someone else's cook.

'I shall have to talk to *tuan doktor* first and if he says it's all right, then you can come.'

'*Baik, mem.*'

He wandered over to where I still stood, custard powder tin in one hand, spoon in the other. '*Apa bekin, mem*? What are you doing?'

'*Sahaya bekin kussitard*. I'm making custard.'

He gently elbowed me aside . . . ' I do, *mem*,' and proceeded to toss custard powder, sugar and milk into a saucepan.

'No, no, Cookie . . . it says here . . . you must take out two tablespoons of milk and blend smoothly with the powder . . .'

'*Tidak mem* . . . I do . . .' He put the pot of combined ingredients on the fire and stirred gently until the mixture thickened. 'There *mem*, easy!'

I stood in wonder and amazement. How simple! No fuss, no lumps! I was humbled and since then I've never made custard any other way. Why custard manufacturers tell us to go through all that rigmarole I don't know. The only time you get lumpy custard is when you try to amalgamate the smooth paste with the rest of the milk. With Cookie's method there are never lumps and my mission in life now is to convert all the women I meet.

This was the first of dozens of occasions when the Chinese showed me that three thousand years of civilization have taught them to do everything under the sun in the simplest, most efficient and most logical way.

Who invented drip-dry clothes? The Chinese don't wring out their laundered garments thus making hundreds of wrinkles which then have to be ironed out. They just lift a garment from the water, thrust a stick through the arm or leg holes and push it out of the window to drip.

Who cuts holes out of the backside of their toddlers' trousers?

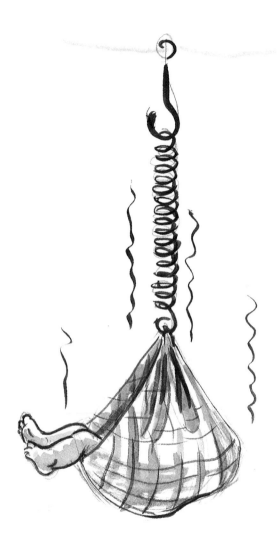

Little baby trots out of the house into the garden or the street and squats down to do his business. No dirty nappies. It's marvellous!

Dozens of years before baby-bouncers were invented in the west, I saw an infant lying in a *sarong* hooked onto a strong metal spring which rocked him effortlessly while his mother got on with her work.

The average working-class Chinese family eats at a circular, scrubbed wooden table (no table mats or napkins to wash). Each person has his own rice bowl and chopsticks. At the end of the meal each person rinses his bowl and chopsticks at the sink and leaves them to drain. Mum has virtually no washing-up to do and plays with her kids all day! Western women can learn a lot from their Chinese sisters.

But I digress. Cookie and Amah came to work for us despite Dr Ozimek's initial dudgeon. They took up residence in the room under the house with their two sons and two daughters, a cat and a horde of chickens and ducks. Amah was in her thirties, I suppose, very placid and sweet-tempered. Her youngest child, aged about two, was still at the breast. As was usual with Chinese couples, she did the lion's share of the work. Cookie shopped, going off to market every morning on his bike, a large woven basket on each handlebar and his old brown felt hat squarely on his head. On his return he did a bit of gentle cleaning and cooked the evening meal. Amah was up before dawn attending to her children, then sweeping through the house, squatting on her hunkers Chinese fashion, before setting and serving breakfast. While we were eating she made our beds, cleaned the bedroom and bathroom and removed dirty clothes and shoes. When she'd washed and dried the clothes, she ironed them and did any mending. After helping Cookie with the dinner, she cleared and washed up. Had we had children, she would have baby-sat until the early hours, then snatched a few hours rest before getting up again before dawn.

She was helped by her daughter Sue Moy, aged about ten, but the two boys went to school. Ah Moy minded the baby so that her

mother could get on with the work and I still have a mental picture of her, thin and spindly, carrying a large baby on her hip, idling through the waist-high grass in the garden or crossing the flimsy bamboo bridge across the swamp into the edge of the jungle. She was a plain little girl with her straight black hair pulled back with a pin and her skinny body outgrowing the faded tight cotton dress she wore. She was very intelligent and it grieved me that the boys should go to school and not Ah Moy. There was no Government

English school so I made some enquiries at the nearby Convent School and then tackled Cookie.

'Ah Moy very clever girl, Cookie. Best she go school, learn reading, writing.'

'*Tidak, mem.* Ah Moy help Amah do work. Boys go school.'

'If Ah Moy go school, Cookie, she learn English, learn reading, writing, get good job, make a lot of money.'

The Chinese understand the language of money. It worked. After a lot of talk it was agreed she could go to school if we paid the fees. So Ah Moy went to school where she quickly absorbed instruction and was wildly happy. Her sullen little face became lively and responsive and she applied herself with enthusiasm to her homework when she came home each afternoon.

After one term Cookie came to me.

'Very sorry, *mem.* Ah Moy no more school. Better she stay home and help mummy, mind baby, do ironing . . .'

Ah Moy's tearstained face was eloquent. I was horrified but all argument was useless.

My next essay into the field of labour relations was also a failure. As an egalitarian Australian, I deplored the way servants worked every day of the year except for their three or four days holiday at Chinese New Year.

'It's not right,' I said to Brian. 'They should have some time off every week. Besides, it would be nice to have the house to ourselves.'

'Okay, let them have Sunday off. We can get by for one day.'

I summoned Cookie and told him he and Amah could have every Sunday off after breakfast. Came the weekend, there was much activity below-stairs and at eleven o'clock Cookie rode off on his bicycle in his good shirt and shorts. Amah and the four children, their best clothes stiff with starch, left the house to walk to the nearest bus stop.

With smug satisfaction I watched them go and started to make our Sunday lunch.

At three o'clock I beheld a sad little procession returning. Amah and the children trailed disconsolately into the house.

'*Mem* . . . I no go holiday. Too tired. Too hot. Cookie go holiday. Children and I stay house, get *tuan's* dinner.'

•　　•　　•

My *tuan* meanwhile was proving most wonderfully domesticated. Compared with my father who was a bookish academic, incapable of driving a nail, Brian could seemingly do anything. Never happy unless he were busy, he would look around the house for things to do. Shoeracks appeared in the wardrobes, a rack for the mugs was fastened to the wall, eggtongs were made from twisted wire and a lovely breadboard appeared at mealtimes. He proved to be knowledgeable about gardening and he was absolutely wonderful with lamps! This really inspired a reverent feeling of adoration in my bosom as the dreaded nightly lamp-lighting ritual threw its shadow over the afternoon. When he was home in the evening he lit our lamps quickly and efficiently, but when he was on night shift I had to do it. There were three of the brutes. Two were Sunflame pressure lamps . . . infernal, complicated things with unscrewings and pumpings and counting ten and more screwings and more pumpings and keeping one's thumb over a hole and counting 25 and trimming the wick and filling a thing with meths and lighting it and waiting till it burnt and then opening a valve, whereupon the whole thing would roar like an express train and flare into glorious light . . . or should. Then there was the Tilley which was also a pressure lamp but not as bad as the Sunflames. With it one just pumped a bit, dipped a kindler in meths and clamped it on the lamp and lit it and it flared away and heated the mantle and then, on opening the valve, it glowed nicely too. With me, however, it always shot a column of flame skywards while smoke belched and the room reeked of fumes. I'd frenziedly turn it out and start all over again. Cookie and Amah would look at me pityingly or sit despondent in the blackened kitchen waiting to cook the dinner. Brian could manage these diabolic monsters without turning a hair.

My command of Malay was improving rapidly under Brian's tutelage and I was soon able to converse with Cookie and Amah. Brian had a far more academic knowledge of the language and had even learned to read and write Jawi script while in Singapore. There seemed to be no end to his accomplishments. Like astronomy. We would go into the garden at night and with heads bent back painfully, study the brilliant array of stars. He knew most of the constellations and would point out the planets and the brightest stars. I knew only those of the southern hemisphere so I welcomed his teaching.

He was studying for his qualifying Radio exam and spent all his spare time and most of the night watch poring over his books. We consequently lived quietly. After his return from work at five o'clock, we bathed and then, clad in *sarong* or dressing-gown, sat on the floor of our bedroom with our backs to the door reading aloud from favourites like Cornelia Otis Skinner's *Our hearts were young and gay* and Jerome's *Three men in a boat*. From the Batu Tiga police station came the sound of bugles playing 'Taps'. It gave me a feeling of security and tranquillity.

Then the furniture arrived! Our own beds, a wonderful dressing table with triptych mirrors so I could see the back of my head, a double wardrobe for me, a single wardrobe for Brian and a very large chest of drawers all made in teak, now filled our bedroom. The dining room had an expanding teak table, chairs with green padded seats and two matching carvers, a sideboard with glass sliding doors in front to display our glass and crystal and a drinks cabinet. The shelves of the latter were too close to hold bottles so we used it as a china cabinet. In the living area were a settee and two armchairs with loose cushions, a bookcase with glass doors which we used as a drinks cabinet and the beautiful carved camphorwood chest which Pete had given us as a wedding present.

The little entrance alcove contained the teak kitchen table at which we breakfasted with the sun pouring in, a long cane lounge and two rattan armchairs. Our furniture had been supplied according to the official 1890 Cable and Wireless standard list of furniture for expatriate staff and included a hat rack and umbrella stand, though they had the decency to delete a commode and washstand, but overwhelmingly they provided us with twenty chairs. As two of us couldn't possibly rush around all day sitting on twenty chairs, I toyed with the idea of putting them all out in the garden, erecting striped umbrellas and serving teas, but with the grass so high it didn't seem an attractive proposition. We therefore scattered the chairs through the house, two in the bedroom, ten in the dining room, five in the alcove, two in the kitchen and one in the tiny spare room.

The living room was really a very wide hall in the centre of the house and was rather dark, having no windows and being panelled in *seraya* wood, so I chose material to cover the settee and armchair cushions in a chequerboard arrangement of bright yellow, forest green and tan. I got a quote from a Chinese tailor for the making of the loose covers but Brian said: 'Why don't you make them?'

'I wouldn't have a clue how to start.'

'It shouldn't be too difficult. I'll make them.'

My God, was there nothing he couldn't do?

He measured the various sections of the cushions, cut out paper patterns, hacked into the fabric and then stitched the pieces together on my wind-the-handle machine.

Along one wall hung six Martin Boyd pottery mugs in different colours. Next to them was a print of Van Gogh's 'Fishing Boats at Ste. Marie' hanging over an open bookcase full of World Books in their bright jackets. It wasn't till much later that we discovered our mistake in having an unglazed bookcase. In the tropics mudwasps delight in crawling up the spines of books to make their compartmented nests, laying their eggs and stuffing lots of paralysed insects inside as a living larder for the developing larvae.

Some months later I'd take out a book and be showered with dried mud, larvae, eggs, legs, wings and all sorts of débris. As well as mudwasps, other insects ate the glue in the binding and mildew spread its horrible patchy stains across the covers.

On a low round table was my Martin Boyd circular tray of multi-coloured *sambal* dishes. A coloured woven grass mat covered the floor and local clay pottery jars of red croton leaves and yellow foliage brightened the room, together with empty Chianti bottles from the *Surriento*. In their natural raffia baskets with candles in them and wax coursing down the sides, they added a cheerful touch.

One very strange feature of the house was the fact that in every room except the bathroom there were wooden towelrails around the walls. Our landlord, when tackled on the subject, merely laughed genially and said that it was good to have plenty of room to hang things.

The house stood in an acre of ground. Someone had made a lovely garden at one time and there were a lot of shrubs and fruit trees, but it had run to ruin and the long *lallang* grass was strangling most of the plants. With the house in order, we turned our attention to the wilderness outside, working each evening when it was cool. Brian taught me how to dig and prepare the ground but we learned about tropical plants together. We planted lots of flowers which friends had given us (*Russellia juncea*, a Mexican plant which formed large tussocks of spiny leaves and produced swags of vivid scarlet bells, Java violets, cannas), and took turns with the *changkol*, a Chinese hoe, and the *rembas*, that delightful grasscutting implement shaped like a hockeystick which the Dusuns swing so gracefully and effortlessly. It never ceased to amaze me how *lallang*, the coarse tussocky grass which deterred so many from making a garden, became positively lawn-like when cut regularly.

We uncovered frangipani, hibiscus, yellow allamanda, red croton, gardenia and – joy – a rambling pink rose! For all the splendour of flamboyant tropical flowers with their heavy, heady perfume, I pined for the delicate scent of a violet or a rose.

At the back and sides of the house were many banana trees, *papaya* and *durian belanda*. This was not the infamous evil-smelling *durian*, famed as an aphrodisiac (*'Durian jatoh, sarong naik'* – When the durian falls, *sarongs* rise), but soursop, a fruit very similar to custard apple and absolutely delicious iced for breakfast. Cookie peeled the large irregular-shaped fruit, wrapped it and put it in the freezer compartment of the refrigerator. In the morning he brought it out, unwrapped it and put it on the breakfast table where it gradually thawed with a lovely crystalline bloom. We cut crunchy slices off it and found it a most refreshing sweet-sour breakfast dish.

We also had lime and mango trees, a bush which someone identified as coffee and a cascara tree with its long beans hanging like brown icicles.

Beyond our borders was the swamp with mangroves standing on tiptoe in the mud, crabs and probably crocodiles. At the back of the house a little bridge crossed the swamp which at high tide was full of seawater. The servants' lavatory was in a hut built over the swamp and consisted of a hole in the floor. A simple enough arrangement when the tide went out taking with it all excreta, but until that happened the water became rather littered. On crossing the bridge for the first time Brian slipped and fell through, only saving himself by his arms from an unpleasant ducking.

Once a month we had a king tide when the water level in the swamp rose and spilled over the road in front of our house. A friend of ours, driving to Tanjong Aru one night, was slowly crawling along the flooded road when he met another car approaching on the same side. He swerved to avoid it and abused the driver.

'Admiralty Rules, old man!' came the cheery reply.

•　　•　　•

Our own stove now stood in the kitchen, a shining Florence oil stove with four burners and a separate oven which stood on top of the burners for baking. The snag was that saucepans and oven could not be used simultaneously. I don't know how Cookie managed to cook a roast dinner. The oven would have to be heated first, the joint of meat put in and cooked till it was half done, then the oven removed so that the vegetables could be cooked in saucepans. After that the joint would be cooked some more and finally the vegetables reheated and the gravy made.

Now the kitchen was completely functional and Cookie came into his own. He operated simply with a few basic kitchen tools . . . the all-important Chinese cleaver which could cut, shred, chop and mash; a pair of wooden chopsticks which combined the functions of the western eggbeater, cooking fork, mixing spoon, draining spoon, wire whisk, spatula and fish slice; a simple Chinese wooden-sided sieve and a home-made grater – the lid of a tea tin with numerous punctured holes. Thus equipped, he proceeded to demonstrate why he was known as the best cook in Jesselton. His pastry was a dream, his desserts inspired and his curries were famous. On Saturday afternoons he would go along the foreshore, picking a leaf of lemon grass, shreds of pandan, the seeds of cumin and coriander, a stalk here, a piece of bark there. In the refrigerator on Saturday night there would be a saucer with a spoonful of paste on it, the sum of his labours, the product of his pounding and mixing. Sunday morning he would make the curry.

I pestered him to teach me how to make a curry. His secret was simple.

'*Mesti ada wangi, mem!*' (It must have perfume.)

His curry always did. It was never just a peppery-hot mess. It was fragrant and full of juices, essences, herbs and spices. Delicious!

First he made the curry base with onions, garlic, fresh ginger, cardamom seeds, sultanas, sour green apple, lots of tomato and the curry paste, adding stock and then the meat, fish, prawns or fowl.

Two teaspoons of brown sugar and the juice of a lemon (the empty shells sliced and thrown in to give a wonderful scent) completed the sauce and there were always halves of hard-boiled eggs, small round onions, chunks of cucumber and hunks of potato. This was surprising as one wouldn't expect potatoes as well as rice, but Cookie always included them. (Useful, too, if the curry is too hot as they will absorb a lot of the flavour.) At the last minute the gravy was thickened with ground peanuts and *santan*, coconut cream. The rice was cooked Chinese-style in a small amount of water, steaming dry until each grain was separate and fluffy. By the time a generous helping of curry was heaped on a mound of rice and topped with spoonsful of up to twenty *sambals*, there was a formidable pile on the plate. Conversation ceased as spoons were raised, an appreciative silence being all the comment needed.

When we were well settled, we asked the Gatfords to dinner. This was our first attempt at entertaining in the grand manner and I was nervous. Being almost totally inexperienced as a cook, I could only throw out tentative suggestions to Cookie about the menu. I supervised the laying of the table with our best Chinese embroidered linen, Gatfords' dinner service, silver candlesticks, Mr Barnes's silver cruet, sparkling wine-glasses and other wedding presents. Amah arranged some pink and white periwinkle in a green Carlton pottery bowl and put a spray of pink corallita in each finger-bowl.

Our guests arrived and admired the house and its furnishings. Brian offered them drinks.

'Whisky soda please,' said Mrs Gatford.

'Make that two!' said Harry.

Brian poured the whisky and took up our shining new soda siphon, a present from the Colony geologist. He squirted soda into the glass and swore in dismay as a stream of mud wasp débris was expelled from the spout. Any cavity offers a delightful home to wasps. After that episode the first squirt of soda always went out of the window.

In due course our guests took their places at the dining table. They complimented me on the elegant table and didn't appear to notice the wheezing Sunflame lamp on the sideboard. Soup was quickly disposed of, then a handsome chicken and mushroom pie arrived and every succulent morsel was devoured. I suddenly realized that I had no idea what was planned for dessert. What on earth had Cookie made? Why hadn't I checked? I sat agitating until, in an expectant hush, he appeared at the door, resplendent in snowy shirt and shorts above bare brown legs, bearing a large platter. On it was an annular mould of pink ice in which were frozen pink and white periwinkle flowers. Icecream and tropical fruit were banked around the outside of the ring and out of the centre arose a burning candle. My eyes thanked him and I sat back preening myself on having such a treasure.

Cookie had other virtues. He was much in demand as a packer and I was thankful that when it was time for us to leave Borneo, our precious possessions would be safely packed and crated as only an expert Chinese can do it. Chinese packers disdain wrapping each article in layers of newspaper as we do. They merely use a few wisps of straw in between breakables and nothing is ever broken.

A less prestigious but equally gratifying talent was his ability to clean shoes. He had a secret formula which produced shoes gleaming like black glass. It was something to do with water, I recall, and was possibly a method akin to 'spit and polish'.

Whatever the secret, Brian went off to work each day in starched whites, polished shoes and darned socks and so, completely freed from domestic chains, I started work with Sime, Darby and Company, one of the big merchant firms of the Far East. (My place with C.D.C. had been filled when I went to Australia.) I rode my Corgi into Jesselton each day and Brian rode his two-stroke motorbike to the Cable and Wireless station at Tanjong Aru. As he was travelling against the flow of office workers going to Jesselton, he rode at a constant half-salute, greeting everyone he met.

John Stagg was my new boss, a tall, languid young Englishman, an ex-Army officer, blond of hair and moustache, who dressed elegantly and openly expressed disbelief when I told him Brian possessed three shirts.

'No man,' he said loftily, 'can make do without at least two dozen shirts, preferably three dozen.'

'But why so many?' I demanded. 'How can you wear so many?'

'Well, you need at last a dozen best white shirts and a dozen or so sports shirts, and evening shirts and tennis shirts and . . .'

I was cowed and raced home to ask Brian if he wanted more. Did he feel hard done by?

'Of course not. I can only wear one at a time. As long as I have a clean change, that's all I need.'

However, I bought him three or four more (trying the new nylon ones that didn't need ironing) as it soon became evident that my dear man had a predilection for oil, acid and grease of all sorts. Of course it was ridiculous to wear starched white clothes whilst crawling through six foot high grass taking bearings, or climbing masts, or dismantling engines or carrying carboys of acid. Maybe it was considered *infra dig* for Europeans to wear navy blue overalls, so white clothes it was and I soon became used to grease-splotched clothes and acid holes in the most revealing places.

We were sitting on the Mess verandah having drinks one evening and conversation turned to Brian's disreputable shorts. Jerry White, a sturdy man of about forty, got up without speaking and went into his room, reappearing with a pair of very large but intact grey drill shorts.

'Here Brian,' he said, tossing them onto the table. 'Try these!'

I was mortified and they all laughed at my discomfiture.

But to return to Sime, Darby, the staff comprised two Chinese, the senior salesman Lim Kian Sam, a dear Buddha-like man with a round moon-face in his late thirties and a younger one, Simon Lee; two Dusuns, Clement Yap and Peter Govilon; and a Brunei Malay messenger boy, Matussin, who was very smart and willing. Johnny

Wong drove the Land Rover. Simon and Clement had a smattering of typing and could cope with stores lists and inventories but I did all the correspondence and was left in charge of the office when John Stagg went on tour. As Sime, Darby dealt largely with machinery – generators, outboard engines, motor cars, tractors and earth-moving equipment, time switches and refrigerators – I was frequently out of my depth and many times I sent off a requisition to Singapore office with a desperate *cri de coeur* pinned to it: 'After looking at the manual, I cannot decide whether the part our client wants is No. 236A or 315. Can you help?'

After an initial wariness on the part of Lim, Simon, Clement and Peter, who had had little contact with European women, we soon became very good friends and had hilarious times in the office. I didn't go over the road to the coffee shop with them. They would have been embarrassed. Instead, a waiter brought a tray with our drinks, his wooden clogs clattering on the road. Exquisite curry puffs and the slaking sweet-sour taste of Fraser and Neave's grapefruit soda are for ever associated in my mind with those sweltering days in Sime, Darby's office. Lim drank only tonic water and urged us to try it. For some reason I was reluctant, perhaps because it was called quinine water, but I remembered it later and drank it all my years in the tropics.

As we munched our pungent curry puffs, Lim would relate his domestic worries concerning wife and children, Simon responding with stories of his courting and Clement, who frequently over-indulged in *tapai*, the local rice beer, would come complaining that he had fallen over and 'broken my bloody trousers'. Peter was an unintelligent storesman, often incurring John Stagg's wrath, but one day he presented himself with a request to buy a Morris chassis for conversion to a bus. All the native buses were acquired on hire purchase in this way. A carpenter would build the wooden super-structure and the owner would thereupon start operating his bus. When he had paid off the cost of the vehicle he would buy another one. Peter seemed a most unlikely bus operator but he had done his calculations well and had a partner who was providing the deposit, so John Stagg could not refuse him as a customer.

●   ●   ●

'Darling, the K———s have asked us to drinks on Tuesday night. You're not working that night, are you?'

'No, but I don't want to go. I can't stand that woman!'

'But I've said we'll go.'

'You can but I'm staying home.'

'But . . . what shall I say? I've *said* we'll go!'

'You'll have to think of an excuse. You should've asked me first.' Troubled silence.

'Well, I'm sorry, but as I've accepted can't we both go this time?' Pause.

'All right then, but consult me next time, right?'

On dear! It was the first lesson I'd had to learn. I was too used to leaping through life, taking other people for granted and expecting their reactions to be the same as mine. I hadn't realized that marriage doesn't make two persons one. It makes one person two. I had to learn to consider two people and act for two people. The sea of matrimony might look calm and benign but there were sharp rocks lurking underneath. Constant vigilance was the password.

●   ●   ●

In those days before the permanent shop-houses were built, European women were hard put to it to replenish their wardrobes. Sun and frequent washing soon drained the colour from bright cottons and perspiration rotted the fabric. But there were no ready-to-wear women's clothes, not even underwear. Perhaps some tiny women could have found garments in the Chinese shops but not large-framed Australians like me! There were plenty of shops selling material and Mary Pang was an excellent dressmaker if one couldn't sew oneself. I had brought with me from Australia a Frister and Rossmann wind-the-handle sewing machine, a wedding present from my parents. There were no electric machines and treadle machines were too big to move about. It was quite an art to manoeuvre cloth one-handed under the foot while turning the wheel rapidly with the other hand. When Diana had to mend sheets at the Rest House, she used to get one of us to turn the handle while she used both hands to feed the cloth through. However, many women couldn't or wouldn't sew so Mary Pang was in great demand.

She lived in a wood and *attap* bungalow across the railway line at the foot of the range. Inside her small house were piles of fashion magazines which we pored over in search of a suitable style. Neatly dressed in *saam fu*, she was quick to grasp what we wanted, even when we tried to explain it in halting Malay. Once she understood, there was no problem and the dress was always beautifully finished with tiny hand-sewn stitches. Zips were always put in by hand and never machined.

About once every six months the news would fly around that Gordon Dunn was in town. He was a representative of the large Singapore emporium Robinson's. Like a rather superior pedlar he would start at Kuching and work his way northward through Miri, Lutong, Kuala Belait, Jesselton and Sandakan. He would appropriate some empty shop or a room in the Rest House, unpack his crates and soon tables would be covered with heaps of merchandise. Fashion-starved women poured into his shop and grabbed dresses, slips, bras and shoes to try, nearly weeping with chagrin if they didn't fit or departing triumphantly with their bags if they were satisfied.

Gordon was another Scot. How that nation has spread across the world! After shutting his shop in Kuching one afternoon, he went to the Club. In the billiard room a game was in progress. One man he knew, the other was a stranger. He looked at the board where the initials of the players were chalked.

'Who the hell's H.E.?' Gordon demanded.

'I'm H.E.,' replied the stranger.

'Oh, I thought it was the bloody Governor,' joked Gordon.

'I AM the bloody Governor!'

It was Sir Antony Abell, the new Governor of Sarawak who had come to replace the murdered Governor Stewart.

• • •

One afternoon about three months after our wedding, Brian and I were sitting idly in the cool inner hall of Hemlock Cottage. I looked speculatively at his face. He had stopped shaving the morning after his arrival in Jesselton. What did he look like without his beard? I held it back under his chin and tried to imagine but his moustache was still there. I must have kept on about it for suddenly he stood up and went into the bathroom, closing the door behind him. I flew after him, protesting that I hadn't really meant it.

'You asked for it, you'll get it!' he said firmly.

'Well, leave the moustache on and show me what that looks like.'

At this agonizing moment of suspense Monica arrived. I didn't tell her what was happening but tried to make polite conversation.

In a few moments Brian called me to the bathroom. The beard had gone from his jawline but the moustache still graced his upper lip. It looked silly by itself so I told him to take it off. But my heart sank. Already it was evident that he had no chin.

I went back to Monica and five minutes later my new husband emerged. I was stricken with shock. The aggressive thrust of the beard had gone leaving a white nothingness, pallid as a fish's belly by contrast with his sunburnt face. Chin flowed into neck without the definite border of hanging hair. He was a different person. It was a sobering moment.

Monica surveyed him for a second and pronounced her verdict.

'That's much better! I like it!'

I adjusted to the change, of course, but I didn't feel comfortable with him for several days. The Malay staff who had previously called him *Tuan Janggut,* Mr Beard, now called him *Tuan Budak,* Mr Little Boy. He did look terribly young. There was a brief flurry of gossip about Wendy Suart riding pillion behind a strange young man, her arms hugging him tightly around the waist, and then everyone got used to him.

•   •   •

In March, Mrs Gatford's Rangers were commissioned and sent out to take their own Guide Companies. Kathy Ferdinands captained the 1st Jesselton Guides at St. Agnes Church of England School, I organized an open Company at Tanjong Aru made up of Malays, Chinese and two Europeans. Vicky and Rosie Perkins took the Company of girls from the Sacred Heart Convent School and other Companies followed.

My friendship with Suwindar had developed. She used to send me sweet little letters written with stubby pencil on torn pages of exercise books. She had given me a photograph of herself with a bunch of roses which was quite charming. I went to see her and told her about the new Guide Companies.

'How would you like to join?' I asked her.

'I should love to but my uncle will not allow it. He is very strict with me.'

Kishen Singh came into the shop and I pleaded my cause. I told him that Mrs Gatford had trained hundreds of Guides in India, I told him that Pushpam was a Ranger and she was Indian but he smiled politely and refused pointblank. As Suwindar had said, her uncle exerted very strict control over her.

My Guides wore a deep petunia pink tie and I divided them into three patrols, *Bunga chempaka* (frangipani), Rose and Orchid. It was no use naming them after unknown English flowers but we could only get Patrol patches with English flowers on them. I therefore chose English flower patches which resembled local flowers.

Only the two European girls spoke English. There were nine Malays and two Chinese. The Chinese spoke Mandarin but like most people living in Borneo understood Malay so our meetings were conducted in that tongue. I spoke only Bazaar Malay which is devoid of the intricate prefixes and suffixes of Rajah Malay but the girls understood me. It was not easy trying to instruct them in the complexities of sheepshank or fisherman's knot, of tracking signs and stalking, constellations in the sky or the dangers of haemorrhage in a foreign language. Fortunately I received a Malay translation of 'Be Prepared' from Singapore in which a lot of the terms were available. I was soon able to call Mrs Gatford down to enrol my girls.

It was very hard running my Company. How I longed for better communication and for greater numbers to enable the Patrol system to work. The two Chinese girls seemed uninterested and sullen but the little Malays were as keen as mustard. We were the first Company to produce a 2nd class Guide. To get my numbers up, I had roped in Sue Moy and her quick intelligence soon made her invaluable. She would grasp what I was trying to get across and then explain it to the others. One day, some months after starting the Company, I heard two of the Guides talking to her. She shushed them and they subsided into giggles. I asked what was the matter and despite Ah Moy's remonstrances Halimah said something about someone being rescued from drowning.

'Where? Who?' I demanded.

'Ask Ah Moy!'

I was astonished. 'What happened?'

Ah Moy gave the details in a flat, matter-of-fact way. She was walking along the beach when she saw a child in difficulties in the water. She dragged him out, laid him face down on the sand and proceeded to give artificial respiration as she'd been taught.

I was filled with excitement and gratification and rushed to tell Mrs Gatford. She was delighted and wrote off to Guide Headquarters in London. When an illuminated certificate arrived commending Ah Moy for her prompt action, there wasn't a happier little girl in Jesselton.

•   •   •

At Easter our Australian friend Major Wikner invited us down to Beaufort. Tall and slim with an erect, military bearing, iron-grey hair and clipped moustache, Wik was the Railways Superintendent of Ways and Works. He had been the Australian Army engineer in charge of the railway as the liberating Australians advanced up the line to Jesselton from Weston on Brunei Bay. His men had to repair the track, erect temporary bridges and salvage what rolling stock was available. At the end of the war, Wik stayed on under contract to the Colonial Government and despite almost insuperable difficulties, got the railway operating again.

Brian and I packed a small case and took the morning railcar to Beaufort. Someone once wrote that in Borneo 'roads and railways are both short and laughable to those who associate such things with speed and sprung cushions',* but I loved that railcar. It was very pleasant running through the long green tunnels of jungle or through an open expanse of brilliant jewel-green new rice, watching the antediluvian mud-caked buffalo wallowing in puddles or passing native villages where dusky naked babies spilled out of the doorways to wave as we passed.

It was almost two years since I'd gone to Beaufort for the opening of the new Club. It looked no different. There was the lush valley with houses dotted on the hillsides, the railway line coming in from Jesselton to the north and disappearing around a curve on its way to Tenom. Once the morning train had come and gone, the silence dropped down on the valley again. I remembered the cool night and misty morning on my previous visit. Now there was the heavy heat of noon.

---

* 'Borneo, Past, Present and Future' – The British Survey, Feb. 1951

Wik's pleasant bungalow offered shade, a colourful garden and a surprise – a two-year-old female *orang utan*, beautiful in her lustrous red long-haired coat. Inevitably Wik called her 'Blue'. (Australians perversely call all red-haired people or animals 'Blue'.) The ape took Wik and me by the hand and walked around the garden with us, then climbed into my arms and nestled like a child. She was young but tremendously strong. We watched her, sprawled on the floor, stretch out a muscular arm and grab a heavy blackwood chair by the bottom of a leg, her wrist resting on the floor. A twist of her wrist brought the chair crashing down. Although she had a cage in the garden, Bluey had the run of the house when Wik was there. At teatime she joined us at the table. A banana was peeled and eaten and then Wik placed a cup of tea in front of her. A sip from the cup and her lips curled back from her teeth in a snarl of disapproval.

'Too hot?' said Wik, and added some milk.

Again she sipped the tea, again the snarl.

'Oh, I forgot the sugar.' A couple of lumps thrown into the cup produced the right taste and the *orang utan* lifted the cup and drained it.

These beautiful animals are threatened with extinction. Hunters supplying zoos, and the destruction of their habitat by timber companies have drastically reduced their numbers. Wik had found Bluey orphaned while still very young. Now she was growing too big to be a pet and he was planning to return her to the jungle. Would she adjust to freedom without her usual cup of tea?*

●   ●   ●

As we were sitting at breakfast one day, a white and tan mongrel appeared at the table. I recognized him as Mr Faulkner's dog from

---

*There is now an *orang utan* sanctuary at Sepilok where rescued animals are prepared for their return to the jungle.

the next house across the swamp. He was in a dreadful state. His coat was dull and staring, he had some kind of eczema and he carried one of his rear legs. Mr Faulkner said he had been hit by a car. I knew I shouldn't feed him but I couldn't resist his pleading eyes. I gave him some of my Marmitey crusts of toast. Inevitably he reappeared every day at breakfast. He got some Marmite every day and a miraculous change occurred in his appearance. His eczema disappeared, his coat grew sleek and shining, his eyes became lively and he bounded with energy. He spent more and more time with us so eventually Mr Faulkner said we had better keep him. We called him Little Joe and he became a great joy to us, especially after Jeep returned to the Wookeys. His leg strengthened and although he still carried it sometimes, he could outrun any other dog, his tan ears flying out behind him like pennants.

He had his failings. Groping my way into the bathroom early one morning, I picked up the dipper and dipped into the stone trough. We had had plenty of rain and the tanks were all abrim with clean rain water. I dipped lower but still met no resistance. I opened my eyes and looked into the tank. It was bone dry. Aghast, I saw that the bung had been pulled out by Little Joe and all our precious water had run away.

Jeep was a splendid dog. Brian enjoyed teasing him and he would curl himself round into a horseshoe, growling with delight, talking to us. Nell Wookey had a lovely tale to tell about him. When Keith had been appointed District Officer Tenom, she had accompanied him on a week's tour of their new district. On returning to their house they were met by Jeep who greeted them ecstatically. He followed them from room to room, growling and wagging. A little later the cook-boy came in and stood nervously before them.

'*Tuan, mem* . . . while you away, everything good, no trouble. But I must tell you . . . I *did* sit in your chair here and I *did* open your book and look and I *did* take a cigarette from your box and smoke it. I tell you this because I know Jeep already tell you all this. I very sorry *tuan!*'

Jeep's one shortcoming was his delight in chasing cars. I suffered many a sleepless night listening to the sound of oncoming cars and waiting for the vociferous barking as he dashed out to intercept them. There'd be a squeal of brakes then silence until the hum of the next approaching car.

We never had a cat. Both of us preferred dogs and the Borneo cats were not attractive. They were particularly yowly and they all sported a stumpy, kinky tail with a disjointed bend in it. Local legend explained this with the story of the princess who, while swimming in the river, removed her ring and tied it up in the tail of a cat. A passing crocodile snapped at the cat's tail, amputating it at the knot and leaving it crooked.

'Body' Barnes was one of those people who cannot stand the presence of a cat. Back from Korea, he asked us to dine with him one night and I saw the door behind him open as a cat entered the room. A minute later he stiffened, snuffed the air and said:

'There's a cat in the room!'

He turned in his chair and looked about him. 'Has anyone seen a cat?'

I said that one had come in a moment before and surely he'd seen it.

'No, is there one here? I thought there must be. I can't stand the things. Amah, put it out!'

I was astonished that he could sense one without seeing it.

•　　•　　•

At about this time I became Jesselton correspondent for the *North Borneo News*, a small, unpretentious magazine with a circulation of only five hundred which was published weekly in Sandakan. My identity was supposed to be a secret and to further confuse the issue I was fed copy by Terry de Souza about the Anglo-Burman community, many of whom worked at the Secretariat. Besides writing a column of 'Jesselton Jottings', I began to add a 'Thought for the week' – pieces of verse drawing attention to any matter which was exciting public concern or interest that week. This bit of doggerel describes an experience I had on one of my early trips to the market.

Sing hey for health and hygiene and hurrah for Pure Food
  Acts!
Come gather round me, children, and listen to the facts:
Let's go to Api-Api, in the market there's a treat,
For in the fly-screened meatshop there are blowflies on the
  meat!
They're most well-bred about it, their blood could not be
  bluer,
They enter by the door 'Masok' and leave by one marked
  'Keluar'.
'The reason' -- and the vendor smiles – 'is that we're always
  hopin'
That more folk will come in to buy if doors are kept wide
  open!'

Another piece dealt with Jesselton's perennial problem, the power supply.

Sandakan has a power supply and Tawau hasn't any,
Kudat uses candles which they claim appeal to many,
But Jesselton progresses and we think it rather nifty
To divide the power quite equally between us, fifty-fifty.

It's really very simple, all you have to do is know
Which night and on which side of street the light is going to
  glow,
But it always seems to happen, for I'm not extremely bright,
That whenever I have guests to dine, there isn't any light.

Now this sounds quite romantic, soft lights and music
  sweet,

With shining silver candlesticks at table when you eat,
But this old lamp, a Sunflame, no eye could ever gladden.
I fear I'm going MAD! Please, who can lend me an Aladdin?

John Stagg lent us an Aladdin lamp and the joy of it was quite overwhelming. The silent, radiant, silver light replaced the roaring Sunflame banshees and brought serenity to our dining table.

One week the Editor of the *News* asked me to cover the Empire Day Race Meeting, especially the fashions of the ladies. Brian and I were not interested in the races at all. To stand around in the blazing heat all afternoon with only a two-minute flash of excitement every half hour was not our idea of fun. The racecourse was not unlike the rough and ready tracks at Australian picnic race meetings with nothing in the way of a stand or shelter from the sun. As for the horses, Borneo ponies were so small in stature that the jockeys' feet almost touched the ground. Later on, Australian horses were imported and this no doubt increased the attraction of the races, but at the time I am speaking of, only the keen punters went. On this occasion the women were particularly dowdy! Blouses and skirts and faded print dresses just about summed up the fashion scene. The men though . . . that was another matter! They couldn't have obliged me better had they known my task. This is the piece I sent my editor.

'The dullness of the weather was offset by the brilliance of the frocking. Mr G. Chettle, Chairman of the Turf Club, was most tastefully dressed in a dove-grey jacket, blue shirt with maroon tie and dazzling white trousers and hat. Mr James Wright chose a fine check mauve silk shirt with a darker toned spotted bow tie and an olive-green porkpie felt. Panamas were the most popular item of the day being worn successfully by Mr J. Robinson (with an attractive Paisley tie and matching cigar) and Mr J. Macpherson. With his jaunty wide brim and contrasting band, Mr Macpherson teamed a vividly striped tie in purple, black and white silk. An interesting fashion note was struck by Dr A. Ozimek who achieved an opera cloak effect with a black raincoat thrown nonchalantly over his shoulders, and Mr Macartney looked neat in all-white, relieved by a soft green felt and a green cane umbrella under his arm. Jewellery was not plentiful but Mr A. Fairleigh featured a touch of gold at each wrist to offset his beige shantung shirt and rich American silk tie patterned with scarlet, grey and maroon. There were many attractive ensembles of shorts and long stockings. Mr R. Buckland was most striking in a green check shirt, darker green tie, contrasting shorts and brown suede shoes, while Mr Ian Mackay was original in a black and white check shirt and black shorts. However, Mr Bernard Stidston was the most beautifully dressed. With his shorts Mr Stidston teamed a green, white and pink large-checked shirt worn loose around the waist and hips, long white stockings, a white Panama and a fine linen bandage around his knee. This exquisite ensemble drew murmurs of admiration from the crowd . . .'

The *North Borneo News* printed little international news but articles of interest about economics or agriculture sometimes appeared as well as a lot of interesting snippets from the East and West Coast Residencies. I rather liked this letter to the Editor.

Sir,
    I have collected you some Kudat news. I hope you will have it published as soon as there is space. What I am going to write about is the marriage of the well-known breeder's son to a girl in Bandau.
    I shall now describe a few brief outlines about it, and in which I hope you, Sir, will write some more additional sentences such as the enjoyment, things moving, etc.

1. Mr Chee Fook Min is an old Kudat Root, having stayed fifty-five years in Kudat. Thirty-five years ago he was an Agricultural Inspector and now is a chief registered breeder for Kudat. His son, Chee Chon Len, has just married Miss Young Len Fa, the queen of Bandau.

2. On the occasion of the marriage, many many guests were invited to dinner. There were about two hundred persons to join the celemony.

3. The District Officer and his wife with many others were also present at dinner and had given lots of laughable movement and tricts to the bride.

4. The very last minute of the bride-playing were Mr Tai Yun Min and Mr Chung Ah Cheon to be appointed as Mosquito-net Hangers. (According to Chinese accustom, no one of the relation of the marrying couple is allowed to hang up the mosquito-net for the Bride and Bridegroom.)

5. We hope this couple live happily ever after, and we expect to see their first child at this day of next year.

The mention of the 'bride-playing' refers to the custom of submitting the bride to all sorts of embarrassing provocation, both verbal and physical, which she must suffer with equanimity and a straight face.

•　　•　　•

In June 1951 there was a ripple of excitement as the Chartered Bank Manager's house neared completion. Heads of Government departments and managers of commercial firms mostly lived in pre-war houses dotted along the range of hills overlooking Jesselton. The rest of the expatriates lived in *kampong orang puteh* at Tanjong Aru or in bungalows along the beach. The Chartered Bank house was the first permanent building to be completed since the war. Rumours had been circulating for months about various features of the house – there was even supposed to be a long bath in it! – and everyone was agog. Then Mr and Mrs Macpherson sent out invitations to a drinks party to be held in their beautiful new home. Eyebrows were raised as it was discovered that both European and Asian guests had been invited for the first time. It was wonderful to step out of *kajang* and *attap* into a civilized atmosphere of tasteful furnishings, soft crimson carpets and the luxury of ceilings. In Hemlock Cottage, as in every other building in Jesselton, the rafters rose above our heads into the gloomy, dusty, cobwebby thatch. The *bilian* shingles of the front part of our house contrasted with the *attap* at the back. Spiders and friendly little *chichaks* were always with us (it is said that a house without *chichaks* is not a happy house), and occasionally the dark shapes of swamp rats would creep along the beams like black blots. It was better not to look up!

Some months after the completion of the Bank house, a wonderful story began to circulate. Mr Macpherson was a member of the Legislative Council and therefore a very important person. Because of its luxurious appointments, the Bank house was used as an extension to Government House whenever V.I.P.s visited Jesselton, and overflow guests were bedded there. Betty Macpherson was a gracious lady whose flower arrangements and domestic appointments were impeccable. Came yet another important visitor to the Bank house. Mr and Mrs Macpherson entertained him to drinks and then retired to their room to bathe.

'Have a hot bath, Mr ———. There's plenty of hot water. Dinner will be at 8 o'clock.'

When they reassembled, Mrs Macpherson asked her guest if he had enjoyed his hot bath.

He looked at her for a second then burst out: 'Well, no I didn't.'

'Oh dear!' Mrs Macpherson's eyebrows knitted. 'Wasn't there enough hot water?'

'Nothing came out of the taps,' her guest said flatly.

'But that's impossible!'

Betty picked up the skirts of her long dress and ran upstairs, through the guest bedroom into the attached bathroom. There was the gleaming new long bath, the pride of Borneo! Two huge chrome taps bristled at the end. She turned the taps. Nothing came out. She looked behind the taps. Nothing was attached to the taps, no pipes at all.

Her embarrassment and chagrin can only be imagined as she thought of the number of departed guests who had not been brave enough to complain.

●   ●   ●

There was only one drawback in my new life. I had no music, no wireless, no gramophone and, worst of all, no piano. There were only a few pianos in Jesselton, Surveyor-General Smallfield's, Nell Wookey's, Ken Summers' and that of Mrs Lee Yun Shu who lived in the *kampong ayer*. I longed for a piano of my own and, talking to Bandmaster Cox one day, he said he had connections with the Chappell Piano Company in England and could probably get me a discount on one. He wrote off and duly received a quotation for a fully tropicalized piano, including freight to Borneo. Brian and I did long calculations and decided we could afford it. We placed an order and then sat back in great impatience to await news of delivery. We eventually received the invoice which stated that the piano was to be shipped on S.S. *Benrinnes*. The Ben Line's ships plied regularly between Britain and the Far East so we enquired from the agent and found out that the *Benrinnes* would arrive in July. As the date came nearer we became increasingly nervous, dashing into the agent's every time we were in town to check the E.T.A. and asking Ted Cox how we were going to get it off the ship. Anything larger than the small coastal Blue Funnels had to lie off-shore.

'Don't worry!' said Ted reassuringly. 'I'm going to see to it! I've organized a lighter which will bring it to shore.'

'But how will you get it off the lighter up onto the jetty?'

'It's not coming to the jetty. We'll bring the lighter in to shore further along by the rice *godowns*. A truck can pull in close there and we'll transfer the piano onto the truck.'

'But it'll have a terrific buffeting on the truck, Ted!'

'Not to worry!' Ted went through life with a smile. 'I've arranged to have it cushioned on a lot of mattresses and I'll get several *mata mata* to hold it steady. She'll be right!'

Everything was done according to Ted's plan and the piano in its padded bed on the truck arrived safely at Hemlock Cottage. There was a moment's anxiety as it was manoeuvred around the angle in our outside steps and through the front door but then it stood there in its packing case.

'The Captain told me when I went on board this morning that his manifest listed 2,000 tons of cargo and THE PIANO,' said Ted.

'Quick then! Let's get the crate off!'

By lunchtime the gleaming Chappell stood in the only suitable place . . . by the front window of the alcove where we had previously breakfasted and waved to friends going past on their way to work.

'Try it!' said Brian.

I lifted the glossy lid, my eyes devoured the ivory and ebony keys. It was a solemn moment. I sat down and played.

Trained as a classical pianist, I had been brought up with a magnificent Lipp grand piano with carved ornamentation on its Italian walnut case. It had been a part of me until I left home. During my travels around Australia I had only honky-tonk pianos in dusty country halls, with an occasional good instrument in private homes. Never had I played such a new piano and never had I played the very first notes on a new one. It was exhilarating!

Brian was already thinking ahead.

'We should have a lamp inside it. Otherwise it will become damp and the keys will stick.'

'Well, we can't have a lamp without power. What about those bags of silica gel that Ken uses?'

'Useless! All you'll be doing is trying to dry out the entire atmosphere of Borneo.'

There was nothing to be done. We just hoped that with plenty of use the piano would not be affected by damp. It certainly got plenty of use. Three months later Pete had business in Labuan, only half an hour away by plane, so he came over for the weekend and celebrated Brian's birthday by christening the piano at a party. The lively jam session and sing-song which ensued rivalled the Chinese Opera in its tent down at Tanjong Aru.

Chapter 11

Makan Angin

C able and Wireless's land consisted of seventy acres along
Tanjong Aru. Governor Twining with the C. & W. Manager of
Singapore and a bottle of gin were said to have made an aerial
survey of possible areas.

'That looks a good flat place!' our man is reputed to have said as
they flew over Tanjong Aru. 'We'll buy that!'

Flat it certainly was. Swamps usually are. It was also pock-
marked with bomb-craters and foxholes in which the bones of Japanese soldiers mouldered. When Brian arrived as Branch Engineer,
his job was to get Jesselton Station working. This meant clearing the
land of six foot high *lallang*, having *sungeis* dug to drain the water
into the sea, levelling and surveying the land and planning aerial
layouts, raising the masts and installing the engines in the engine
room and the equipment in the Instrument Room when these had
been built.

'Body' Barnes, a superbly competent man with the incisive mind
of a lawyer, was in the meantime working in the hut in Jesselton
which served as Town Office, buying land, having discussions
with Government, getting the temporary Mess built and planning
the Engineer's house and the permanent Mess which would eventually be built along the shore. George Pope, that drily comical
man, was mechanician. He had to see that trenches were dug from
Tanjong Aru to Jesselton, a distance of four miles, and cables laid

198

to connect the Town Office and the Instrument Room at Tanjong Aru.

By the time we were married, 'Body' had gone to Korea and Jerry White and 'Tosh' Parriss had arrived to join George and Ag Hill in the Mess. The outlines of the permanent brick Office were taking shape at Tanjong Aru. The bamboo scaffolding for the Engineer's house and the permanent Mess was also being erected. Permanent buildings were still a great novelty in Borneo after the *kajang* and *attap* structures used for houses, shops and offices. I was interested to see that, contrary to practice in western countries, the Chinese builders put the roofs on first, after the basic framework had been erected. How very sensible! They could then get on with building walls and making floors in any kind of weather. Why do Europeans put the roof on last?

One day Brian encountered a serious problem. Right in the path of one of his projected aerials was a huge banyan tree, its branches supported by myriad props caused by hair-like roots dropping from the branches, taking root in the earth and thickening to small trunks. He called the *mandor*.

'Duraman! Get the men to cut this tree down!'

'*Tuan*,' acknowledged the foreman but didn't move.

'I want it done today, as soon as possible,' said Brian.

'*Tuan*, this tree *hantu* (haunted). *Ta boleh potong*. No can cut.'

'Duraman, this tree must be cut.'

Duraman went away and for a quarter of an hour he and the coolies squatted on their haunches debating the matter. Then he returned.

'*Tuan*, coolies no cut tree. That tree *hantu*. Big trouble if we cut down.'

Brian argued. Duraman returned to the men. More discussion ensued. He came back.

'*Tuan*, if Demam put axe in tree, maybe O.K. Demam not Moslem, *tuan*. If axe still in tree next day, that means *hantu* gone away. Then we cut tree.'

Brian agreed and secretly resolved to make sure the axe was driven in very deep. However, the coolies didn't tell him when the experiment was to be made and next morning Duraman summoned him.

'*Tuan*, come see!' He led Brian towards the malignant tree. There was the deep gash in the bark made by the axe of the pagan Demam but the axe itself was lying twenty yards away in the scrub.

'*Hantu* still in tree, *tuan*. Very bad *hantu*. Much bad luck. *Ta boleh potong*. *Tuan* want tree cut, *tuan* can cut.'

There was nothing for it. Brian, George Pope and a workman called Jalleh cut the tree down, all thirty trunks of it. Jalleh was ostensibly a Moslem but not a good one. Almost always inebriated, he had presumably blotted his copybook irredeemably. If the money were right he'd do anything. So the tree came down. Brian felt that the superstition about banyans was very convenient. They are the devil to cut down!

A few days later the major radio transmitter blew up. Then the heavens opened and feet of rain fell over several days. The landline to the main cable failed and on inspection proved to have several holes in it. The paper insulation inside was sodden and the cable unusable. George Pope's language smoked.

Brian inspected the damage followed silently by Duraman, tracing patterns in the mud with his large toe.

'That very bad *hantu*, *tuan*.'

Salt was rubbed in Brian's wounds when he discovered that for the modest outlay of five dollars he could have summoned the local *imam* to exorcise the *hantu*, but how could he account for it on the Company's books?

•   •   •

We were constantly being reminded that although Borneo was a stagnant pool, life was rushing on in the outer world. Miracles of modern science were brought to our notice nearly every week.

'Tosh' Parriss, newly arrived from England, had some of the new long-playing gramophone records in their brightly-coloured jackets. Records had always come in drab beige jackets covered with tiny red-printed lists of other records. What genius dreamed up artistic and photographic designs for record covers? As for the discs themselves, we were still playing 78s for our dances at the Club so we were intrigued by the thought of being able to play eight dance tunes without having to change the record. And to think that a whole symphony could be fitted on one record instead of eight heavy discs, a whole opera on two discs! The mind boggled. 'Tosh' was not so elated. His precious records, brought all the way from England, had warped in the intense Borneo heat and were unplayable. The only cure was to lay them flat in the sun, weighted down by heavy books, until they resumed their intended shape.

The Wookeys came back from their long leave with news of a miraculous new washing-up substance. It was called detergent and had the property of cutting grease. Horrid frying pans and saucepans now emerged dazzling bright from the washing-up bowl. I had always refrained from frying anything on Cookie's day off because I couldn't face the appalling job of cleaning the pan. There was even a detergent for washing clothes. I thought of poor Amah scrubbing the filthy grease stains on Brian's white shorts. What an exciting time we were living in!

My aptitude for cooking had hardly improved. Why should it when I had a superb cook in the house? Sometimes I experimented, as on the day I decided to try my hand at flaky pastry. Cookie was a wonderful pastrycook. His short pastry shivered into crumbs and his flaky pastry dissolved richly on the tongue. I opened my recipe book and prepared the ingredients. If I followed the directions exactly, I should be able to achieve the same result.

Flaky pastry is made by rolling out dough and spreading it with a generous amount of butter, folding the dough over and rolling again, spreading more butter and repeating this process several times. My recipe directed me to spread a quarter of a pound of butter on each layer. The author of the book had reckoned without the Borneo sun. As I folded each layer over, melted butter oozed out of the sandwich and ran over the pastry board. I shook showers of flour from the sifter to dry the board and spread another slab of butter on the dough, scooping it up as it melted and endeavouring to insert it into the dough. It was a melancholy and infuriating experience which reduced me to tears.

It always took one of Cookie's meals to restore my good humour. His *ikan kunyit* for example, succulent fillets of fish simmered in rich *santan* (coconut cream) in which was dissolved a quantity of turmeric, the whole garnished with chopped lengths of spring onion and served with rice. Delicious!

•   •   •

John Stagg departed to England on leave and a short, lively, blunt-mannered little Scot arrived as his locum. Jock Davidson could not have been more different from his predecessor. A no-nonsense, get-things-done man, he lost no time in rearranging the office, inaugurating a completely new filing system, reorganizing the spare parts in the *godown* and giving the long-suffering staff new instructions. Like many small men he was a tremendous extrovert, delighting in fancy dress football matches, water carnivals (he was an expert high diver) and of course Scottish country dancing. His lightness of foot was extraordinary.

As is expected of all new arrivals, Jock signed the Governor's book. One was also expected to sign it on leaving the Colony, on King's Birthday and as a 'thank you' after receiving Government House hospitality, it being a rule that the Governor and his wife could not be asked to dine away from Government House as a reciprocal gesture.

Several days later he received an invitation to dine at Government House. As manager of a merchant company, he rated a dinner whereas we lesser beings only merited a cocktail party. I typed out an acceptance and entered the date in my diary. I reminded him on the day and he duly left for G.H., dapper in his Highland kilt and white mess jacket.

Next morning I asked him about the dinner.

'Well, it was rather strange. No one seemed to know who I was. It was a small party of about twelve people and it was a farewell to some bloke who's going on leave . . . Bryant, I think his name was.'

Mr J.C. Bryant was a leading planter and a member of the Legislative Council. An icy hand clutched my heart and I rang the Private Secretary to the Governor.

'Your Mr Davidson wasn't supposed to come till next week!' he said coldly. 'Last night was a private party of Mr Bryant's most intimate friends. Lady Hone was very good about it. She said not to tell him as it would embarrass him, but there weren't enough chops to go around. Lady Hone had to go without one. What's that? No, we shan't be expecting him next week.'

I was appalled. It was my mistake. I had entered the date on the wrong page of my diary. The vision of this abrasive little Scot whom no one knew entering the reception room of Government House with his kilt swinging is one which still makes me blanch. After this, Jock was always known as 'the man who came to dinner'.

Government House was a strange mix of formality and informality. The furnishings were tasteful and even luxurious but I could never grow accustomed to the 'boys', clad in their starched high-buttoned jackets and white trousers, padding silently over the deep-piled carpet with bare brown feet. Strict protocol was observed. Jack Boles,* a young cadet in the Secretariat who doubled as an *aide-de-camp* to the Governor, would quietly do the rounds of the reception room, tactfully suggesting Mrs Smith should now go and talk to Mr Jones or telling Mr Black that he would be taking Miss

---

* Later Sir Jack Boles, Director-General of the National Trust.

Brown in to dinner and showing them on a plan where their seats were. At the end of the evening he would approach the Senior Lady and tell her it was time for her to make her departure. Once she had risen and thanked Lady Hone, the other guests followed suit so that the room cleared magically in five minutes.

Contrasting with all this formal ritual, when the ladies went upstairs after dinner to Lady Hone's bedroom, the men were taken out into the garden by H.E., where they would all solemnly line up facing a hedge, their white sharkskin jackets gleaming in the dark. This was known variously as 'planter's privilege', 'going out on the coral' or 'inspecting the cannas'. Ministers of State for the Colonies, the Commissioner-General of Malaya, visiting Governors of other territories, the Archbishop of York, even the young Duke of Kent visited Jesselton during these years. I wonder if they, too, were marshalled on the lawn after dinner?

•   •   •

In August 1951 Monica's tour of duty came to an end. For two years she had lived at Tomposik in her native hut with the water buffalo snuffling and rolling underneath, making forays up-country to study the Dusun who lived in the interior. I accompanied her on one of these expeditions, carrying packs on our backs as we walked along narrow paths overlooking tumbling rivers or climbed ridge after ridge of the continuing tree-clad mountains, staying overnight in Dusun houses. I remember sleepless nights as we lay on the split bamboo floors, besieged by mosquitoes or suffocated by a smoky fire, while a group of aged black-clad crones sat up into the night talking endlessly and chewing betel nut. Monica, the spirit of scientific enquiry always strong, made detailed sketches of the architecture of the house, drawing rafters, ridge poles, methods of lashing the *attap*, listing dimensions of the walls and so on. She never really liked the Dusun, much preferring the Bajau, but her instructions had been to study the Dusun and so she did, eventually publishing a scientific paper.

Now she gleefuly packed her belongings and after a grand fare-well party in her honour given by the neighbouring Dusun and Bajau, loaded all her *barang* onto a cumbersome boat and proceeded to pole it downstream in the best Cambridge fashion. When it ran into a sandbank, she jumped into the shallows, grasped the rope and pulled it savagely into deeper water. On arriving in Jesselton and booking into the Rest House, she went all the way back to Tomposik by road in order to reciprocate the villagers' hospitality.

The *tapai* (rice beer) began to flow at two o'clock in the afternoon and by four the party was in full swing. Several Jesselton friends hiked (the road ended at Penampang) to the village that evening to join in the revelry and as we stepped over her threshold, we were greeted by a deafening beating of gongs and drums and the smell of rice, pork and chicken. We sat around the walls to watch the dancing and it wasn't long before we were lured into the charming, graceful mazes of the *dindang*. The springy bamboo floors of Malaysian houses make excellent dance floors and you don't have to exert yourself at all. Standing on the same spot, you extend your arms sideways, bouncing and undulating gracefully to the rhythm of the gongs. As this kind of party proceeds until the last jar of *tapai* has been emptied, usually in the small hours of the morning, it was a very tired anthropologist who returned to the Rest House next day. Monica was made of stern stuff. One of the few women who climbed Kinabalu in those days, she made a special Centenary ascent in March 1951 within a few days of the original ascent in 1851 by Sir Hugh Low.

January to March are the best months for climbing the mountain so when Brian and I planned our January wedding, an ascent of Kinabalu seemed the obvious choice of a honeymoon, but with only three days holiday it had to be postponed and we earmarked January 1952 for the assault.

In the meantime life continued as hectic as ever. The next amateur dramatic production was being rehearsed. *Fresh Fields* by Ivor Novello was a vehicle which offered many splendid characterizations. The Chief Justice, Ivor Brace, revelled in his role as a butler while his wife Dorothy was the star of the show, the flamboyant proprietress of the Angel Family Hotel in Brisbane who has brought her daughter Una to London to do the season. I was in my element playing Una, no longer having to look to my vowels but actually having to brush up my Australian accent. Directed by Mike Saville, it was a lovely romp and played to capacity houses in September.

•　　•　　•

Brian was an accomplished carpenter and cabinet maker and soon after we were married began to talk of building a boat. I had no experience of boats but with the beautiful coastline and offshore

islands waiting to be explored, I was eager for him to start. He spent several days drawing up detailed plans and then began to see what materials he could find. He bought some very hard *selangan batu* for the frame and tongued and grooved *seraya* planks to cover it. The only available place big enough for this building project was the Company's temporary Instrument Room at Tanjong Aru. Desks and equipment were moved to the walls, leaving a large empty space in the middle of the floor where the 13-footer could be built. We have an amusing photograph of the half-completed boat taking shape in the middle of the floor while our Chinese operators are seated against the walls punching out messages. In the background is a wall with a commutation board and a looping black snake of cable coming through the wall. This was the main Hong Kong/ Jesselton cable which emerged from the South China Sea a few hundred yards away, having been relaid into the temporary office by the Company's Cable Ship *Recorder* in April. To me this photo sums up the whole spirit of Borneo. Business was pushed aside while the more important things were attended to. Whenever we had visitors from Hong Kong (who all thought it was the navel of the Far East if not of the whole world), Brian would casually take them into the Instrument Room and show them the boat and the Hong Kong cable disappearing through the wall, thus demonstrating a correct sense of proportion.

At last Brian's boat was finished. Trim in its dark green coat of paint and proudly bearing its name *Aïsah* on prow and stern, it was carried down to the sea by Duraman and his men and ceremoniously placed in the water. *Aïsah* was Mahomet's favourite wife and also the name of one of my Guides but the name was onomatopoeic, suggesting wind and water shushing against the bows. She floated buoyantly in the slight swell.

Brian had designed her as a 'coral creeper', very shallow of draught with vertical sides and a V-shaped keel in section. Broad in beam, she was very stable and it was impossible to capsize her. He had made a pair of oars but we intended to use her as a motorboat and had bought a tiny $\frac{3}{4}$h.p. outboard engine. It took only a pint of fuel to fill its tank and we carried spare fuel in a gin bottle. It was wonderful to putter along in *Aïsah*, floating effortlessly on the oily-calm sea, and to be able to look through the crystal water at the marine life below. Quite often a cumbersome turtle would surface in our wake before submerging again.

We made one trip south from Tanjong Aru to the mouth of the Patagas River, accompanied by Jerry White in his floating bathtub. Not for him the scale drawings of *Aïsah*. He had merely hammered up a long, rectangular box like a coffin and then added a pointed bit at the front! With an outboard engine on the back it managed to keep up with us and we pulled our craft in to a delightful deserted beach some miles south, boiled the billy and picnicked.

This might have been the forerunner of many a pleasant excursion but one night disaster struck. We kept *Aïsah* tethered to an *aru* tree over the weekend and one Saturday night a gale arose and heavy seas drove her in to shore, pounding her against the *arus*.

Brian was aghast next morning to see his beautiful boat with her bottom stove in. To my astonishment he was reluctant to mend it.

'I like planning and building, not repairing.'

'Body' Barnes, back from Korea for some time, had gone on leave and our new Manager, John Tyson, formerly Commodore of the Royal Gibraltar Yacht Club, looked at the wreck with us. Very tall with a grizzled thatch of curly hair, he walked around the boat, his brown eyes shrewdly appraising the hull. Taking his pipe from his mouth, he made a stimulating suggestion.

'Why don't you change her design so that you can use her for sailing? If you're going to mend her bottom, you may as well put in a centre-box and a hinged centreboard. Then you could put in a mast and a boom and we'd get some sails from somewhere . . . '

Brian's eyes lit up. He would enjoy doing that.

He altered the lines at the back of the boat, making the transome rectangular instead of five-sided as it had been. The centrebox and centreboard went in, the latter hinged so we could still creep in over the belt of coastal coral. Then he made a splendid laminated mast and boom. But what about sails? There was nothing available locally.

Again Tyson came to the rescue. When he'd passed through Singapore, one of our staff there had two sails for sale. Perhaps if Brian sent him a signal?

Promptly on the next ship arrived an intriguing large parcel which revealed a huge canvas mizzen and a foresail from a 27-foot whaler! The mizzen was quadrilateral, so Brian cut it down to a triangle and spent long hours laboriously sewing the cut edge and affixing brass eyelets. The foresail needed no attention.

Thus rigged, Aïsah took to her heels. I remember coming home from Pulau Sapi one afternoon with stormclouds gathering and a rising wind. Like a surfboard rider we belted home to the quiet shelter of Tanjong Aru. On subsequent occasions John Tyson raced Aïsah in competition against GP14s and other yachts and did very well.

The only seasonal variations in the weather were in the direction and character of the prevailing wind. From October to March the north-east monsoon blew steadily from late morning to sunset and it tended to be slightly wetter then (Borneo having only two season, the wet and the wetter). Jellyfish suddenly thronged the sea and we had to be careful swimming. From April to September it was a little drier, the south-west monsoon producing sudden strong squalls. The typhoon belt passes north of the Colony so typhoons are unknown, hence the native name 'Land below the wind', but severe rainstorms and high winds sometimes occurred and thunderstorms were frequent. They could be quite dramatic.

When I lived in the Rest House I would see the rain approaching as a dark line from Gaya Island. The skies darkened, visibility decreased, bird-song ceased and apart from the excited shrieks of children down in the *kedai*, a portentous silence descended. Gaya was blotted out. Then the first huge raindrops fell and within seconds a deluge was on us. There was no need to rush around closing doors and shutters. The rain never blew into the room. I could stand there safely watching the sheets of water streaming down. In the town, people scurried about with oiled-paper umbrellas, their bare legs thrust into wooden clogs.

At Tanjong Aru it was different. I had gone to the beach to swim one evening when I saw the signs of an approaching storm. There were some enormous claps of thunder and flashes of lightning which lit up the lowering dusk. Then I heard the rain. I gathered my clothes and started to run for the Mess. From far away down the beach I could hear the approaching roar of rain in the trees and see the casuarinas lashing in the wind. Then it was upon me. It was only a fifty yard sprint to the house but I was drenched before I could reach it. Rain was an almost daily occurrence. It came swiftly and passed on over the hills, very seldom spoiling a whole day, but the amount of rainfall was enormous, ranging from sixty to a hundred and eighty inches a year so the large storm drains in the town were indispensable.

The climate was tropical but equable, day temperatures on the coast ranging from 70°F in the morning to about 88°F at noon, but the nights were comparatively cool and in the early morning I was glad to pull up a flannelette blanket from the bottom of the bed. Brian only had to unroll his *sarong* from around his waist and pull it up over his shoulders when he got chilly.

•　　•　　•

The Sports Club was the centre of the Europeans' social life. Strictly limiting its members to Caucasians, it was the cause of some underlying discontent and embarrassment. Whenever the A.G.M. came around, someone would be sure to move a motion that Asians could be admitted as guests of honour. It was always overruled.

'But the Recreation Club lets us go there!'

'What they do is their business. This Club is a Europeans' Club.'

The backbone of the Club were the *dahulus*, those who had been in Borneo before the war and who wanted to retain the *status quo*. One day I heard the Chief Justice holding forth to the effect that if he wanted to come and play a game of billiards and have some drinks and perhaps let slip a few inadvertent swear words, he didn't want the locals observing him. So it continued as a closed Club, despite the embarrassment of having to deny entrance to such educated and respected men as the Indian doctors at the Hospital.

The Recreation Club on the other hand continued to welcome us in a spirit of magnanimity. Their dances were always very lively affairs and bazaars and canteens for visiting ships' companies were always held there.

We went to the Sports Club for films which were shown by a keen, perspiring member. Rows of chairs were arranged on the badminton court which also served as a dance floor. There was always an hiatus between reels when lights were turned on, drinks fetched from the bar, cigarettes lit and dozens of sandalwood fans agitated. The sweet overpowering scent of sandalwood still evokes for me those hot nights watching old films.

There was a monthly Club dance as well as Race Night dances, Games and Quiz Nights, Treasure and Scavenger Hunts. At one of the latter the list of items to be collected included an elephant. Most hunters searched for children's toys but Paddy Heaton, a mad Irishman, devoted all his time to persuading the proprietor of a visiting circus to let him have a live elephant to take to the Club. He finally got consent to take the animal after the conclusion of the evening performance at 10.30 but unfortunately the Hunt ended at 10 o'clock. Paddy reckoned the evening would have been well spent if he could have taken an elephant up the steps of the Club to confront inebriated members.

As well as these functions there were all the celebrations associated with the many holidays on the Malayan calendar – Malay, Chinese, Indian and British. It always piqued me that Cable and

Wireless got only the six British holidays so Brian would be working when everyone else was free.

January opened with a burst of festivity on New Year's Eve, followed by Burns Night and Australia Day. Chinese New Year made a large hole in January or February, St. David's Day and St. Patrick's Day in March were often overrun by Easter, and Hari Raya Haji was a movable feast some time in the early months of the year. King's Birthday was in June and a couple of Bank Holidays brought us up to August, but the end of the year was particularly hectic. Liberation Day, which commemorated the freeing of North Borneo from Japanese occupation, came in September and was followed by Hari Raya Puasa, the Moslem celebration at the end of the fast of Ramadan and the Double Tenth, the tenth of October, when the Nationalist Chinese commemorated the founding of the Chinese Republic in 1912. Armistice Day and St. Andrew's Night were in November and then came the build-up to all the Christmas festivities. We had a few days back at work trying to pick up the threads before New Year disrupted us again.

There was a large Scottish contingent in Jesselton as there always seems to be in overseas communities. Anyone who could boast a Mac before his name or a burr in his accent counted the days till St. Andrew's Night, known locally as Hari Raya Jock. In 1951 it came as a welcome diversion from the interminable discussions about the British General Election which had just returned the Conservatives with a narrow majority.

The Club was festively decorated with flowers and masses of heather flown in from Scotland. On the walls and columns were representations of large purple thistles and the insignia of various clans. Each doorway was guarded by a pair of crossed halberds giving the atmosphere of a baronial hall. The celebrations commenced with a splendid dinner of Scotch broth, smoked salmon, haggis, neeps and tatties followed by dessert. The haggis was traditionally piped in, followed by the Whisky Bearer. By ten o'clock dancing was under way, a long line of kilted and betartaned couples extending down the room to Strip the Willow or sets of eight dancing reels.

Brian and I arrived with other Sassenachs in time for the dancing. I had decided to get some use out of my wedding dress and in order to make it less nuptial in appearance, I'd looped a length of scarlet georgette around my hips and tied it on one side. As we entered the Club my heart sank. Fool that I was not to remember that all the Scottish women were wearing white with a tartan sash over one shoulder and fastened on the opposite hip.

Chip Plunkett was standing by the door and joked: 'Your sash has slipped a bit, Wendy m'dear!'

Dear Chip was the clown of Jesselton. A highly efficient policeman with many years of service with the Palestine Police and also in the Caribbean, he was Deputy Commandant of the North Borneo Armed Constabulary. An Irishman, he sported a very wide handlebar moustache and his shining bald head was ringed with a horseshoe of dark curly hair. He was an essential guest at any party, usually providing the entertainment for the evening with his jokes or his spirited rendition of *'Rasa Sayang'* or his uninhibited dancing. This lovable man was married to the most exquisite lady I have ever met. Beautiful, elegant, cultured, artistic, Lucille Plunkett was of French extraction and came from Barbados. When I first arrived in the Colony, a brash and unsophisticated Australian, Lu seemed to me the epitome of the gracious European woman. Most Australians had an inbuilt sense of inferiority having been brought up in the belief that nothing Australian had any true merit and that Europe was the source of all things cultured and worthwhile. After speaking with Lu, I always made a renewed attempt to control my vowels and to restrain my exuberant movements. For a while I would use the door of the Rest House instead of swinging my legs over the low window sills.

Not surprisingly the Plunketts' St. Patrick's Day party was always the highspot of March. Their *kajang* was transformed into an Irish pub, the walls decorated with posters and an ornate motto reading 'A little usquebaugh makes you frusquebaugh'. A fine oil painting of the proprietor hung over the bar and sketches of St. Patrick hunting snakes, a locality map of Ireland and a huge barrel of potheen were also on display. About seventy guests assembled and the chatter and laughter were deafening until the Proprietor rang his bell and demanded silence for the Shillelagh Singers who performed some fine Cox arrangements of popular Irish tunes. Chip, eating bangers impaled on the tip of a *parang*, would then oblige with 'Phil the Fluter's Ball' and 'MacNamara's Band', in which Chuck Sventon portrayed the only Swede.

Even the strong Welsh contingent in the Colony couldn't rival that singing on St. David's Day although their rendition of 'Lloyd George' could be heard a mile away. Invitations in Welsh were sent out by 'Flywheel' George but Mr and Mrs Evans, the hosts of the party, were stymied when some of the acceptances came back in Welsh. Leek soup followed by tripe and onions were on the menu that night.

Surprisingly nothing was ever done about St. George's Day in April, but one 25th April Dorothy and Nancy were sitting on the Rest House verandah when Chuck Fenton and Bob Kirkwood came up the steps. It was the anniversary of the disastrous landings at Gallipoli in the 1st World War when thousands of Australians and New Zealanders were killed, the most sacred date on the Australasian calendar.

'It's Anzac Day!' said Chuck. 'What are we going to do about it?'

Little Bridget Colquhoun, the Irish Health Visitor, turned to them with interest.

'Who is St. Anzac?' she asked. 'I've never heard of him.'

Chuck Fenton was our Postmaster General. A small, rotund, ebullient man with an utterly cherubic face and curly brown hair, he was an Australian leprechaun with a puckish sense of humour. A panegyric in the *North Borneo News* on the occasion of his 41st birthday described him as '*bon vivant* and famous host, epicure, equestrian, athlete and archetype, after whose birth in Australia

Fate broke the mould.' No respecter of persons, he tackled Lady Hone one day. Chuck's *kajang* which he shared with Bob Kirkwood, the Director of Telecommunications, was built on the foreshore and had a wonderful view of the sea beyond his garden. Unfortunately a small *sulap* (hut) had recently been built on the beach so that the Governor's family could change for swimming.

'Now look here, Sybil!' said Chuck to Lady Hone with asperity. 'Don't you think it's time you moved your *jamban* somewhere else so I can have my view back?'

Chuck and Bob practically ran the Turf Club unaided. Before one race meeting Chuck arranged for a small radio to be sent to the Convent so that the Sisters could listen to his commentary. All went well until the main race. For some reason the barrier wouldn't work properly and in his commentary box Chuck was getting agitated. The cruel sun blazed on the horses lined up at the start. No one made a move to remove them despite Chuck's pointed comments about the heat and the strain on the animals. Mother Eugenie didn't waste time. Quickly she summoned her pupils.

'Into the church, children! We need your prayers!'

Suddenly the barrier jerked up, the horses leapt forward and Chuck's horse won. What it was to have a direct line to the Almighty!

His personal charity, though he rarely spoke of it, was the welfare of war orphans. He saw to their education and at Christmas gave them a slap-up party. The only trouble was that with the passage of years Chuck's orphans were growing up.

'The youngest is five and the eldest are sixteen to eighteen. What sort of presents do I give an eighteen-year-old?' he complained, puzzlement wrinkling his brow.

Chuck always seemed to run into trouble at dinner parties. A child of nature, the acquisition of social graces did not come easily. Trying manfully to be polite to the Acting Governor's wife one evening, he inclined his head to speak into her ear trumpet, forgetting that he had a tankard of beer in his hand. Down the trumpet

whooshed the beer! Then there was the formal dinner at Government House attended by some visiting English Peers and the Governors of neighbouring territories. Chuck had never learned to tie a bow tie so he made use of a clip-on tie. While conducting an animated conversation during the first course, his tie came off and dropped into his soup. Quite unabashed, he fished it out, wrung it and clipped it back in place.

The only time I ever saw him disconcerted was at another dinner party. He was seated next to Nan whose napkin dropped to the floor. She bent to retrieve it at the same time as Chuck. Under the tablecloth she kissed her own hand with a resounding smack, exclaimed, 'How dare you, Mr Fenton!' and emerged, dimpling prettily at Chuck's astonished confusion.

When I first went to live amongst the expatriate English in Jesselton, I felt very self-conscious about my Australian accent although it wasn't very marked. I decided to broaden my As. However, after assiduously saying 'cahstle' and 'dahnce', I'd hear Mancunian Sister Jones saying 'castle' and 'dance'. It was very confusing. I eventually got myself into a tangle one night and mentioned playing in a 'dahnce bahnd'. Enough was enough! English was too inconsistent a language and I reverted to my familiar speech.

It did surprise me that Brian with his beautiful 'standard English' voice pronounced 'apparatus' with a hard third A and 'zebra' with a hard E. I couldn't believe it.

'"Apparaytus" is so American!'

'You do hear apparahtus in England but it's considered rather Oxford.'

I was also amazed to hear the English saying they'd 'taken' a decision, whereas we'd 'make' a decision. It was very interesting to anyone interested in comparative language.

Whereas in Seria there had been an experience gap between me as a single girl and the married women, in Jesselton it was quite different. I felt separated from others by gaps of seniority or nationality. We young people were rarely invited to the homes of the senior Government officers. We knew them and nodded to them in the street but that was as far as it went.

As for nationality, I found an annoying condescension on the part of many of the British and a surprising lack of knowledge of Australia, all the more marked by comparison with the Australians' wide knowledge of Europe. After all, we were taught from an early age about our heritage and 'the old country', we studied the geography and history of Europe (having very little history of our own), we memorized British poetry and read British novels. So it came as a jolt when an Englishman was unable to say how many States we had or what was the capital of Australia, when he'd never heard of Henry Lawson or Burke and Wills and thought Melba was a fruit dessert. It seemed to reinforce the delusion we entertained that we had nothing of value in our country. It wasn't just that they knew so little about us, it was the galling impression they gave that there was no need to know. They were very nice about it of course but it was maddening all the same.

Nancy, too, had problems with the English residents. One man expressed surprise on learning that she was Australian.

'You don't speak like an Australian,' he said.

Nancy patiently and gently explained that not every Australian had an abrasive accent. When one was brought up to speak correctly and to care about language, one spoke 'educated Australian'. It was only the uncouth, uneducated Australians who spoke carelessly.

'Yes,' said he. 'My wife's an Australian and she's got an appalling accent!'

On another occasion Nan was invited to take tea with a senior Government official's wife. She wondered why she had been so honoured and after sipping her tea and nibbling a thin cucumber sandwich, she learned the reason.

'I suppose you want to know why I've asked you here,' said the *mem*. 'Our son is in Australia, you know, and he has sent us this beautiful boomerang, so we decided to ask you down here to show us how to throw it.'

Nan blinked in utter astonishment. She was nettled by the woman's condescension and by her ignorance. Should she explain that 95% of Australians had never seen an aborigine, let alone a boomerang? Should she sweep out in high dudgeon?

She did neither but, smiling sweetly, stepped out into the garden which faced the South China Sea through a thin screen of casuarinas. Grasping the boomerang she took up what she hoped was the correct stance and hurled it. It whizzed away in a graceful curve, through the casuarinas and over the sea. It didn't come back.

'What did you say!' I exclaimed in horror when she told me.

'Well, I apologized. I said that it wasn't a very good boomerang. It couldn't have been made properly, it didn't have the right curve, and so on. She was most put out, of course. I felt sorry later. It was really a very nice boomerang . . . '

There was a great deal of excitement in November when we all received invitations to a cocktail party on board the Blue Funnel Line's new coastal steamer *Kimanis*. This addition to the fleet had been eagerly awaited ever since the blueprint stage and now here she was on the Borneo run. Comments and criticism filled the air.

'It's just a bigger version of the *Rajah Brooke*!'

'The cabins are wonderful . . . so different from the *Kajang*.'

'Yes, but why don't these Straits boats have enclosed lounges? Why must we sit out on deck?'

'Wonder what the food's like!'

In the middle of the celebrations Tom Prentice came on board in a state of exhilaration to announce that Peggy had just given birth to a son, Hamish, so the champagne flowed anew. The Prentices had been posted back to Jesselton, much to Peggy's joy.

I visited her in hospital next day and found her walking around as spry as an ant. She told me she had arrived at the hospital and was just settling into her room when the baby began to arrive and she just made it to the bed in time, while Tom bellowed for the nurse. It had all been so quick that she was in no way incommoded and was ready to come home.

We had no plans to have a baby. Although we would naturally have a family in due course, I couldn't imagine starting one yet. Life was too full and anyway, we had to climb Kinabalu.

A more pressing decision was waiting. Our year's lease on Hemlock Cottage would expire in January and there was serious doubt as to whether it would be renewed. The roof was leaking badly and we soon ran out of buckets and bowls to catch the water. The landlord showed no sign of carrying out repairs. But what to do? Our permanent house at Tanjong Aru, though taking shape nicely, would not be ready for several months. Once again the Gatfords came to our rescue. There was a vacant Railways quarter which we could have until our new house was ready. So just before Christmas we moved house. I felt no pang at leaving Hemlock Cottage. Its shortcomings were becoming more numerous and I hankered after some mod. cons.

Our new home was nearer to Tanjong Aru but 'on the wrong side of the tracks'. It was in a street of wooden bungalows built up on piles in the usual fashion. In the other houses lived the Anglo-Burman railway workers. There had been a flow of immigrant Eurasians from Burma and India after the war. They were highly-skilled workers experienced especially in the running of railways and proved invaluable to the efficient working of North Borneo trains as the native Bornean was an agriculturalist, not an artisan. Kathy Ferdinands, our Ranger lieutenant, lived in one house a little way along and we knew several of the other families.

As our stay was to be short we didn't set out to make a home. There was a combined living area and dining room, two bedrooms off a hall and a primitive *dapor* (kitchen) and servant's room to the rear. There was only one lavatory so it had to do for us and the servants, although they were accustomed to an Asian 'squatter'. Most important of all, the house had electricity and I marvelled at the way light would flood the rooms at the flick of a switch. We were also able to put a lamp in our piano and heaters in the wardrobes. Our shoes stopped growing fur coats of mould and our clothes lost the sickening smell of mildew.

We spent our first Christmas in the house and later in January the Gatfords and Father Rusted came to celebrate our first wedding anniversary. Rusty professed himself well pleased at the efficacy with which he had tied the knot and the Gatfords beamed on us as though we were their own children.

As January progressed we began to talk about the Kinabalu trip. We felt we ought to do a trial run to get ourselves into trim. There was a moderate 3,700 foot mountain, Bukit Porrein, not very far from Jesselton, which would give us practice. A preliminary visit to the nearest village, Kampong Moyog, a talk with the headman to organize a porter and arrange for a *sulap* to be built on the summit and we were all set to go the following weekend.

Very early Saturday morning we crept out of our house. Monica had lent us a *bongon* (a native 'back-pack' made of light wood and bark, strangely top-heavy to European eyes as its widest part is at the top on a level with one's head tapering to a narrow base) and this was stuffed with our change of clothing, food and bedding. The engine of Brian's motorbike exploded into life, shattering the early morning calm of the sleeping street. Somehow I clambered on the pillion carrying the *bongon*, its weight almost pulling me backwards off the bike. We set off, swaying and steering an erratic course down the dusty road, roaring with laughter, and once equilibrium was established, drove through Batu Tiga and out on the Penampang road. It was delicious travelling in the fresh

cool morning but the *bongon* straps cut painfully into my shoulders. When we reached the village of Moyog I climbed down thankfully and handed the *bongon* over to the waiting porter. Watched by a curious crowd of villagers we set off into the jungle.

The jungle! What evocations of mystery, of danger, of menace are conjured up by that word! As a child I had feasted on a diet of Edgar Rice Burroughs so as I peered around me I almost expected a huge python to unfold from a branch above and loop me in its coils or a large ape to swing down on a vine and carry me up to a platform in a tall tree. I laughed at myself. We were not far from a village and between the trees was a lot of secondary growth, evidence of man's encroachment on the wilderness. Trees are cut down, paths are made and as the sunlight penetrates, secondary growth springs up – ferns, wild orchids, flowering plants, vines, sensitive grass and a lot of anonymous 'bush'. The transition from hot sun to cool shade was welcome and we padded along easily in the wake of the porter.

I knew there were small elephants somewhere in Borneo. Might they be here? Rhinoceros too and apes of all sizes, from the beautiful large *orang utan*, the man of the forest, to the excitable gibbons, the *wah-wahs*, with their long slender limbs. There might be entrancing animals like the slow loris, its eyes like moons, or the *pelandok*, the delicate mousedeer prancing on its matchstick legs, and the *musang* or civet cat. I'd have expected the jungle to be full of noises, rustles, snarls and screams but all was quiet. No brilliantly-plumaged bird flashed through the dappled shadows. No heavy beating of wings ruffled the heavy curtain of silence. Were we three alone?

Something bright caught my eye.

'Look Brian, coleus!' It was indeed our domestic coleus, a beautiful plant with multi-coloured leaves

And then a Dusun woman came down the track towards us, breaking the spell. She came to a halt and stood respectfully.

'*Tabek tuan, tabek mem*!' she greeted us. '*Pergi mana?*' (Where are you going?)

'*Makan angin . . . naik Bukit Porrein.*' (Eating the wind – that is to say, walking for pleasure. We're climbing Mt. Porrein.)

'Ah, *makan angin.*' She spied the coleus in my hand. '*Chantek itu mem. Tidak boleh mati. Tidak boleh mati.*'

It cannot die. I have always remembered those words, in subsequent years, in many countries, as I took cuttings to propagate coleus.

'*Selamat jalan!*' (Go safely!) She continued her way down the path.

Now we were climbing. Our sturdy guide's bare brown legs plodded on indefatigably in front of us. Whenever we paused for breath he looked around wonderingly. The path followed the river Moyog at one stage and we paused for a drink by a beautiful rock pool. A waterfall fell into it and another out of it. All around the jungle pressed privately, silently. We were hot and tired. A swim in the pool was tempting but we had to keep up our pace.

'Perhaps on the way back,' said Brian.

As we climbed higher the secondary growth disappeared and the trees grew closer and higher, soaring up, up towards the sun, straining towards the light. Between the trees was only moss now, the flowers were up on the forest canopy. The trees dripped, there was a chill dankness in the air and our perspiration dried cold on our bodies. Despite a break for lunch we were tiring. Towards the end of the afternoon Brian began to experience a shortness of breath and had to stop frequently, panting.

'Do you think it's a shortage of oxygen?' I asked him, wondering how he would cope with Kinabalu's 14,000 feet.

'More likely I'm out of condition.'

I began to hate the muscled calves of the porter ahead, unflagging, untiring. Around five o'clock we pulled ourselves up the last steep pinch of the path and reached the summit . . . quite a small summit, no more than ten yards long. An area of undergrowth had been cleared and a rough *sulap* built, merely a roof of leaves supported by rough-hewn poles. We couldn't even be rewarded with a view as trees grew up the sides of the mountain. In one place Brian lifted me and through a gap I glimpsed jungle reaching to the horizon. Someone once wrote: 'Borneo has few people and many trees.' There were the trees, a tapestry of infinite gradations of green unrelieved by any other colour or any man-made structure. Was there really nothing under those limitless trees or did they conceal undiscovered settlements, unheard-of animals and mysterious tribes?

The sun was dropping fast behind the trees and the evening chill made us rummage for sweaters. The porter made a fire and we ate a frugal meal. By half past six it was dark. With nowhere to go and nothing else to do, we went to bed. Snuggling under blankets Brian and I listened to the noises of the night and tried to guess how many times the tok-tok bird would call. Internees in the P.O.W. camps used to bet on it. Tok, tok, tok. Completely unpredictable, the bird called. Tok, tok, tok, tok, tok, tok, tok. It was maddening. Tok. I tried to shut my ears to the monotonous sound but inevitably found myself counting. Tok, tok.

The ground was hard, our legs ached with weariness but I felt wrapped in warmth and love as we lay together on the mountain top.

I was used to sleeping on hard surfaces but Brian had a restless night trying to find a hip-hole. The porter fell asleep immediately and rose before dawn. The crackling of twigs and the delicious smell of wood smoke woke us. The air was cold and damp.

We started off down the mountain and made a rapid descent, almost eager to reach the hot foothills. The porter went ahead to his village and we took our time, pausing at the rock pool for a swim. We took off our sweaty clothes and dived into the icy water. All around the jungle crouched, silent except for the hum of cicadas and the occasional honk of a hornbill. Ill at ease, I sensed eyes surrounding us but no rustle of leaf or crack of twig betrayed any observer. The jungle merely watched and waited till we, the intruders, departed.

•   •   •

On reflection we decided that we needed more practice before attempting Kinabalu but once again fate intervened. I discovered I was pregnant and went to see the gynaecologist, a wonderful large lady with strong, capable hands. She was married to a planter down the line and came up once a month to hold a clinic. I mentioned that we wanted to climb Kinabalu.

'Kinabalu? Oh, I wouldn't recommend that, would you, Sister?'

Sister 'Pete' Peters agreed, despite my desperate look of appeal. I have always found it difficult to accept harsh rulings of fate. I beat my puny fists against obstacles and if I cannot overcome them, I have to rationalize. I overcame my great disappointment about Kinabalu by mentally trading it for a child, although it didn't help when I subsequently learned that Joy Gay had climbed the mountain when she was three months pregnant!

Chapter 12

Anak Laki-Laki

P regnancy was the most astonishing concept to grasp! Doctor
MacLaren seemed to understand.

'It can't happen to you! Is that what you think?'

That was it exactly. Other people had babies, my sister Marj,
loads of women in Seria, occasional women in Jesselton, but *me*! I
didn't even understand how it could've happened. We certainly
hadn't planned to have a child. I couldn't imagine our twosome
becoming a threesome. I wasn't sure if I were pleased or not. Brian
in his usual realistic way said:

'Well, there's nothing to do about it if you're not. We want a
family, don't we?'

Of course we wanted a family . . . some time.

My sister Marj's advice to me on leaving Melbourne had been:
'Have plenty of children! They're the best insurance. My health
isn't good enough and your sister Noël's too poor, but you're going
to have a comfortable life with servants, so have lots of kids!'

As the idea grew on me I became excited by the prospect and a
host of questions crowded my mind. What sex would it be? Whom
would it resemble? I then became caught up in what was to be the
first of the many Causes which have engaged my enthusiasm over
the years. Grantly Dick Read's wonderful method of Natural Childbirth was beginning to attract wider attention although his patients
in England had been practising it for over ten years. I sent off to

Singapore for his *Revelation of Childbirth* and *Introduction to Mother-hood* and devoured them. Brian read them too and encouraged me. I started the exercises and practised relaxation. My fanaticism gave me confidence but I realized I had to tackle Dr Ozimek. Many doctors were opposed to these new-fangled ideas. I explained to him that I wanted to have my baby by natural childbirth and that I didn't want anaesthetic. I wanted to see the baby born.

The big Polish doctor laughed at me.

'What are you worried about? We've delivered thousands of babies.'

'I'm not worried about you! Don't you see . . . I want to do it the right way the first time otherwise I'll have unpleasant memories next time.'

'Yes, yes, yes,' he humoured me. 'You don't want anaesthetic.'

'That's right. Even if I say I want it, I want you to talk me out of it and help me.'

'Yes, yes . . . but of course, if there are any complications you realize we would have to interfere.'

'Of course,' I agreed and promptly forgot about it. There would be no complications. I was exuberantly healthy and intended working up to a month before the delivery.

At this time another difficulty arose. Poppa Gatford needed the Railway house for one of his staff and although the Engineer's house at Tanjong Aru was still not ready for us, a small weather-board house nearby, destined to be the home of an Anglo-Burman supervisor, had just been completed. Set back from the road leading to the fine new Cable and Wireless station, it was smaller than the temporary Mess but it would do us for a couple of months.

I christened it the Rabbit Hutch. From a tiny garden steps led up to a verandah only wide enough for a couple of chairs. The front door led into a small living/dining area, off which led two bedrooms separated by a bathroom. Steps from the back of the living room led down to the kitchen and servants' room. Once more we moved our belongings although a lot of the furniture had to be stored. Once more we brought with us a few treasured plants taken from the garden of Hemlock Cottage, putting some into the ground and leaving others standing around in tins.

Now that we were even farther from Jesselton and its shops, I sent off to Robinsons, the big Singapore emporium, for extra kitchen equipment (for the days when I cooked) and a pair of hair-cutting scissors and hair clippers to save Brian having to go to town for a haircut. I was used to cutting women's hair but learning to taper his hair from crown to nape of neck was difficult and mastering the use of hair clippers on his neck was a painful business for him. In an effort to get to inaccessible corners around his ears I'd drape myself around him and inevitably end up giving him a big hug.

'Funny,' he'd say, 'my barber never does that.'

Tanjong Aru was a delight! The actual *tanjong* was still composed of untouched jungle. The two remaining Harrisons and Crosfield bungalows and the Steel Brothers bungalow were ranged along the beach on one side of the point, while the C. and W. land extended along the other side and inland as far as the Jesselton road. In the remaining jungle were monkeys and lots of unknown birds although one day I identified the brilliant flash of jewelled peacock blue as a kingfisher swooped down and alighted on a branch. Every evening we heard the screaming of flying foxes, the *kluang*, that streamed in thousands from their roost on Gaya Island to feeding grounds inland. Mango trees, *papaya* and other crops would be plundered before they returned in a dark silent cloud at dawn, fluttering into the trees on Gaya and hanging upside down like old black umbrellas to sleep till evening.

Shortly before 'Body' Barnes left Jesselton, he came in looking very pleased with himself. There had been a lot of interest shown at that time in the immigration of about 1,500 Cocos Islanders. When groves of palm trees had been felled on one of their islands in order to build the war-time airstrip, their source of livelihood disappeared. Sir Ralph Hone conceived the idea of bringing them up to

North Borneo to ease the desperate labour shortage. They were Malays by race, they spoke the same language and should be able to integrate easily into Borneo society. Favourable conditions had been offered to them and whole families left their idyllic home in the Indian Ocean and came to work the C.D.C. *abaca* plantations at Tawau and the tobacco estates at Lahad Datu on the East Coast. The transplant didn't work at first. The Islanders pined, sickened and died in dozens. 'Body' heard that one Henry bin Kalwie was over there. He had known him when stationed in Cocos.

'The best engine man I ever had!' he told us.

He promptly put in a request to transfer the man to Jesselton and Henry duly arrived. His wife and two children had died in Lahad Datu but he brought with him two daughters, Libya and Phyllis. They joined my Guide Company and Henry proved invaluable on the Station. As well as being an experienced engine man, he was a skilled carpenter and presented Brian with a most beautiful *parang* or jungle knife in a finely-fashioned wooden sheath.

Now that I was living at the beach, Guide meetings became more adventurous. We did tracking and stalking through the trees along the beach, practised swimming and lifesaving and used knots for practical purposes like tying up boats and throwing lines. Brian helped me to test the girls in visual Morse Code, both arms extended at the side for a dash, one arm for a dot. One afternoon we were doing Scouts Pace, twenty paces walking, twenty paces running, a fairly easy method of covering a long distance quickly without undue fatigue. Libya, an ungainly girl of about fifteen years, was trailing behind the others and I chivvied her along, my eye on the watch.

'Come on, come on! The others have finished! You're supposed to do a mile in twelve minutes.'

She didn't look too bright. 'Are you all right, Libya?'

'*Sahaya sakit Kaptan. Ada demam.*'

I placed my hand on her forehead. The sweat on her skin should have been sizzling. I ran home and got the thermometer. She had a temperature of 105°F! Good God, and doing Scout's Pace!

With the beach so close, I swam daily for exercise. As my girth increased I wore a *sarong* for swimming, like my little Guides. In the daytime I wore Jerry's voluminous shorts with a smock on top. There was no source of ready-to-wear maternity clothes and my ideas of what pregnant women wore went back to my sister's clothes during the war, but they were austerity styles and little did I know what progress had been made since then. While I was wearing my home-made gathered drawstring skirts which made me look enormous, the newly-arrived vet's wife appeared in slenderising pencil-slim skirts.

'How can you wear such slim skirts?' I demanded. 'Where do you put your bulge?'

She lifted her neat jacket and showed me the hole cut out of the skirt, through which protruded her bulge. Ingenious! No more would there be the unsightly riding up of the front hem of a dress.

Now that I was becoming bulky I stopped riding Bess and with great sadness sold her to a planter down the line. What happy times I had had with her! But Brian still had his motorbike (which he had unsuccessfully tried to teach me to ride) and we were allowed to borrow the Company van occasionally. John Stagg, recently re-turned from leave, now lived in an H. & C. bungalow at the beach with George Cameron-Douglas and they picked me up each morn-ing in a Land Rover and took me into Jesselton to work. One day when John hooted, I ran out to the Land Rover and saw no Cameron-Douglas.

'I'm afraid he's met with a slight accident,' said John, embar-rassed. 'He's broken his leg.'

When George reappeared a few days later, his right leg encased in plaster from thigh to ankle, the account of what had happened spread rapidly. Apparently he and John had left a party very much the worse for drink. John climbed into the driver's seat of the Land

Rover and George stood behind the vehicle to watch him back. Somehow John had run him down and then, on George telling him in an aggrieved voice that he had reversed over him, John had driven forward over him again.

•   •   •

Shortly after moving to the beach, Brian began to have severe migraines. He would wake up in the morning, drenched in sweat, with a blinding headache and intense photophobia. The flimsy little print curtains at our windows did little to impede the bright tropical light and he would seek refuge under the bedclothes where he sweated even more. All I could do was to give him a hot water bottle to ease the pain and wait for the attack to pass.

On one of these mornings I awoke and to my dismay found a show of blood. I knew that in the early months a pregnancy is at risk and that I should go to bed or to hospital. Brian was sweating away in our bed, we had no phone, no car and the office was 300 yards away. Could I walk 300 yards safely? I didn't know how long it took to miscarry. I lay down on the small settee in the sitting room but it was too short for comfort and I was too worried about Brian to relax. I prowled around unhappily until he awoke from a deep sleep, free of pain, then told him my problem. He dressed quickly, borrowed the Company van and bumpily drove me to the hospital.

Dr Ozimek didn't mess about. 'You must come straight into hospital.'

I burst into tears. 'But I can't leave Brian. He's sick!'

'Well, he'd better come in too. I can give you adjoining rooms.'

So we were both admitted, I for treatment by injections to save the baby and Brian for observation.

Jesselton Hospital was extremely primitive, built of *kajang* and *attap* with little in the way of privacy or sound-proofing. Sister 'Pete' used to enthral us with tales of operations conducted by torchlight when the power failed and the resourcefulness of Doctors Herbert and Dickie Wyile in overcoming the lack of essential equipment.

However, a beautiful new first class ward had just been opened with large, airy rooms, glazed windows and ceilings. Brian and I were given adjacent rooms and as he was a walking case he sat by my bed in his *sarong* and kept me company. He annoyingly produced no symptoms to be observed and after twenty-four hours was sent home. I was discharged after three days and Brian promptly went down with another attack. This time Dr Ozimek came straight down to see him and prescribed some pills. I couldn't help wondering why he was continually sick in the Rabbit Hutch but not when he went to the hospital. Was he perhaps allergic to something at the beach? Dr Ozimek thought there might be something in this and suggested we go away for a holiday.

Nan and Ken had been married in London in June 1951 and were now living in Sandakan. We threw ourselves on their mercy and flew over to the East Coast to stay with them in their new home. For some reason it did the trick. Brian had no attacks there. As an added bonus, as our plane left Sandakan and headed for Jesselton, I happened to look out of the window and frantically grabbed his arm.

'It's Kina! How fantastic . . . the summit's absolutely clear!'

We were flying right alongside the magnificent mountain whose craggy granite slopes fell away into the depths below. We could actually see the sacred pool near the summit. I felt wildly happy. The baby was saved, Brian was better and we had seen the summit of Kinabalu after all.

On returning to Tanjong Aru Brian experienced no more migraines. I think we had finally got rid of the *hantu*. In fact, while we were having lunch one day, little Joe started barking at the approach of a visitor. I went to the verandah and saw an itinerant Indian fortune teller standing on the steps. (Why did Indian salesmen always come at meal times?) By nature I resist salesmen, perhaps because I was one for several years myself and recognize all the tricks. This one had the usual smooth flow of patter delivered in the high-speed manner of southern Indians which makes their speech sound like a machine-gun.

'You have very lucky visage, *memsahib* . . . very lucky. Just like Queen Victoria! This is your lucky year, *memsahib*.'

I didn't relish being likened to Queen Victoria, a resemblance which had no justification whatever, but I agreed that it was my lucky year. I had a wonderful husband and was expecting my first baby. What more could I wish?

Brian and I were eagerly looking forward to the birth of our child.

'We must buy some good children's books,' he said one evening. 'Plenty of them.'

'What were your favourites?' I asked.

'Oh . . . Lewis Carroll of course and A. A. Milne and Kenneth Grahame's *Wind in the Willows* and *The Golden Years*, and all the fairy tales . . . Grimm, Hans Andersen and Aesop's Fables . . .'

'I want *Snugglepot and Cuddlepie* . . . it's an Australian classic about the bush and all the flower babies, gumnuts and blossoms. And Norman Lindsay's *The Magic Pudding*, *Seven little Australians* and *Peter Pan* of course, and the Deerfoot series and *Hiawatha* and the Biggles books.'

'Have you ever read Don Marquis's *archie and mehitabel*? You'd love that!'

'And we must get some Arthur Ransome books later on.'

We sat down and made a list.

Then we remembered Owen Rutter's *Dragon of Kinabalu* and T. S. Eliot's *Old Possum's Book of Practical Cats*, but it wasn't till years later that we discovered the delightful collection of Borneo stories called *The Meeting Pool* written by Mervyn Skipper, himself a C. and W. man.

When we couldn't think of any more, we wrote off to Kelly and Walsh in Singapore. Tim & Ed didn't sell very many books and certainly not specialized ones such as we wanted.

Back came an answer.

'Regret we are unable to supply from stock *Old Possum's Book of Practical Cats*. The only books on Cats we can supply are: Kit Wilson's Cat Encyclopaedia, *Siamese Cats* by Phyllis Lauder, *Ordinary Cats* by Charles Duff.'

Brian collapsed, helpless with laughter.

'They thought we wanted a book on cats! Practical cats!' he hooted. 'Oh dear oh dear, and they've offered us one on ordinary cats!'

We managed to find *Old Possum* some years later and then bought a record of Robert Donat reciting several of the poems. It was a great favourite.

• • •

In April Tuaran held its annual Agricultural Show. It was a beautiful day and people had come from many miles around to watch the inauguration of the new *tamu* ground by the native chiefs. This was a ceremony rarely seen and enthusiastic photographers pressed forward to be nearer the *tamu* stone and the half-circle of chanting chiefs. I was upset to see a tethered buffalo nearby. Its purpose was obvious. As the chanting grew to a crescendo, a long spear was driven into the ground next to the stone and then the buffalo's throat was cut and its blood smeared on the stone. Many of us were feeling decidedly shaky at this stage and were relieved when the Governor officially opened the Show and judging of the exhibits took place. A holiday atmosphere prevailed and after a round of the stalls, people made for the river with picnic baskets.

Papar's *tamu besar*, the big event of the year for towns and estates along the line to Beaufort, followed closely and this year I was able to go as Sime, Darby was participating. I travelled down with John Stagg in the rail car and was delighted to alight at Papar, having always gone through it on previous trips. On each side of the line were the billiard-table smooth green fields, buffalo-cropped, alternating with squares of *padi* fields, their flooded surfaces reflecting the clouds which drifted across a brilliant sky. The *padang* was crowded with tents and stalls and a typical Borneo gathering, multinational, multilingual and colourfully dressed. Sime, Darby's stand consisted of a tarpaulin stretched over a rough structure of round poles. Inside was an assortment of the products for which the firm was agent – paint, milk powder, galvanised window frames, outboard engines and a refrigerator stocked full of beer and soft drinks to comfort us. John Stagg was most solicitous for my well-being and after lunch, as the afternoon sun blazed down on the canvas roof and raised the temperature within, he commanded me to go up the hill to the District Officer's house and lie down. This was a dubious remedy as by the time I'd climbed the hill to the bungalow I really needed a bed.

I came down to the Show around four o'clock as the shadows were lengthening and was just in time to see the Beauty Competition. Papar is known for its beautiful women and four charming Dusun girls in their native costume were drawn up for the final judgment by the Governor.

I remembered Kidman Cox's dissertation on the Dusun costume and looking at these girls began to change my mind. Certainly the flamboyant florals in conflicting colours of the Malay *sarong kebaya* now appeared garish and undisciplined. These neat black pencil-slim skirts, calf length, with their tightly-fitting black velvet jackets were elegant in the extreme. A demure high-necked white blouse showed under the V of the jacket and the starkness of the black costume was only relieved, but how splendidly, by gold piping and gold buttons and the highly prized belt of Hong Kong silver dollars. The girls' neatly-braided hair hardly showed under their conical 'lamp-shade' straw hats. Not the wide, conical coolie hat of the Chinese but small hats extending to only two inches beyond their ears. At the other extremity their brown feet were bare.

There could be no doubt about the final decision. The same exquisite girl won who had gained the prize the year before. Rumour had it that her bride price was so high that she stood little chance of marrying.

* * *

With the launching of *Aïsah*, C. and W.'s temporary Instrument Room once more operated normally. During the day the Chinese operators typed out messages as they arrived by radio and cable or punched up outgoing messages. One of the Europeans stood watch until 11 p.m. then closed the circuit down. After this the men slept unless called out by an alarm bell to attend to something urgent. The night watch could be uneventful and boring or full of drama if a cable developed a fault or the only transmitter broke down.

One night when Brian was on duty he was sorely troubled by mosquitoes. They danced in a halo around his head, dive-bombing his nose and whining away out of reach. One zoomed close to his ears and in a fury he swatted it with his hand. Instead of flattening it he only succeeded in knocking it inside his ear where it buzzed and maddened him with the noise inside his head. Hopping around and shaking were useless. He bore it as long as he could and then rushed to the Mess, woke up 'Tosh' and told him to squirt some Flit into his ear. That fixed it. It killed the mosquito but gave Brian a very sore ear. At the hospital next day Dr Herbert Wyile listened to his story with great amusement.

'You bloody fool! What did you do that for? All you had to do was fill your ear with water and the mosquito would float out!'

Brian ruefully reflected that a mosquito inside the ear isn't conducive to logical thought.

The office became operational again at 6.30 a.m. Brian used to go over before breakfast, start the engines and warm up the transmitter. He was still busy working at half past seven one day when George Pope pushed open the door and came in wearing his impassive morning face. He sat down moodily on a box, breathed heavily and stared into space. Brian went on working. After some twenty minutes George sighed deeply and got to his feet.

'By Christ, Brian, it's a long day . . .' he muttered lugubriously and marched back to the Mess for his first gin.

Maurice 'Joe' Oates had relieved Jerry White. He was a tall fair young man on his first tour of duty. Woken by the alarm bell in his bedroom at 5.30 one morning, he rolled out of bed. There was an urgent message on the line requiring immediate attention and it was his turn to deal with it. He dressed sleepily, went over to the office, opened the circuit, typed out the message and mounted his motorbike. It was raining steadily and cursing his luck he rode out into the dawn.

The telegram was for a high-ranking Government official. He knew where the house was, a couple of miles away through the rain. Peering through the curtain of water he found the place with difficulty, leaned his bike against a convenient wall and mounted the imposing flight of steps. On the top step he paused, his hand raised to knock, then stared blankly ahead of him. There was no front door. There was no house. Nothing but the flight of steps was left when workmen demolished the old house several months before. It was a very angry Joe who returned soaking wet to the Mess.

•   •   •

A tennis team from the Panaga Club of Seria was coming to Jesselton. This meant we'd be seeing Pete again as he was singles champion of the oilfield, but this time it was an official visit by the team of a neighbouring territory so Jesselton pulled out all the stops to entertain them.

The Shell plane arrived early on Saturday morning and was met by a large group of hosts. We took Pete home for a wash and change and then drove to the Sports Club for refreshment. The Seria visitors complained later that Jesselton had fielded a very competent non-playing entertainment and drinking team. They also felt that Gordon Lum, one of our players and a former Davis Cup player for China, was formidable opposition. Gordon had lived for many years in Melbourne and sported a fine Australian accent.

The visitors were carried off to a many-course Chinese *makan* by Gordon but this lunch failed to sink them and they turned up on the courts at four o'clock ready to do battle. Jesselton won three out of four matches and the teams had celebratory drinks at the Club before going home to change. There was to be an informal dance in the evening and I was determined that there would be some live music for a change. The nearest piano belonged to Mrs Lee Yun Shu whose *kampong ayer* house was almost opposite the Club. She agreed to lend us her piano if we would arrange the transport. We manhandled it along the narrow bridge from her house to the land and then across the road, along the drive and up the steps to the Club. Now it stood against the wall ready for me.

We had a wonderful evening, interspersing recorded music with Dixieland jazz. Pete was tired after the tennis but if anything can stimulate him it's music. We played till 1 a.m. when recorded music was resumed. Brian and I took Pete home to sleep but the dance went on till the very early hours, the last survivors even turning out for a swimming party at the beach.

On Sunday morning everyone arrived at the wharf at eight o'clock for a launch trip to Gaya Island where once again the Jesselton hosts tried to exhaust the visitors with lots of swimming, sun, beer and curry. They needn't have troubled. The Seria team said they had never felt better and in the afternoon won two games out of four.

When we entered the Club in the afternoon, I was aghast to find that the hot midday sun slanting through the windows had blistered the highly-polished lid of Mrs Lee's piano. What could I possibly say to her! How could we repair the damage?

Brian had the answer. A first-class master carpenter from our Hong Kong Branch was in Jesselton making furniture for the new office. Perhaps he would repolish the piano lid in his spare time. This he did, although I still had to confess to Mrs Lee and explain the delay in returning the piano.

Strangely enough, the same thing happened to our own Chappell very soon afterwards. Our piano was set against an inner wall of the Rabbit Hutch but the lowering sun found it and this time the entire fascia board was peppered with blisters. Again our carpenter came to the rescue.

When the fascia board was removed, for the first time in a year, I was dismayed to see that the green felt of the hammers was covered with clusters of eggs and green fluff. Brian lifted the lid off and began to remove the keys, laying them in order on the dining table. Each key rested on two pins, each wearing a green felt washer. Every washer was eaten or clustered with eggs. We realized that moths had been attracted by the electric lamp burning behind the footboard as a drying agent, creeping in the pedal holes to find a warm, dry place to lay their eggs. We had laboriously to brush each washer and replace it, then brush each hammer and every felt strip which underlay the strings.

As Brian replaced the keys he sighed deeply.

'Well, that settles what we do every Sunday morning in future! Piano fatigue!'

And so it was. We'd remove all the front panels, sweep up dead moths and other insects lying around the lamp and then spray all the felts with insecticide. Tropical living has its drawbacks and I think the worst is the teeming, ever-threatening insect life.

We used to have recurrent visitations of different insects. One night it would be stink bugs, those abominable pests shaped rather like a harlequin bug but a dullish green in colour. If one happened to touch or tread on them, they emitted the most atrocious smell. H_2S. Appalling! Attracted by light like moths, I have seen huge piles of them swept up under the neon strip lights outside

Jesselton's solitary cinema. Another night we would have rhinoceros beetles. These were large, black, horned, prehistoric-looking creatures which hurtled through the air only to collide with the wall or a lamp shade and drop heavily to the floor, there to lie on their backs waving their legs forlornly in the air before rolling over and taking off again. They were not actually harmful, but if you happened to be in their flight path, it could be quite painful to be forcibly struck on the temple by one of these creatures. Another night there would be flying ants – actually, swarming termites which arrived in droves and coupled stern to stern tottered around all horizontal surfaces, one dragging the other. Mating completed, they dropped their wings in neat pairs and disappeared. I was told by a distraught *mem* of the day she found that termites had eaten their way straight up from under the house, through the floorboards into the linen cupboard, up through the many folds of a pile of white sheets and out through the roof. They seemed to love anything white. When the sheets were unfolded, there were dozens of neat round holes distributed across them.

We soon formed the habit of not switching on our lights until as long as possible after sunset, sitting outside on the verandah with our evening drinks. The theory behind this was that all the insects would flock to other lighted bungalows leaving us in peace. It seemed to work, although we always had mosquitoes with us and had to burn a 'fish'. This was a coil made of some mysterious substance by the ingenious Chinese. It was balanced on a small metal stand and then lit. The glowing end gradually consumed the concentric coils over a period of about six hours and the not unpleasant smoke kept mosquitoes at bay. The most popular was called 'Fish Brand', with a picture of a voluptuous veiled goldfish, so the coil was always called a fish.

Our most exciting experience was the discovery one night of an Atlas moth on the wall of our verandah. This creature, the largest of all moths, measured nearly twelve inches across its beautifully-patterned wings. It was gone by morning.

Centipedes and scorpions were about but I never saw any. Brian, however, was sitting on the lavatory one day when he saw a large centipede about ten inches long and as thick as his thumb on the floor between his bare feet. He told me later that he had risen vertically in one bound to stand on the seat before seizing the Flit gun. Scorpions were like fresh-water crayfish (the Australian 'yabbie') but black, their menacing tails arched forwards over their bodies. I was told that in the event of being stung by a scorpion I should mash up the body and apply it as a poultice to the wound as therein lay the antidote to the poison. I never had to put this to the test.

As for larger creatures, one was always aware that there were venomous snakes about but I never saw one although they were fairly frequently encountered on C. and W. land by Brian and his workforce. One of the labourers, Abdullah, would then be summoned. He was the local snake man and would quickly approach the snake from behind, grasping it behind the head, and then despatch it. It would then be sold to the Chinese who put it in a jar of wine for medicine.

Behind the Railway house there was a path leading into the jungle. It was about five feet wide at first, narrowing further along. Looking out of the kitchen window one day I saw a large reptile emerge from the trees and cross the wide path. Its head was already in the shadow on one side and its tail was still on the other side so it must have been a monitor lizard about seven feet long.

The weirdest and most unnerving animal was surely the king crab. Brian, bent over his books studying while on night shift, heard something scraping and clanking along the wooden floor behind him. Turning around in alarm he saw what resembled a German helmet or an upturned metal bowl dragging itself awkwardly across the floor. This prehistoric creature has hardly changed in millions of years. Its horny, domed carapace precedes a frightening spiked tail about two feet long, attached by a universal joint which enables it to swivel in any direction. Fortunately its harmless nature belies its horrendous appearance.

•   •   •

Sleepy little Borneo was emerging from its cocoon and dragging itself laboriously into the modern world. A new automatic telephone exchange of four hundred lines had been installed. No longer did we wind the handles of our telephones and ask the operator for the numbers we wanted, only to fume with frustration when we were connected to a wrong number or disconnected in the middle of a conversation. However the new exchange handled only Jesselton numbers. Tanjong Aru was still without a service.

The Bryants of Menggatal Estate held a big party to warm their new house, the first post-war permanent estate house. In Jesselton a block of new shop-houses was nearing completion. H.E. had laid the foundation stone on Liberation Day 1951 and now, nine months later, they were nearly ready. Gangs of carpenters and decorators were working industriously on interiors and shop fittings. Instead of the old flimsy shops with living accommodation on one floor above, roofed with *attap* and patches of rusty corrugated iron, there now arose on one of the bombed-out blocks sturdy constructions of reinforced concrete and brick with two floors of accommodation above. Designed by Brian's Best Man Robbie, they set the standard for future shophouses. Steel-framed windows replaced the old shutters and roof tiles the *attap* covering. There was even a rumour that a sewage system might be installed.

The new Police Station was finished and occupied and repairs and renovations were carried out to the Post Office building, a gaunt, barn-like structure through which the swifts swooped, pausing momentarily at their nests up in the rafters or under the eaves before flashing down again.

Beds of vibrantly coloured cannas appeared along the central grass strip between the shady poinciana trees.

A new Government rice *godown* had been built on the waterfront. Large and noisy machines were preparing the ground on the sites for the two banks' new buildings, there was a new home for the Geology Department in the Penampang Road, a new railway station was operating at Tanjong Aru and there was persistent talk of a hotel to be built somewhere along the beach.

The dilapidated *kampong orang puteh* was being vacated at last as senior Government staff moved into the row of new asbestos houses built along the southern end of the beach. Also designed by Robbie, they were comfortable houses and miraculously dry in rainstorms but many thought the tiny windows were not suitable for the tropics. New junior staff quarters had already been built, backing on to the main Tanjong Aru road. This puzzled us until we learned that they would eventually face a new complex of access roads as yet unbuilt. For many months therefore, residents had first to cross a ten foot wide drain and then a four foot bamboo fence to get their shopping to their doors.

The most impressive piece of news was that the new Papar Bridge was finished at last and would be opened by H.E. the Governor. This bridge, the seventh of its kind, took the place of a temporary structure which had been in use since the war, and had been under construction for many many months, considerable difficulty having been encountered in clearing submerged obstructions from the river. Papar went wild with excitement when the day of the official opening arrived and H.E., after cutting the ribbon across the northern end of the bridge, mounted the footplate of the locomotive *Gaya* and drove it and its train across the new bridge, pulling up with a triumphant whistle at Papar station.

•   •   •

I was now seven and a half months pregnant and stopped working with Sime, Darby. John Stagg came round one day with the good news that the firm had given me an *ex gratia* payment of $750 for services rendered. He shuffled and looked embarrassed because he thought it was a trifling amount.

'But John, that's over £100!'

I was overjoyed and put it away to buy an engagement ring.

I had left the last six weeks free for sewing so that the time would not hang heavy on my hands. There was no source of baby clothes in Jesselton so everything had to be imported or made. I bought a book called *Mothercraft in the Tropics* which proved invaluable to me over the next twenty years. From it I got a list of items needed for the confinement and the baby's first year. Thus armed I wrote off to Singapore for Harrington's gauze napkins and cross-over vests. From the Medical Hall I bought Evenflo bottles and Wright's Coal-Tar Soap. (I slavishly followed the recommendations and bought this brand of soap and I must say when I got to hospital I enjoyed its refreshing, slightly medical scent. Whenever I smell it now, it is redolent of hospitals and childbirth.)

I bought some cream Viyella and made two carrying blankets, one edged with white ribbon and one with blue. These, together with some bootees and matinee jackets (which Mrs Gatford asked the Carmelite nuns to knit) were all that was necessary for a tropical baby. With no air conditioning one rarely had to worry about cold but bootees were essential for little feet.

Looking ahead still further, I was lamenting one day that I couldn't buy a christening robe in Jesselton. A Chinese friend, Ernest Low, who came from Hong Kong, said he'd write to his mother.

'She'd love to find one for you. She'll probably go to Swatow Lace . . . they have beautiful embroidered stuff there.'

In due course, not one but two exquisite long dresses arrived, one rather feminine with sprays of flowers and lace, the other more masculine with neat tucks and bows. I was delighted.

I had already written to Monica in England asking if she'd be the baby's godmother. Her reply surprised me.

'What do you mean by a godmother? Someone who sends him a present on his birthday each year or someone who makes sure he's brought up in the Church and is confirmed at the appropriate time? I ask because I remember that in the census Brian stated that he was a heathen.'

She had me there! I had had no formal religious upbringing and thought christening was just name-giving. I went to Mrs Gatford.

'What on earth shall I say? Brian isn't religious but I can't say I just want a present each year!'

Mrs Gatford calmly solved the problem.

'I don't think you need worry. When the child goes to boarding school he'll receive religious instruction and be confirmed. Tell Monica you want her to be a proper godmother.'

So I did.

There was a unanimous belief at the hospital that I would have a male child. Chinese divination asserts that if the baby is carried to the front forming a point, it is a boy but if the mother is broad at the sides it is a girl. I waited excitedly to see if they were right.

We had finally bought a wireless and by listening to Radio Australia we were able to catch up on international news and saturate ourselves with music. We heard for the first time Alistair Cooke's 'Letter from America' and as I sewed I delighted in hearing the splendid Scottish singer, Kenneth McKellar, singing 'Scotland the Brave', 'Green grow the rushes' and other ballads. But I was astonished to find that the popular song scene had radically changed. Bing Crosby was still around, of course, but there was a strange sort of music called bebop, or was it rebop, and there was a male vocalist, Johnny Ray, who 'cried' his songs. I quite liked him, especially his 'Walking my baby back home' but I couldn't understand bebop, much less play it. Anyway big bands were on their way out and something called skiffle was all the rage. I actually knew about skiffle as some talented Anglo-Burmans had formed a group and I played piano with them sometimes. Rudy d'Cruz played excellent rhythm guitar and provided vigorous vocals while Terry De Souza operated the 'box bass', a tea chest with a broomstick and a piece of string to twang . . . a cheap and easy way of making music. With a drummer and some other instrumentalists we made a good sound.

•　•　•

One day Cookie and Amah asked if they could go off to a relative's funeral. They left cold meat and a salad ready for lunch but half an hour before Brian was due to return I decided to whip up a batch of scones. The temperature had dropped by a degree or so, a variation which in Borneo sends one running for a cardigan, and I thought something hot should go with the cold lunch. I had never made scones in my life but I remembered how my mother would make them and have them on the table in about fifteen minutes flat. I fetched my recipe book, a *Malayan Book of Cookery*, which included English, Chinese and Indonesian recipes as well as Malayan ones. The scone recipe looked simple enough. I found the Jacob's Cream Cracker tin in which Cookie kept the flour to guard it against weevils although it still had to be sieved three times through a silk stocking. I measured out the flour, worked in the knob of butter and then added the milk. Even to my inexperienced eye the result- ant mix looked distinctly odd. Instead of being cream-coloured and dusty like dough, it was pure white, enamelled and shiny, thrust- ing creeping pseudopodia in all directions when I attempted to roll it. Too wet. I added some more flour. It crumbled into dry gravel. Too dry. I added more milk. Now before my fascinated gaze viru- lent specks of emerald green and cyclamen pink appeared in the mix. It was five minutes to one. I couldn't mess around any more, I must get something into the oven. Desperately I rolled out the dough, cut out circles with a tumbler and slapped them on a baking sheet. After fifteen minutes in the hot oven I brought them out. Each scone was about a quarter of an inch high. I took one in my hands and broke it. It split reluctantly and pulled out into long viscous threads. In frustrated fury I wrapped them in newspaper and hid them at the bottom of the rubbish bin where Cookie wouldn't find them. We had salad for lunch.

On another cool day I asked Cookie to make a steamed roly-poly jam pudding. He looked troubled and said that he couldn't make one that day as he had no banana leaves to wrap it in. Brian exploded when I told him.

'Tell him that millions of people in England eat steamed puddings and they've never seen a banana tree!'

•   •   •

A chastening experience occurred when I decided to give a farewell Chinese lunch for the Sime, Darby men. I invited Lim, Simon and Clement, Johnny and Peter. In the *kedai* I had bought some attractive rough pottery bowls about six inches in diameter and three inches deep. They looked primitive and cottagey and I told Amah to use them for the *nasi goreng* we were to eat. An hour before the guests arrived she came in to see me and tentatively proffered some assorted china rice bowls of the usual size, about three inches in diameter and two inches deep, obviously begged and borrowed from neighbouring houses. (This was a favourite ploy of servants and many a *mem* has sat down to dinner in someone else's house and found her own dinner service being used.)

'More better you use these, *mem*. Big ones for coolie. Not good.'

Unthinking in my obstinacy I insisted she use the large ones. When my guests sat down and Amah served the rice, she delivered what was obviously a lengthy apology and explanation in Chinese. My dear friends, polite as only Chinese can be, dutifully ate their meal from the large rice bowls. It is only with the benefit of hindsight and twenty years' acquaintance with the Chinese race that I can now realize the enormity of my gaffe. The Chinese have their rigid class system too. Coolies are at the bottom end of the scale and coolies eat their rice from large bowls. How my heart bleeds today for the insult I offered my friends although after Amah's explanation they no doubt excused me as an ignorant barbarian.

• • •

On the 1st of October I awoke with an unmistakable contraction. Soon after there was another. I lay in bed timing them. They were coming at five minute intervals. I was astonished. In the maternity book it stated that labour started with contractions about every hour, increasing in frequency until they were coming every five minutes. By this time one should be in hospital. I roused Brian and soon we were bumping our way into Jesselton in the Company's van. Every time a contraction came he pulled into the side of the road so I could do my special breathing and relaxing. At the hospital I was put to bed in a large airy room and I sent Brian home. Neither of us thought to ask if he could stay. Giving birth was woman's work and a father would only reappear when everything was over to share in the congratulations and general rejoicing. Besides he had a busy day ahead as the new office building was nearing completion. There was nothing he could do to help me. I knew what I had to do and was tremendously excited by the prospect. Sister Sattler promised to send for him when something was happening.

I continued to have five-minute contractions during which I did my abdominal breathing and shortly before noon I went into second stage. I knew this to be nearing the time of birth and began pushing with exuberant delight. What a fantastic evacuative feeling! I went on pushing and never stopped to think that this stage is not normally a long one. At 2 o'clock Dr Ozimek arrived and I was moved into the delivery room. I told him what had been happening, that I was feeling wonderful and . . . not to forget . . . I didn't want any anaesthetic. I also stressed to both doctor and nurse that they were *not* to tell Brian the sex of the child when it was born. It has always annoyed me that a doctor will rush out and say to the husband 'It's a boy!' Surely the news should be given to him by his wife.

When Sister told the doctor the membranes had not ruptured, he examined me and broke them. Then, to my utter astonishment, he said:

'Give her the mask!'

I looked at him reproachfully, feeling betrayed.

'I don't want any anaesthetic. There is no pain!'

'No, no, no,' he said as though humouring a small child, 'but you'd better have the mask.'

Sister Sattler produced a small mask on which she had dripped Trilene and placed it firmly over my nose. My hands clawed at her starch-smooth gown, my bare feet felt the rough prickle of blankets, I had no head and as I kicked and protested darkness descended.

I opened my eyes and saw Brian coming into the room. I was still lying on the delivery table. I felt warm and comfortable. I smiled at him and he smiled lovingly at me. We greeted each other and he asked how I was. I remembered that he wasn't to be told something.

'They haven't told you, have they?'

'No darling, they haven't told me.'

'And you still don't know?'

'No, I still don't know.'

Full realization dawned. 'My God, I don't know! Sister, what have we got?'

Sister Sattler came to us with a bundle in her arms. 'It's a lovely boy,' she said.

Together Brian and I looked at our son. A beautiful boy of eight pounds, he looked up at us, calmly, appraisingly, his steady blue gaze wondering what sort of parents he had. Is there any moment in life to compare with that when a father and mother look for the first time on their first-born?

When I was back in my room Dr Ozimek came to see me. In his blunt manner he came straight to the point.

'We had to act fast. The child might have died.'

Apparently our baby had a prolapsed cord wound around his neck. All my exhilarated pushing was only constricting the cord. I was overwhelmed with gratitude that he had saved our child but why hadn't he explained that there was an emergency? Perhaps he thought that I might have panicked but I would have gladly accepted the mask had I known there was something wrong. The sense of betrayal and frustration at not seeing our baby born stayed with me until the birth of our second child.

We called our son Phillip after my Antarctic explorer brother and John after many generations of Suart. I was kept in bed for two weeks but it was a happy time. The nurses were Chinese and Eurasian, some of them fellow Rangers and the hospital could never have been called institutional. The friendly atmosphere made it more like a very comfortable hotel.

I was woken just before six every morning when the nurse brought Phillip for his feed. It was still dark at that hour and as the nurse folded away my mosquito net the air was fresh and cool. There were windows on both sides of the room and on the eastern side I could see Kinabalu, a ragged black shape edged in gold with the rising sun behind it. Sister 'Pete' had told me that was the time to see the mountain, when it was a symphony of green, silver and gold. It was always a magical hour.

Later in the day Dr Ozimek made his rounds and on one occasion almost reduced me to tears by holding little Phil by his hands and, ignoring my protests, swinging him in the air.

'Babies are strong,' he said. 'It will do him no harm. What are you going to call him?'

'Phillip.'

'That's a dom zilly nom,' he said gutturally. (His name, I might say, was Andrew Maximilien.)

'What should I call him?'

'I don't know . . . call him anything . . . John, Jan, Jean . . . anything, but Phillip's a dom zilly nom.'

A stream of friends visited me. Mrs Gatford, in her role of proxy grandmother, reported back to Brian on my condition. ('Don't worry, they always cry on the third day!')

There were other distractions too. In the next room, separated only by a flimsy wall, was a senior officer of the Medical Department who was suffering from delirium tremens. His frequent cries of 'Boy, *stengah*!' resounded through the wide-open windows. His wife and various Government officials came and stood outside on the verandah in worried consultation. He was flown out soon afterwards.

Of closer concern to us was Joe Fong, a C. and W. operator, who was brought into hospital suffering from a perforated gastric ulcer. His condition deteriorated and the surgeon, Dr Mehta, called for a blood transfusion. Joe's Chinese relatives were loath to oblige so Brian volunteered. His blood matched Joe's and a direct transfusion was made. It is the only time in his life that Brian has fainted and his donation was to no avail. Joe died next day.

•   •   •

To circumcise or not to circumcise, that was the question. My mother advised it. The mothercraft book emphasized how meticulous care should be taken to ensure cleanliness in the tropics. I sought advice from another young mother.

'It saves a lot of trouble if he's circumcised, but if you do decide on it, get Dr MacLaren to do it! I took my son to Dr Ozimek and when we went back to the hospital a week later to have the dressing removed, I was aghast! "What has he done to my son!" I yelled at the nurse. Instead of cutting the foreskin around neatly, the doctor had merely made a small slit and turned the corners back like a dog-eared book. I reckon he probably disapproved of circumcision . . . maybe something anti-Semitic in his Polish upbringing. Anyway I went rushing off to Dr MacLaren and she was very sympathetic. "You want it done the usual way, right?" So my son is probably the only baby to have been circumcised twice!'

•   •   •

At the time I was expecting to leave hospital the Duchess of Kent was due to arrive on an official visit to North Borneo accompanied by her sixteen-year-old son, the young Duke. I had been fascinated by Princess Marina ever since her marriage to the Duke of Kent. He was supposed to have come to Australia as Governor-General and our exercise books at school bore their portraits for many months. They never came. His tragic death during the war made us sympathize with the elegant, solitary Duchess and I was eager to see her. There was to be a great gathering at the pier to welcome her, with all the Guides, Scouts and other youth groups on parade. I naturally expected to lead my Guide Company but Mrs Gatford with great cunning (which I saw through) asked me to lend my Officer's hat to Nancy who was leading the Sandakan Guides. So I did not stand for hours in the blazing sun on the day of the Royal party's arrival. Instead I listened to Chuck Fenton's colourful reporting of the scene on newly-established Radio Sabah, even though I was a bit worried lest he should forget he wasn't at the Racecourse and lapse into a 'coming up the straight' commentary.

I insisted on going to the Garden Party on the *padang* although the usual perplexity over what to wear was complicated by my enlarged waist measurement. What could I possibly wear?

There was a lot of amusement in the town over a cutting from the London *Sunday Empire News* which was being passed around. Concerning the visit of the Duchess of Kent it said:

> In Jesselton, the capital of British North Borneo, they are also preparing for the Royal visit. The dress shops are filling up with Paris-style evening gowns imported by enterprising merchants with an eye to making money from the 'big

day'. They hope to reap a golden harvest from the women who come down from lonely jungle outposts. For many a woman will sit under the palm shelter in a canoe fitted with an outboard motor while her husband ferries her into town to buy her beautiful gown.

What a laugh! I promptly sat down and wrote my 'Thought for the week'.

GETTING A GOWN

'I say, a soignée evening gown, *ada*? . . .
Something suggestive of Dior?
No? Then maybe a dream of a frock
To cause a simply tremendous furore
As over the *padang* the multitudes flock?'

'Sorry , better try Kim Seng Hock.'

'Oh Kim Seng Hock, I wish to ask . . .
I believe from the papers that you are stocking
Rack upon rack of exclusive frocking,
And that by the last boat you brought in
Taffeta, velvet and georgettes thin.
What? Not here? Who? Bang on Hing?'

'This looks like it . . . say, listen *towkay* . . .
I've brought my wife in a *perahu* from Talang
To buy her a chic little cocktail hat.
She also needs stockings and long kid gloves
And a handbag fashioned of water rat.'

'*Tid'ada tuan*, but Ah Soong Fatt . . .'

'Well, here we are – what a glorious day . . .
Why Minnie dear, I adore your frock!

Where *did* you find it? I walked every block.
Such fabric! Such fit! So chic, so nifty!
It's not like you who are always so thrifty . . .'

'I whipped it up, Bet, for seven-fifty!'

I finally decided on a dress from my trousseau, a butter-yellow satin-striped dress of ample waist, its black patent belt notched on the last hole. Long black gloves and a black Dutch hat borrowed from Lu Plunkett completed the ensemble.

The *padang* was thronged with more-smartly dressed women and men looking ill-at-ease in unaccustomed jackets and ties. Flamboyant Malay *sarongs*, colourful Indian saris, Chinese *cheong saam* and Filipino butterfly-sleeved dresses were visible here and there. There was a great patchwork of colour on the sloping Club lawns which provided the usual public grandstand, and the schoolchildren were massed around three sides of the *padang*.

There was a stir of excitement and craning of necks as the Royal Standard was glimpsed fluttering on the beautiful black car (our Director of Public Work's Armstrong-Siddeley) preceded by its Police motorcycle escort. There was a murmur from the women as they glimpsed the Duchess in her crisp white organdie dress and small fitting hat of burnt-pink feathers. The Governor escorted her to the saluting base while the police, resplendent in their splendid ceremonial uniforms (white with pompons on their red pillbox hats) marched past to the impeccable music of Ted Cox's police band.

Then the Duchess began to receive the guests. The Native Chiefs, elaborately dressed and dignified as usual, were greeted with the respect due to them and then we lesser mortals filed past. Afternoon tea was served at flower-decked tables and, wonder of wonders, in fine china cups instead of the usual coffee-shop thick, chipped ones.

Then came the entertainment: dances from the Convent girls, gymnastics from the All Saints boys, agile dancing and tumbling by

children from the Chinese schools and a charming retinue of tradi-
tionally-clad Malay girls and boys from the Vernacular School.
Next we had native dances by modestly dressed Dusuns and scant-
ily clad Muruts, their dark red *chawat* or loin cloths passing between their legs and dividing their buttocks before hanging down
in a cascade of cloth at the back. As the last gong sounded and the
last drum beat faded, the Duchess and the Governor drove around
the *padang* in the open car as dusk was falling.

As we all repaired to the Club comments flew thick and fast.

'She's got green eyes . . .'

'No, they're not, they're amber!'

'Doesn't she look GREEK!'

'Hong Kong cakes weren't they?'

'I'm as dry as a bone. Boy, *stengah*!'

'Must say the Club looks nice . . .'

'Why weren't the bachelors asked?'

'Don't you think we made a good job of the Armstrong-
Siddeley?'

'I do like the Police Officers' new uniforms . . .'

'Well, thank God that's over!'

Chapter 13

Selamat Tinggal

While I was settling little Phil into a routine back in the Rabbit Hutch, Brian was working twelve hours a day putting the finishing touches to the new office. The Governor was coming to open it officially at the beginning of November and our big white chief, the Divisional Manager of the Far East, was coming down from Hong Kong to host the celebrations. Mr Tyson, our splendid Manager and worthy heir to 'Body' Barnes, was kept busy in the Jesselton office while Brian, Tosh, Joe and a newly-arrived bachelor called Terry Cashmore were under engines and inside transmitters at Tanjong Aru. All this had to be done whilst maintaining a normal service in the temporary instrument room where we'd built *Aïsah*.

The architect of the new Cable and Wireless complex was a Swiss called Minutti. An elderly man, he had retired to live in Jesselton but did a little work on the side. Whenever he visited the site to inspect the building work he would come and have a drink with us. Sitting on our tiny verandah he chain-smoked incessantly and one morning after one of these visits, I picked up thirty-seven butts below the verandah rail, each one two inches long. (Brian, too, was a heavy smoker though he never actually lit a new cigarette from an old one. Dr Terry Abbott, who had recently sworn off smoking, said the medical evidence of a connection with lung cancer was too convincing to ignore. He wasn't able to convert Brian to his viewpoint.)

Mr Minutti had also been responsible for designing the eight-story Mercury House in Hong Kong for Cable and Wireless and told us ruefully about the problems he had encountered. Our Divisional Manager, a notorious ladies' man, had a penthouse on top of Mercury House.

'That penthouse,' said Minutti mournfully, 'gave me more trouble than all the other floors put together. One week it would be Tudor beams and inglenooks. The next week . . . a new girl friend . . . and pffft! All chromium and glass!'

The redoubtable Divisional Manager arrived at the end of October and, not content with having a wonderful new office which far outshone anything in North Borneo, determined in the few days remaining before the official opening to turn the 72-acre estate into Kew Gardens. Brian muttered some pithy comments on the subjects of D.M.s, especially after he'd been supervising the burning of some dense clumps of *lallang* and a terrified bitch ran out of the thicket leaving her litter of pups to die in the flames. He had to remove the charred remains of the little creatures and was greatly distressed.

It was also decreed that, as neither the D.M. nor Mr Tyson had a wife on the station, I was to be hostess for the reception following the ceremony and would therefore entertain the guests in the new Engineer's house. So while Brian was supervising Duraman and his gang in Allen-scything the rough *lallang* grass and erecting a new flagpole in the square enclosed by the three arms of the building, I had to move house yet again. Our new house was only five hundred yards from the Rabbit Hutch so most of the move was done on foot. But a move is a move. The new house had to be cleaned of builder's dust and grit, furniture taken out of storage and disposed in the much larger house, drawers had to be lined before receiving their cargo of clothes, curtains had to be made and hung, and of course the baby had to be fed every four hours.

Our splendid new house was better than anything else in Jesselton and I was full of pride for the Company. Cable and Wireless, with almost one hundred years' experience of foreign service, had shown Jesselton what staff quarters should be like. Basically one room wide, the house ran right along the shore of a small inlet of the sea. Although the water right around the coast of Borneo is generally shallow (the embryonic Yacht Club had to moor its yachts in Jesselton by the main jetty), we were able to keep *Aïsah* moored right in front of the house in a convenient pool. A thirty yard belt of foreshore separated our verandah from the lapping sea.

We now had three bedrooms, two bathrooms and one large living room entered through the front door on the landward side and leading onto a wide verandah on the seaward side. Alongside the living room was a good dining room and off it a pantry and the kitchen, from which steps led down to the servants' quarters. Unfortunately the floors were only of concrete but the Company had promised to lay chipboard tiles in the sitting room.

Access to the house was by way of a circular drive around a large lawn. There were as yet no flowers or trees on that side but the outlook towards the office was very pleasing with what would soon be lawns separating the house from the large office block, the Mandor's house and the coolie lines. In the distance were the Rabbit Hutch and the temporary Mess. John Tyson, as keen a golfer as he was a yachtsman, had a pet scheme to turn all the land under the aerials into a golf course. From the front verandah we could see the imposing shape of Kinabalu behind a group of coconut palms. About a hundred yards along the shore from us was the almost-complete permanent Mess. Later, a Manager's house would be built along from the Mess and then the station would be complete. Perhaps the man who had bought the site after an inspection from the air hadn't made such a mistake after all. It was really rather lovely.

At last the great day arrived. Brian went to the office early to raise the Company flag on the new pole and to check on the cleanliness of the lavatories and the efficient functioning of the office equipment. The roads and paths were all swept. Through half-closed eyes one could imagine the grass was lawn.

Amah had cleaned our house till it shone and had done several flower arrangements of the ubiquitous periwinkle. Cookie was in charge of the *kechil makan* and the champagne.

My worry was fitting little Phil into the arrangements. The Governor and Lady Hone were to arrive at eleven o'clock. The Opening Ceremony would take place soon afterwards. The Governor would send a congratulatory message to our Head Office in London and would receive a reply within minutes. The visitors would be shown around the office, the Instrument Room and the engine room before coming to our house at noon for refreshments.

I had briefed Amah the day before.

'Many people come house, I very busy, Amah. You must look-see baby! I don't want to be bothered by baby. If he cries, take him outside in pram. Go walk, do anything, just don't bother me for one hour!'

It was ten o'clock. I went to feed little Phil but he was fast asleep. Good! The later he was fed, the better. I showered and dressed as far as my slip. Still he slept. I did my face and my hair. He was still sleeping but it was half past ten and I could delay no longer. I woke him and began to feed him. He sucked away for a few minutes then the nipple fell from his mouth and he drowsed off. I jogged him up and down and tried again. He wasn't interested.

'You'll have to leave him and come!' said Brian, his eye on the clock.

I tried a little longer but at a quarter to eleven I had to give it up as a bad job and pull on my dress.

'Philly no eat, Amah. I give milk when I come back. If he cry, don't forget, take outside!'

I raced over to the office and stood with the D.M., Mr Tyson and Brian, ready to receive the Governor. The sleek black car with its crown arrived, Sir Ralph and Lady Hone got out and climbed the steps. Mr Tyson introduced them to the D.M. and then to us. Little Phyllis, in a new print frock, her hair braided around her head,

came forward and presented a bouquet to Lady Hone. The ceremony began.

While all the visitors were inspecting the new building, I ran to
the house to be ready to receive guests. I expected to hear the angry
wail of a famished child. All was still. I hurried to the nursery and
there was Philly lying on his back in his Moses basket, fast asleep. I
called to Amah.

'Baby OK, Amah?'

'*Baik mem.* No trouble.'

I marvelled and ran to comb my hair and wash my hands. Out of
the window I saw Lady Hone approaching with the D.M. Sir Ralph
and Mr Tyson were following and all the other guests behind them.
I just made it to the front door in time.

Throughout the reception peace reigned. Cookie and Amah dis-
pensed the champagne and *makan kechil* and a loud babble of conversation came from the room full of people. In a corner, Chuck
Fenton was crouched over our radio straining to hear a Radio
Australia broadcast of the Melbourne Cup. He emerged beaming
with delight, having backed the winner.

I kept an ear cocked for sounds from Philly but all was quiet. I
simply couldn't understand it. He hadn't been fed since seven
o'clock in the morning. Normally he would be yelling vociferously.

The photographer came to take photographs of the party. I took
him to the nursery and had several pictures taken of little Phil.
Friends asked to see the new baby and duly admired him. Eventually the guests departed, Brian took off his jacket and tie and it was
after two o'clock when I lifted Philly for his next feed.

'How lucky that he behaved himself today of all days!' I said to
Brian.

I related this episode to a friend some months afterwards. I
showed her the photos of the baby drooping in my arms. He looked
like a wax doll, his face showing an extreme pallor, his closed eyes
underlined with shadows and his arms and legs hanging like those
of a rag doll.

'Opium!' my friend said succinctly.

'Opium?' I shrilled.

'Opium! It's a favourite trick of the amahs. Keeps the kids quiet. They put a tiny bit under the finger nail and the baby sucks it. Wham! Bye byes!'

I was horror-stricken and surprised that something of that sort hadn't occurred to me. However, I'd given Amah *carte blanche* . . . 'Do anything, but keep him quiet!'

Philly was a difficult baby. Not a night went by without our walking the hard concrete floors for hours. I took the first shift, hoping to get him off to sleep without having to wake Brian, but when I was ready to drop with fatigue I'd call him to take over. He had a line of nonsense songs which he sang to Philly's delight and in due course the little eyelids fluttered up and down like roller blinds before clamping shut. There would be the agonizing suspense as we tried to lay him in his basket without waking him and then we'd collapse on our beds exhausted. We thought he was colicky and got through bottles of gripe water but looking back, I realize that he was probably perpetually hungry. Once a fortnight I took him to the hospital, gave him a test feed, chatted to the nurses and went home. The scales revealed that he was taking only two to three ounces of milk but no one ever suggested I supplement him with bottled milk. He was forever falling asleep at his feed and we all assumed he was getting enough. An hour later he'd be bellowing. Sister 'Pete' would have diagnosed the trouble but she was on leave. It was only when Mrs Gatford suggested giving the four-month-old child a little cereal that our life improved. Amah could have told me months earlier had communication been better.

'*Mem*,' she said one day as she watched me doggedly feeding Phil, '*Mem, punia susu tiada bagus!*' (Mem's milk is no good.)

She lifted her tunic, withdrew one heavy breast and squeezed the nipple. A jet of milk described a snowy trajectory across the room.

I sat mournfully, drooping over my baby. I squeezed my nipple. Nothing came out.

'*Tiada bagus!*' she said again and left the room.

I dissolved into tears and resolved to wean the baby.

Life at the beach was idyllic. I played with Philly in the shallow inlet in front of our house while little Joe dug for crabs in the sand. Brian came home for lunch. Rumours of the occasional robbery or crime of violence came but faintly to our notice. Jesselton was still laughing about the prisoner who, whilst engaged on grass-cutting fatigue in Atkie's garden, had entered the house and helped himself to the Commandant's drinks cupboard. But one Sunday morning, as we sat on our verandah having breakfast, we were discussing the latest police man-hunt.

Eight o'clock in the morning was a delicious hour. The air was still cool but with the silent overtone of heat to come. Not a breath moved the palm trees along the beach nor the patch of jungle on the point. The sea was dead calm with that heavy oiliness of the tropics. Patches of brilliant turquoise joined with ultramarine blue far out to sea where the emerald shapes of Sapi and Gaya lay. In our pool the water was the palest duck-egg blue and *Aïsah* rode peacefully at anchor.

I sighed contentedly as I squeezed lime juice over my *papaya*. Life was wonderful.

Suddenly a loud whistle shrilled and the whole landscape moved. Dozens of little *mata-mata* jumped out of trees, from behind bushes, emerged from the long grass, slid down coconut palms. They had apparently been lying in ambush but a new trail had been discovered and they dashed away clamouring excitedly. We stared in absolute astonishment. Then peace descended again and it was as though nothing had happened.

•   •   •

One of Mr Tyson's yachting friends was an eminent though eccentric judge. Stories about him were legion. He was nicknamed 'Harpic' as it was reckoned he was 'clean round the bend'. Sailing over to Gaya one lovely evening, we saw that the water was thick with large pink jellyfish. Following a discussion as to whether they were harmful or not, Harpic spent the whole voyage scooping them up with his bare hands and throwing them in the air whilst joyously whooping: 'See? They don't hurt! They don't hurt!'

Nan and her sister Nell were walking along the main street in Jesselton one day when Harpic approached.

'Good morning ladies! How charming you look! Fresh and lovely and so beautifully attired! You look as though you were dressed for Henley-on-Thames!'

They exchanged pleasantries for some time and then, turning to go, Harpic said:

'By the way ladies, when I met you . . . was I coming from this direction, or from that?'

'Why, you were coming from there,' said Nell, pointing.

'Oh, then in that case I've had lunch!' said Harpic and hurried on.

John Tyson often went walking with him. On one occasion they were passing some Chinese houses when two pi-dogs rushed out at them, snarling and barking. Harpic stood his ground.

'There's only one way to deal with these dogs,' he said and, dropping on his hands and knees, barked back. The dogs slunk away.

The story I love best was told to me by Betty Macpherson. Apparently caught short in a busy courtroom one day, Harpic reckoned he had just time enough between cases to dash outside to the public lavatory. The old courthouse was situated by the Customs wharf. He nipped smartly out of the back door and along the rickety wooden bridge to the *jambans* situated at the end, over the sea. Unfortunately he pushed open the door of the women's *jamban*, only to be confronted by an outraged Chinese market woman who pursued him back along the bridge, his scarlet robe flapping, his wig askew, belabouring him with her umbrella, vegetables and fish spilling from her baskets as she ran.

Everyone has a stock of lovely stories to tell about life in Borneo in those days. I think it was the combination of primitive living conditions and bizarre happenings which provided the best ingredients. 'It could only happen in Borneo' was our favourite saying.

Take Monsieur Bultot, a Belgian who had started a small but thriving business making concrete bricks. At Government House one evening, the acting Governor's wife who was hard of hearing and always used an ear trumpet, had asked who he was.

'I'm Bultot, ze man 'oo makes ze bricks,' he replied.

Thereafter he was always called 'ze man 'oo makes ze bricks'. He asked Brian to come and look at his machinery one day. Instead of making one brick of a certain size every two seconds, it had gone berserk and was shooting out tiny bricks, four a second. While Brian was adjusting it, Bultot told him about a recent domestic uproar.

Madame, it appeared, was in the garden dressed in the minimum of clothing when she screamed to her husband that a *wah-wah*, a gibbon, was in one of the trees. Monsieur, in the house, snatched up his rifle and discharged it at the *wah-wah* through the window, failing to notice that the window was shut. The glass shattered and the gibbon swung its way up to hide under the eaves of the house. Madame, finding it all too much for her, ran inside and collapsed on a *chaise longue*. Monsieur called for reinforcements in the shape of the *tukang kebun* (gardener), who advanced on the unfortunate *wah-wah* with a *rembas*. The animal left the shelter of the eaves and scrambled up the *attap* of the roof. Monsieur yelled for the *tukang kebun* to give chase. Up the roof he clambered only to crash through the yielding *attap* and fall into the lap of the wilting Madame in the room below. I suspect the *wah-wah* was laughing in a tree.

•   •   •

Brian had just taken Cable and Wireless's General Examination, the major hurdle which its engineers must pass if they are to gain further promotion. Our Manager, John Tyson, had been a tremendous help, taking Brian into the office whenever possible to go over the accounts and Company Law. We heard later from Brian's friend, John Rippengal, who had had the reverse experience on his African station, where the Manager was absolutely obstructive and seemed to resent the fact that young men were coming up the ladder behind him.

John Tyson, like 'Body' Barnes and other T.C.s (telegraph clerks) of his generation, had been trained by the Company to take down incoming telegrams at the rate of 25 words a minute in a small, neat and very legible hand. You can always pick an old T.C. by his handwriting. 'Able and tireless' was a common variant of Cable and Wireless, to which detractors might be heard to mutter 'Garble and careless!'

In the examination there were the usual questions about running a Company Branch, a cash statement to be balanced and then a final broader-based question: 'Demonstrate why the organization of sport on a Branch is to be desired.' Brian, never a yes-man, started by writing 'All sport is anathema to me' and then warmed to his theme. It must be remembered that sport was considered so important at that time that foreign service men, both in the Colonial Service and Cable and Wireless, were often given a particular posting if a good spin bowler or a half-back were needed there to complete a team. Brian left the examiners in no doubt as to his contempt for such matters of policy.

As a break from his long period of study, we decided to go to Keningau in the interior for a few days. Once more we clattered down the line in the 'matchbox' through Papar to Beaufort but then we continued through new territory to Tenom. It was an exciting journey along the river Padas with the jungle pressing around us. We eagerly craned our necks to look for crocodiles basking on the banks in the baking sun but saw none. The railcar bumped along beside the river in the Tenom gorge through a wilderness of rock and thick undergrowth with great creepers and vines looping from the trees. The scenery was grand in the true sense of the word, the tumultuous river on our right foaming over giant boulders or running smoothly and swiftly through deeper channels.

The tremendous potential of the Padas was recognized by British capital after the war. Extensive prospecting and surveying established the fact that a dam could be built across the Padas and a huge hydro-electric scheme could be developed there. There was talk of great mineral deposits which could be exploited. At the last minute the scheme was rejected, mainly because of the chronic labour shortage in North Borneo. The decision came just too late for the printing of a new stamp featuring a map of North Borneo with Tenom marked prominently on it. Philatelists may well wonder now why little Tenom was so honoured. (They may also wonder why the 50-cent stamp in the same definitive issue bore a spelling mistake. Within minutes of the Post Office releasing the new pictorial series, the word swept through town that the 50-cent stamp depicting the clock tower was labelled 'Clock Tower Jess*le*ton'. There was a rush to buy it in case it should become a rarity. By lunchtime the stamps were withdrawn but hundreds had already been bought, too many for the stamp ever to become valuable so it was eventually released for sale again.)

On reaching the railhead at Melalap we learned that the Land Rover which was to take us on to Keningau would not arrive for a couple of hours so a young planter who had been travelling with us invited us to his home to shelter from the fierce sun. We were welcomed by his Malay mistress and their infant son. She was intrigued by little Phil's fair colouring. European babies don't spend much time in the sun, so he was very pale with a fine covering of golden down on his head. Whenever I took him to any public place we would be surrounded by Chinese or Dusun women touching him.

'*Halus!*' (Fine!) they would say in wonder as they stroked his hair.

The planter's son was a bonny, dusky child with a vigorous thatch of dark hair. I wondered if the grandparents in England knew about him. In the early 1950s the moral climate was still disapproving of liaisons with native women. (In fact, in 1949 someone in the Colonial Office realized that the famous Marquis of Crewe circular, *circa* 1909, had never been sent to either North Borneo or Sarawak as these territories only became Colonies in 1946. This was remedied and European men of the Colonial Service in Borneo were duly advised that there was great concern that some officers had been indulging in concubinage with native women thus bringing the Service into disrepute. This behaviour must stop. If further cases came to light, disciplinary action would be taken. The only obvious result of the circular was great amusement amongst the young cadets.)

Planters, however, were not Colonial Servants. The life of a bachelor planter is unutterably lonely and a three or four year tour seems endless. Little wonder then that these liaisons were formed. 'Sleeping dictionaries' was the popular term for concubines as association with a native woman gave a man a fluent grasp of the language as well as providing him with creature comforts. On some estates before the war a woman was allocated to a newly arrived planter, whether he wanted her or not. Sometimes the man married his mistress but the wife was never accepted by the Europeans. More often the bachelor would get married on home leave and many a new bride found, on arrival in Borneo, that she had a ready-made family in the local convent.

One very experienced District Officer was being considered for a particular post of importance but it was discovered that he had a couple of children in the convent. His superiors searched for another District for him but alas, it was found he had progeny in every town.

Cable and Wireless never let things go so far. Should a bachelor develop what was considered to be an undesirable liaison with a native girl, he was whipped out straight away and transferred to another Branch, usually Cocos or some such isolated outpost where he could reflect at length on his transgression. Even at Cocos there were temptations. I remember the day Brian unexpectedly came into my office and asked if we had a second Bentley Code book. I produced it for him and he took a piece of paper from his pocket. It was a coded cable from a friend in Cocos. After turning the pages and making notes for a few minutes he started laughing.

'What is it?' I asked.

He read the translation. 'Please forward quantity rubber goods soonest.'

Still chuckling, he went along the street to the Dispensary and bought six dozen condoms. Thereafter the Chinese salesman treated him with great respect.

The saddest story I know concerned a young man working for a large commercial firm. He was deeply in love with a local girl of good family who felt the same about him. His firm would not allow him to marry her. She became pregnant and was spirited away in good time to Singapore where she eventually gave birth to a son who was immediately adopted. In the meantime the young man left his employer and joined another company which was more tolerant. He married his sweetheart on her return to Borneo and they eventually had several children. I wonder if they ever managed to forget their son, the brother of their children, lost in the millions of Singapore.

•   •   •

Keningau is situated on a wide plain surrounded by distant mountains, the highest being 8,000 foot Trus Madi. On the extensive stretches of grassland cattle were being grazed in a rather disorganized way. It seemed to me that the general standard of animal husbandry was low, the normal practice being for livestock to be left to fend for itself. Cattle often congregated in almost wild herds, wandering freely until the owners drove them back to overgrazed pastures rather than lose them. Ownership seemed to vary from one working beast per family to many hundreds, but sometimes herds appeared to be the common property of a village. With this haphazard method of raising cattle, it was small wonder that the quality of animals brought in for slaughter was poor. The meat was all consumed locally, the only export being hides, and there was no production of butter or milk. David Fiennes had hoped to interest C.D.C. in the idea of a well-run cattle farm but it never got off the ground.

The natives in this area were mainly Dusun and Murut, the latter being the most primitive of North Borneo natives. Not unlike the Dyaks they wore their hair long or knotted on the nape of the neck and were naked except for a *chawat* or loin cloth.

I had seen Muruts only twice before, at the Duchess of Kent's reception and at the farewell in Jesselton to John and Mary Walne of the Police Force. The latter occasion was an evening affair and the final stunning item was the arrival of the Muruts bearing flaming torches. The light from a central bonfire flickered red on their brown skins and the *chawat* which divided their buttocks hung down almost to the ground behind. Their firm muscled bodies leaping and dancing around the fire evoked a vision of primitive savagery that I have never forgotten.

The Muruts, or 'men of the hills' as the Bajaus call them, were for generations hunters, scouring the jungles with their hunting dogs, *parang* by their side, blowpipe in hand, in search of deer, python, wild buffalo, boar or anything edible. The male married only after he had taken at least one human head in battle. As they were always warring among each other, this prerequisite was not difficult to obtain. When warriors returned victorious with their spoils, the longhouses resounded with feasting and dancing all night. Like the Dyak they were proficient in the use of the blowpipe and during the war were encouraged by Allied guerillas to resume their old head-hunting habits. As the Japanese plodded through the jungles, the silent blowpipe stung their backs with sharp poisoned darts. Borneo became highly unpopular with Japanese soldiers and the smoke-blackened skulls in the rafters of the longhouses were not all so old.

When not warring, the tribes cultivated hill *padi* and tapioca on the slopes of the mountains in clearings made by an annual slash and burn, but as they believed the earth spirit set a time limit on these ravages, they shifted to a new site every seven years. This 'shifting' cultivation was the despair of agricultural officers in the '50s as it was very wasteful of land. Trees were felled to enable planting to take place and when the tribes moved on secondary growth sprang up. It might take hundreds of years for primary forests to redevelop.

With the coming of the *orang puteh* to the interior, life for the Muruts changed overnight. Ancient customs were abandoned, the cohesion of tribal life broke apart as men were tempted by the attractions of money, European clothes and consumer goods to go and work on rubber plantations around Beaufort and Tenom or on the railway line penetrating their territory. A census in 1951 showed that the Murut population was continuing a downward trend and in 1953 when we were in Keningau, a doctor from Malaya, experienced in social medicine among aborigines, came to investigate the dying race. The trouble seemed to be that women were simply not having babies. They conceived but rarely came to term or produced a living child. Many women died in childbirth.

Sister Peters had been posted to Keningau to relieve the legendary Sister Hilda Bates. I asked her why the infant mortality among the Muruts was so high. She was convinced that malnutrition and malaria were the main contributing causes although a recent World Health visitor had said that malaria was not a problem. 'Pete' said that the ailment of practically every patient in the hospital was complicated by malaria and it was certainly responsible for miscarriages and premature births.

'So what can be done to improve things?'

'We've got to treat the malaria, improve their nutrition and the standard of midwifery in the *kampongs*,' she said.

She told us how Sister Bates, who had been a Health Visitor at Keningau for years, had started by holding baby clinics, offering prizes for the best-kept baby and the best-kept house in a *kampong*. 'Pete' herself had continued the work, often in very difficult conditions. The only transport she had was a Land Rover which was none too comfortable an ambulance when midwifery patients had to be brought to hospital. When the rough tracks ended, she sometimes had to continue her journey on the back of a buffalo, her Staff Nurse sitting in front of her and her own legs sticking straight out sideways over the *kerbau*'s broad rump.

A child-health clinic was held at the hospital each week and every twelve days 'Pete' went to the *tamu* in neighbouring villages. There the head man would erect a booth and she would hold a baby clinic with a male dresser and a Dusun Staff Nurse. Eventually she was able to overcome the women's distrust and was able to start ante-natal clinics at the hospital. The next step was to ask the head men of the villages for young girls to come to the hospital to be trained in the elements of midwifery. She had to promise that the girls would be chaperoned and protected at all times.

This scheme was most successful. Part of the training programme required each girl to be given a small plot of land at the hospital where she could grow assorted vegetables and fruits. When native mothers brought their children to hospital, they were shown the gardens and told how they could easily cultivate such things as *papaya* (very rich in Vitamin C) and green vegetables to give their children. Low-protein diets were improved with grated coconut and soon a marked change was noticeable in the well-being of the children.

Keningau had no doctor. The nearest one was at Beaufort, hours away by Land Rover and train. 'Pete' couldn't even rely on contacting him by telephone as the line, looped from tree to tree, was often pulled down by *orang utan*. She told me of one maternity patient she had brought in to hospital from an outlying *kampong*. The woman had tuberculosis and 'Pete' was worried about her impending confinement. She went into labour soon afterwards and the foetus *in utero* was extruded. 'Pete' dealt with this emergency by raising the woman's feet high and getting her nurse to exert counter traction on the uterus. The baby was safely born and then the uterus had to be returned to the woman's abdomen.

It couldn't have been easy delivering babies by torchlight in dirty *kampongs* nor trying to teach unlettered native girls to be midwives, but 'Pete' was of that wonderful breed of English-trained midwives who can cope in any eventuality.

There were lighter moments like the time she heard a hissing noise coming from the pit beneath the lavatory seat. It was a cobra lurking in the depths.

'Don't worry *misi!*' said one of the village boys, who proceeded to lasso it. Unfortunately he captured it by the tail and not the head

and went racing off with the cobra trying to double back on itself to get at him.

On another occasion, while under the mosquito net in her Rest House bed, she was woken by a grating noise under her head and discovered mice were eating the kapok seeds in her pillow! The Rest House manager was given an ultimatum that if Keningau were to have a Health Visitor, then he must get new pillows and a cat.

We too stayed at Keningau Rest House and while we were there John Tyson phoned through to tell Brian he had passed his General exam with distinction. We were jubilant. Now he was fully quali-fied and eligible for more senior postings.

•   •   •

Back in Jesselton our thoughts were turning towards leave in July. We were planning to go to Australia first, where my parents were waiting to meet my husband and their grandchild, and then on to England where I should meet the Suarts. The prospect was very exciting.

At the end of our six months leave we would be posted to one of the Company's many stations scattered across the world. Penang perhaps, or Rio? Singapore or St. Helena? Or perhaps one of the less welcome spots like Port Sudan, Bahrain or Accra?

'You're fluent in Malay,' I said to Brian, 'Perhaps they'll send us back to South-East Asia?'

'All the more reason to send us to South America,' he said drily. 'They don't worry about little things like languages. Some Com-pany men have several languages.'

Not knowing where we would be sent made the future even more tantalising.

And then disaster struck. Cookie brought the marketing book to me as he did every day after returning from the shops. I would check his accounts and pay him for what he had spent. This time however there was a slip of paper in the back of the book. I looked at it idly and then realized that it was his own account of that morning's shopping. The amounts shown on his list were different from those in the book. They were less. I had caught him doing a fiddle! I said nothing but handed the book back to him with the money. However, the damage was done. He knew that I knew. His loss of face was so great that a little later he came and gave me notice. I was appalled! The maker of the best curry in Jesselton would no longer please our guests with his magnificent dishes. Worst of all, our priceless treasure who packed for everyone else would not be here to pack for us. It was a daunting prospect.

With only two months to go until our departure, where could I find a replacement? Good servants were hard to find at any time but who would come to work for us for only eight weeks? Just as contractors were chartering Dakotas to bring down unskilled pick and shovel coolies from Hong Kong for their building projects, some people had started importing servants and the experiment was watched with interest by many residents wondering how to break the deadlock of the labour shortage. When the first cooks, houseboys and *amahs* arrived, immaculate in their starched white jackets and wide-legged black trousers, their employers and others gasped at their faultless service and attention to detail. The practice looked like catching on but there was no point in our spending so much money to import servants for such a short time.

There was no use pleading. When there is loss of face, the sufferer departs.

On their last day Amah came to me with various bottles and packets. Here was the soap powder, she said, and here was the blue. And here, giving me a Jacob's Cream Cracker tin, was the starch.

'Starch!' I was aghast. 'Surely that's flour?'

'No *mem*, this starch. Flour in other tin.' She showed me the second Jacob's tin in the kitchen.

I remembered my flat, tacky scones, I remembered the white enamelled pseudopodia flowing. Starch scones! Convulsed with giggles I ran to tell Brian.

So Amah and Cookie left. Ah Moy, Ah Jon, No. 2 son and No. 2 daughter, whose names I never knew, went with them. Amah and Ah Moy, their faces woebegone, looked back as the little family straggled down the road behind the defiant Cookie sitting bolt

upright on his bicycle, his brown felt hat set squarely on his head. I
felt bereaved.

We found a feckless Malay girl, Halimah, to do the washing and
mind little Phil, and a pleasant middle-aged Chinese woman called
Ah King, with a splendid solid-gold tooth in the front of her mouth,
came to cook.

•   •   •

There was great excitement in Jesselton. The whole town, and in
fact the entire Colony, was preparing to celebrate the Coronation of
Elizabeth II. King George VI had died over a year before and it is
odd that I have no record of his passing in my diaries, letters or
newspaper cuttings. His death didn't make a ripple in our quiet
pool. But now, with the new Elizabethan era about to begin, there
was a tremendous flurry of activity. We sensed the turning of a
page, the beginning of a new chapter.

The town was cleaned up, the plantation strip along Gaya Street
had its face lifted. Trees were lopped of untidy branches and
flower-beds were fenced in neatly. Triumphal arches were erected
at points of entry to the town proper. All the shops had been selling
souvenir goods for weeks while dressmakers and tailors shelved all
other work to make dresses and dinner jackets for the Garden Party
and the Ball. The hardworking drycleaner was inundated with rush
orders. A real newspaper, *Sabah Times*, had started publishing in
1952 and would be covering the festivities in depth.

Just in time a new shop opened at Tanjong Aru. Julietta Salon, the
first of its kind in Jesselton, catered almost exclusively for ladies.
Furnished in European style with spacious fitting rooms, chairs
and tables for tired shoppers or perhaps long-suffering husbands,
it made a welcome change from the public atmosphere of a *kedai*
shop. Julietta specialized in exotic Chinese fabrics, brocades,
satins, heavy crepes, fine muslins and silks. She had wonderful
cheongsaam lengths imported from Hong Kong with beaded or

sequined designs rippling from neckline to hem and she made dresses to order. We were overwhelmed by the supply of luxury goods and the availability of smart accessories previously unattainable. With this Aladdin's Cave to rifle, it was no wonder that jaded women were becoming excited. By the time June arrived, the whole town was in holiday mood.

The Coronation Race meeting started the festivities. It was reckoned by racegoers to be particularly good but, not being interested in racing, my pleasure came from the commentary on Radio Sabah which ran something like this:

'. . . the horses are all up at the line . . . Number three is a little restive . . . oh, it looks as if they are off . . .'

Long pause.

'Well, that was a really good race. I don't quite know who won. I'll ask the judges.'

A far cry from the boisterous commentaries of Chuck Fenton!

That night happy punters celebrated their wins at the Race Night Dance. H.M.S. *Maenad* was showing the flag in port and the ship's company provided more partners than was usual at our dances.

On Monday morning there were Water Sports at the Customs wharf. The main part of the wharf was kept reasonably clear for competitors and officials but the transverse section was jammed with spectators. The Governor and his party watched the proceedings from the launch *Malawali* and cruising around the calm water were half a dozen trim sailing boats, some from Jesselton's new yacht club and two from *Maenad*. At half past ten the gun went for their race to start. Strongly handicapped, John Stagg's GP14 *Yellow Peril* was first home. Brian's *Aïsah*, long since redesigned for speed, had been lent to John Tyson, now Commodore of the Jesselton Club. He had raced *Aïsah* before with considerable success but this time she was holed by a submerged stake while coming from Tanjong Aru to the starting line.

Meanwhile, swimming races and novelty events were taking place continuously and there was a Greasy Pole which sent the

townspeople into wild transports of delight. As an unlucky contestant was forced to loose his hold on the pole and began to slip
inexorably to watery ignominy, a great howl of approval went up,
reaching a yell of triumph as he disappeared into the water. Duckdiving and *perahu* races were also very popular and there were
even races for girls and women, something I had been agitating for
in my column for two years.

In the afternoon a Garden Party was held on the *padang*. In spite
of sweltering heat, nearly the whole populace turned out, the
women looking cool and elegant in either national dress or
Julietta's creations. I was reluctant to spend money on one of the
latter so once again I wore my tomato ballerina-length dress, together with the cane shape swathed in flame georgette. Brian, however, had improved the little hat with a side flounce of black lace.
Orang Tua in their splendid ceremonial attire mingled with Malays
in their formal dress of short sarong worn over white shirt and
trousers, and white-suited Europeans with Chinese. 'Warm lemonade and cold tea' was the usual verdict on refreshments at official
parties but on this occasion a special effort had been made. Afternoon tea was served in thin china cups at attractively decorated
tables and the cold drinks were actually cold.

Rain rather dampened the fireworks display at the Turf Club that
night but on Coronation Day everyone lined the decorated streets
to watch the Parade. The news of the successful assault on Mount
Everest had just come over the radio and everyone was simmering
with excitement, especially the New Zealanders.

A naval contingent from the *Maenad* marched through the town
but our Police looked just as fine and marched as smartly as the
sailors. A large crowd of spectators gathered in the Sports Club and
on the Club hill but couldn't hear a word of the Governor's speech
as it was not amplified.

Then came the parade of decorated vehicles. There was a wide
variety of floats, some showing great imagination and ingenuity.
One truck was converted into a dragon, another into a realistic ship

but there was not one Kinabalu which I thought would have been a perfect disguise for a driver's cabin. The only decorated private car was a small one transformed into the familiar bowler-hatted head of Winston Churchill, complete with cigar.

After lunch there was a sports meeting on the *padang*, pools of water from the previous evenings's rain contributing to the fun. There was a Fancy Dress football match against the Navy – rather one-sided owing to the Navy bringing its own goalposts, just wide enough not to let a ball through. Many a 'lady' was flung unceremoniously into the water. Keith Wookey appeared as a Red Cross nurse, Chuck Fenton as a coal-black mammy and Rex Blow as a diapered baby, while Atkie, recently made Commissioner of the re-named North Borneo Police, patrolled lugubriously around the perimeter of the *padang* as a clown. The match inevitably deteriorated into a mud fight.

The culminating feature of the day was the splendid lantern procession from the *padang* to the wharf in the evening. The Chinese have long been masters of lantern making and all the schools and associations in town combined to make the *padang* a twisting, bobbing mass of coloured lights. Inevitably there were numerous crowns and effigies of the Queen and some quite magnificent constructions representing the State Coach, a pagoda and a full-size aeroplane but my favourites were the variegated fish with goggling eyes and waving fins.

Bringing up the rear of the procession was the ultimate in the bizarre. Picture a diminutive Malay girl enthroned as Queen in full regalia, carried through the streets by four stalwarts while around her capered a crowd of schoolboys bellowing 'She'll be coming round the mountain'.

When the long spectacular procession had wound its flickering way to the wharf, H.M.S. *Maenad* gave an outstanding display of fireworks, the reflections in the water of the bursting rockets adding greatly to the beauty of the lights. At the end of the show a great gasp went up from a thousand throats as the whole ship was suddenly floodlit from bow to stern and remained illuminated throughout the night.

For the next three nights the Jesselton Players presented their Coronation play *See how they run* and on Saturday, the Queen's Birthday Parade and the Coronation Ball at Government House brought an end to the festive week. Government House gardens were decorated and floodlit and the buildings were gay with flowers and coloured lights. The police band played light music in the garden and there was dancing indoors to well-chosen records. It was generally reckoned to be the best function that had ever been held in Jesselton.

* * *

In the last few weeks we were kept busy with farewell parties. Two of them I remember particularly. One was at the Macphersons'. We were without any transport at all, 'Tosh' Parriss having failed to take a tight curve on the hill road and put the Company van half-way down the hillside. Then Brian lent his motorbike to Terry Cashmore who had an accident, wrote off the bike and landed up in hospital where he met Sister 'Pete' and started a romance which was to result in a long and happy marriage. We managed to get a lift to the Bank house and hoped to get a ride home with one of the dinner guests. There were a lot of newcomers. Jesselton was changing and the European population increasing rapidly. When I first arrived in the town there were only about two hundred and fifty expatriates. I knew everyone and was welcome in everyone's home. Doors were never locked and if your vehicle broke down, you had only to enter an empty house to use the phone or get a drink from the refrigerator.

I looked around the sitting room. There were only a few faces I knew. I decided to ask Chip Plunkett if he could take us home afterwards. His wife Lu was away from the Colony. He agreed. That settled, I turned my attention to the other guests.

Mrs Macpherson was a martyr to migraine and this was one of her bad nights. She valiantly strove to entertain her guests but I could see she wished us all miles away. Eleven o'clock came but no one moved. Eleven fifteen. Eleven thirty. I kept sneaking covert glances at my watch. Why didn't someone make a move?

I sidled up to Chip and whispered out of the side of my mouth: 'We're ready when you are . . .'

He stood up promptly.

'We've all been waiting for you,' he hissed.

'For me? Why me?'

'Senior lady!' he said.

'Me! Senior lady!' I looked around wildly.

It couldn't be true. We were very junior. But . . . Lu wasn't there. Mr Tyson's wife wasn't there. I didn't know how the other unknown women ranked but protocol demanded that no one should leave until the most senior woman made a move.

Full of contrition I approached Mrs Macpherson.

'I'm afraid we shall have to go . . .'

'Oh must you?' She leaped up with astounding alacrity.

The party broke up.

Two days later we went to Government House. Now that we were leaving, we were invited to dinner instead of the customary cocktail party. It was a pleasant party of about fourteen guests. I sat on H.E.'s left and on his right was the vivacious American wife of the Basel Mission chief. When the meat course was finished, the boys padded in with the dessert. Each carried a dish with a flummery kind of sweet in patriotic colours of red, white and blue. We each took a portion. We all lifted our spoons. From the far end of the table Lady Hone spoke brightly.

'Well, this looks very colourful.'

Her husband said guardedly . . . 'I suppose the red is cochineal. What's the blue, darling?'

'I'm sure I don't know,' said Lady Hone. 'I can't think what it could be . . . maybe Reckitt's Blue!' She laughed merrily.

We all took a tentative bite. The lady missionary opposite me lifted her large blue eyes from her plate and in a whisper which was heard right down the long table said:

'Do you know what I think it is?' Dramatic pause. 'INK!'

Fourteen spoons were laid on fourteen plates and the ladies followed Lady Hone upstairs.

●   ●   ●

Somehow or other we got our packing done without Cookie. The new Engineer arrived and was shown around the Office. He was unmarried so there was no *mem* for me to initiate into Borneo life. We were sick at heart at the prospect of leaving little Joe but the bachelors in the Mess agreed to take him. The relieving Engineer bought our piano and Terry Cashmore bought *Aïsah*.

As our time grew short, I was obsessed with a desire to record our life and family. We bought a movie film and Keith Wookey came down to shoot it on his camera. He had already given us a film of our wedding and this one was a natural progression showing our first-born.

But our romantic Hemlock Cottage is not in the film. Instead there is the luxurious brick and tile permanent Engineer's house. Cookie and Amah are not in it, only Halimah and Ah King. Little Joe is in it but not Jeep. Instead of our lovely tangle of garden with fruit trees, climbing roses, flamboyant cannas and delicate Java violets, there are clipped lawns and formal roads. Although Robin Forster, the Agricultural Officer, had made a horticultural plan of what the Cable and Wireless estate might eventually look like, with a double row of Royal palms leading from the office to the houses, screens of oleander and hedges of bougainvillaea, the site was still very much in its infancy and the coarse *lallang* had merely been cut to resemble lawns.

But Kinabalu is in our film and Kinabalu is North Borneo to me, remote, alluring, exciting and dramatic. North Borneo is now called

Sabah, a part of East Malaysia, and Jesselton has been renamed Kota Kinabalu. If the lovely old name Singgah Mata was not to be chosen for the capital, what better name than that of the magic mountain! I am told that there are skyscrapers in the town now and tourist hotels at the beach. A road runs almost to Kinabalu and ascents to the summit are common. I never did climb it, but it is comforting to know that however North Borneo may change, the mountain will always be there.

POSTSCRIPT

On the 12th of March 1986, Wendy Suart saw Halley's Comet from the summit of Mount Kinabalu.

GLOSSARY

(I have used the spelling which was in common use when I was in Jesselton)

abaca	Manila hemp
ada	Is there any? Have you got? To have
amah	Child's nurse, female servant
amok	One who runs amuck in a thirst for blood
anak	Child
angin	Wind
apa	What
apa khabar	What news?
Api Api	Native name for Jesselton
arak	Native rice wine
aru	Casuarina tree
attap	Thatching made from pandan leaves
ayer	Water
ayer limau	Lime water; fresh squeezed lime drink
ayer panas	Hot water
ayer panas mandi	Hot water for bathing
baharu	New
baik	Well: very well

Bajau	Native of North Borneo
barang	Baggage; things
batik	Cloth dyed by a special wax process
batu	Stone: milestone
bawang	Onion
bekin	To make
berapa	How much?
besar	Big
bin	Son of
boleh	Able to, can
bongon	Native basket carried on the back
bua	Fruit
buang	To throw
buang ayer	To urinate
budak	Small boy; golf caddy
bulan	Moon
bunga	Flower
bunga chempaka	Frangipani
bunga rajah	King of flowers; the night-blooming cereus
burong	Bird
cutch	A product of mangrove bark used for dyeing and tanning
chakap	To speak
chakap perlahan-perlahan	Speak more slowly
chantek	Pretty
chantek itu	That's pretty
changkol	Agricultural hoe
chawat	Loin cloth
cheong saam	Shanghai dress; high-necked Chinese sheath dress
chichak	Gecko lizard
chiku	Malay fruit

chuchi	To clean
dahulu	Before (*dahulus*, name given to to Europeans in Borneo before the war)
dalam	In
dapor	Kitchen
dari	From
demam	Fever
dindang	Native dance
dua	Two
durian	Large odiferous fruit
durian belanda	Dutch durian; soursop
Dusun	Native of North Borneo
Dyak	Native of Sarawak
empat	Four
empat-puloh	Forty
enam	Six
gaji	Wages
gigi	Tooth
godown	Warehouse, store
gula	Sugar
gula malacca	Traditional dessert to follow curry
halus	Fine in texture
hantu	Ghost, haunted
harga	Price
hari	Day
hari raya	Holiday
Iban	Sea Dyaks native to Sarawak
ikan	Fish
ikan merah	Red snapper

ikan tenggiri	Spanish mackerel
imam	Moslem priest
itu	That, those
jalan	Road
jamban	Lavatory
janggut	Beard
jatoh	To fall
kah	Interrogative suffix
kajang	Woven palm leaf used for walls, doors etc.
kambing	Sheep, goat
kampong	Village
kampong ayer	Water village
kampong orang puteh	Name given to locality where Europeans lived in Jesselton
kahwin	To marry
kechil	Small
kedai	Malay bazaar
kelip-kelip	Fireflies
keluar	To leave
kerbau	Water buffalo
keris	A Malay dagger
kerusi malas	Lazy chair; *chaise longue*
khabar	News
khabar baik	Good news
kluang	Flying fox
kopi	Coffee
kopi-oh	Black coffee
kropak	Prawn crackers
kumpit	Small cargo – carrying boat
kunyit	Turmeric

lagi	More
laki-laki	Male
lallang	Coarse grass
laut	Sea
lembu	Ox
lima	Five
lima-puloh	Fifty
limau	Lime
mahal	Expensive
mahu	To wish
mahu makan-kah?	Do you wish to eat?
makan	To eat; a meal
makan angin	Eating the wind, i.e. going for a walk
makan besar	Banquet
makan kechil	Small meal; cocktail snacks
mana	Where
mandi	To bathe
mandor	Foreman of work force
mas	Gold, golden
masok	To enter
mata	Eye
mata-mata	Policeman
mata-mata gelap	Detective
mati	To die; dead
mee goreng	Fried noodles
mem	Married European lady. (Derived from 'memsahib')
merah	Red
mesti ada wangi	It must have perfume
misi	Unmarried European lady; Miss
Murut	Native of North Borneo
naik	To rise or climb

nasi	Cooked rice
nasi goreng	Fried rice
negeri	Country
okra	Lady's fingers (type of vegetable)
orang	Man
orang laut	Man of the sea
orang puteh	White man; European
orang tua	Old man; Head man of village
orang utan	Man of the jungle, red hairy ape
padang	Sports field; plain; open field
padi	Rice plant; unhusked rice
pak choy	Chinese spinach
papaya	Papaw
parang	Native jungle knife
pelayaran	Voyage
perahu	Boat
pergi	To go
pergi mana	Where are you going?
perkakas rumah	Household furnishings
perlahan-perlahan	Slowly
pisang	Banana
pisang mas	Golden dwarf banana
pomelo	Large citrus fruit
potong	To cut
pukul	To strike (*pukul enam* – six o'clock)
punya	Denotes possessive in bazaar Malay
pulau	Island
puteh	White
Rajah	King
Rajah muda	Young king; heir to Rajah
rambutan	Malay fruit

rembas	Grass-cutting implement
rentas	A path cut through the jungle
rotan	Rattan; plant with long, thin pliant stems used for many purposes
rumah	House
saam fu	Chinese pyjama suit
sahaya	I
sakit	Sick
sambal	Side dish served with curry
sana	Over there
santan	Coconut cream
sari	Indian lady's garment
sarong	Malay skirt worn by men and women
sarong kebaya	Malay skirt and jacket worn by women
satay	Malay kebab
satengah	A half; name given to half peg of whisky; 'Stinger'
satu	One
selamat	Peace; safety
selamat jalan	Go safely; Goodbye (to those going)
selamat pagi	Good morning
selamat tinggal	Goodbye (to those staying behind)
selangan batu	A very hard local timber
serang	Head man of a boat crew
seraya	Local timber
siap	Ready
singgah mata	Where the eye lingers; old name for Jesselton
songkok	Muslim man's hat, usually in black velvet
stengah	See *satengah*
suka hati	Content; happy
sulap	Small hut

sungei	Creek
susu	Milk
syce	Driver
ta	Abbreviation of *tidak* – No, not
tabek	Hullo
tamu	Native market
tamu besar	Annual agricultural show
tanjong	Cape, headland
tapai	Native rice beer
tepi	Edge
terang	Clear, bright
terimakasi	Thank you
tiada	Is not
tiada bagus	Is not good
tidak	No, not
tidak boleh mati	It cannot die
tid'apa	It doesn't matter; never mind
tiga	Three
tikus	Mouse
timor	East; eastern
tinggal	To stay
towkay	Chinese shopkeeper
tua	Old
tuai rumah	Headman of a longhouse
tuan	Sir; form of address to European men, Hajis and some Malays
tukang ayer	Water carrier
tukang kebun	Gardener
udang	Prawn
ulu	Hinterland; outback
wah-wah	Gibbon

wayang	Drama; characters from a play
wong ah pak	Chinese leaves (type of vegetable)
ya	Yes